Quantum Computing: Principles Programming and Possibilities
A Complete Guide for Students and Researchers

Anshuman Mishra

Published by Anshuman Mishra, 2025.

QUANTUM COMPUTING: PRINCIPLES, PROGRAMMING, AND POSSIBILITIES – A COMPLETE GUIDE FOR STUDENTS AND RESEARCHERS

DESIGNED FOR BCA, BTECH, MCA, AND MSC PROGRAMS

📚 TABLE OF CONTENTS

🕮 About the Book

"Quantum Computing: Principles, Programming, and Possibilities – A Complete Guide for Students and Researchers" is a thoughtfully curated textbook designed for **undergraduate and postgraduate students** across Computer Science, Information Technology, and related disciplines. It bridges the gap between foundational quantum theory and its real-world computational applications, providing a **step-by-step guide** to mastering quantum computing concepts, algorithms, and programming.

This book is structured into 15 well-organized chapters that gradually build up the learner's understanding—from basic quantum principles to advanced quantum algorithms, machine learning, and practical programming using platforms like **Qiskit**, **Cirq**, and **Q#**.

Key features include:

- **Clear explanations of core concepts** such as superposition, entanglement, and quantum measurement.
- **Comprehensive coverage of landmark quantum algorithms** like Grover's and Shor's algorithms, with intuitive circuit diagrams and practical examples.
- **Hands-on coding tutorials** using Python-based Qiskit to help students simulate quantum circuits and run them on real quantum computers via IBM Quantum.
- **Dedicated chapters on quantum error correction, hardware, and cryptography**, which prepare students for research and industry.
- **Real-world examples, solved problems, diagrams, and code snippets** to aid visual and experiential learning.
- **Future scope discussions** on careers, ongoing research, and the evolution of quantum computing.

Whether you're a **BCA, BTech, MCA, MSc student**, or a **researcher or tech enthusiast**, this book provides the foundation, depth, and skills required to excel in the fascinating world of quantum computing.

🎯 Benefits of Studying This Book

✅ 1. Curriculum-Aligned & Industry-Relevant

- Tailored for university courses (BCA, BTech, MCA, MSc).
- Covers topics frequently asked in UGC-NET, GATE, and interviews.
- Updated with the latest developments and platforms used in quantum research and industry.

✅ 2. Learn by Doing

- Includes coding examples using **Qiskit**, the most widely used open-source quantum SDK.
- Exercises include building real quantum circuits, simulating quantum teleportation, and exploring quantum search.
- Helps transition from **theory to practical implementation**.

✅ 3. Strong Conceptual Foundation

- Starts from the basics of math and physics, making it ideal for beginners.
- Gradual progression to advanced topics ensures no conceptual gaps.
- Explained with analogies and visual aids for better retention.

✅ 4. Preparation for Future Careers

- Prepares students for careers in **quantum computing**, **data science**, **quantum cryptography**, and **AI-quantum hybrids**.
- Includes a full chapter on career paths, certifications, internships, and global research labs.

✅ 5. Suited for Self-Study or Classroom Teaching

- Organized in a modular structure with learning objectives and summaries.
- Each chapter ends with **review questions, coding tasks**, and **mini-project suggestions**.
- Ideal for online learners, university students, and instructors alike.

✅ 6. Multidisciplinary Relevance

- Relevant for students in **Computer Science, Physics, Mathematics, Engineering, and Data Science**.
- Explores intersections with **cryptography, machine learning, and theoretical physics**.

ABOUT THE AUTHOR:

ANSHUMAN KUMAR MISHRA IS A SEASONED EDUCATOR AND PROLIFIC AUTHOR WITH OVER 20 YEARS OF EXPERIENCE IN THE TEACHING FIELD. HE HAS A DEEP PASSION FOR TECHNOLOGY AND A STRONG COMMITMENT TO MAKING COMPLEX CONCEPTS ACCESSIBLE TO STUDENTS AT ALL LEVELS. WITH AN M.TECH IN COMPUTER SCIENCE FROM BIT MESRA, HE BRINGS BOTH ACADEMIC EXPERTISE AND PRACTICAL EXPERIENCE TO HIS WORK.

CURRENTLY SERVING AS AN ASSISTANT PROFESSOR AT DORANDA COLLEGE, ANSHUMAN HAS BEEN A GUIDING FORCE FOR MANY ASPIRING COMPUTER SCIENTISTS AND ENGINEERS, NURTURING THEIR SKILLS IN VARIOUS PROGRAMMING LANGUAGES AND TECHNOLOGIES. HIS TEACHING STYLE IS FOCUSED ON CLARITY, HANDS-ON LEARNING, AND MAKING STUDENTS COMFORTABLE WITH BOTH THEORETICAL AND PRACTICAL ASPECTS OF COMPUTER SCIENCE.

THROUGHOUT HIS CAREER, ANSHUMAN KUMAR MISHRA HAS AUTHORED OVER 25 BOOKS ON A WIDE RANGE OF TOPICS INCLUDING PYTHON, JAVA, C, C++, DATA SCIENCE, ARTIFICIAL INTELLIGENCE, SQL, .NET, WEB PROGRAMMING, DATA STRUCTURES, AND MORE. HIS BOOKS HAVE BEEN WELL-RECEIVED BY STUDENTS, PROFESSIONALS, AND INSTITUTIONS ALIKE FOR THEIR STRAIGHTFORWARD EXPLANATIONS, PRACTICAL EXERCISES, AND DEEP INSIGHTS INTO THE SUBJECTS.

ANSHUMAN'S APPROACH TO TEACHING AND WRITING IS ROOTED IN HIS BELIEF THAT LEARNING SHOULD BE ENGAGING, INTUITIVE, AND HIGHLY APPLICABLE TO REAL-WORLD SCENARIOS. HIS EXPERIENCE IN BOTH ACADEMIA AND INDUSTRY HAS GIVEN HIM A UNIQUE PERSPECTIVE ON HOW TO BEST PREPARE STUDENTS FOR THE EVOLVING WORLD OF TECHNOLOGY.

IN HIS BOOKS, ANSHUMAN AIMS NOT ONLY TO IMPART KNOWLEDGE BUT ALSO TO INSPIRE A LIFELONG LOVE FOR LEARNING AND EXPLORATION IN THE WORLD OF COMPUTER SCIENCE AND PROGRAMMING.

Copyright Page

Title- **QUANTUM COMPUTING: PRINCIPLES, PROGRAMMING, AND POSSIBILITIES – A COMPLETE GUIDE FOR STUDENTS AND RESEARCHERS**

CHAPTER 1: INTRODUCTION TO QUANTUM COMPUTING

Quantum Computing

Quantum computing is a paradigm shift in computation that moves beyond the limitations of classical computers by harnessing the bizarre and powerful principles of **quantum mechanics**. Unlike classical computers that store and process information as definite **bits** (either 0 or 1), quantum computers utilize **qubits** which can exist in a superposition of states, dramatically increasing their computational power for specific types of problems.

Let's break down the key concepts:

1. Quantum Mechanics: The Foundation

At the heart of quantum computing lies quantum mechanics, a fundamental theory in physics that describes the physical properties of nature at the scale of atoms and subatomic particles. Some of its key principles that are exploited in quantum computing include:

- **Superposition:** This is the ability of a quantum system (like a qubit) to exist in multiple states simultaneously. Unlike a classical bit that is definitively 0 or 1, a qubit can be a combination of both 0 and 1 at the same time. Think of it as being in a probabilistic state where there's a certain probability of being 0 and a certain probability of being 1.
    - **Example:** Imagine a coin spinning in the air. Before it lands, it's neither definitively heads nor tails; it's in a superposition of both possibilities. Similarly, a qubit can be in a superposition of the $|0\rangle$ state and the $|1\rangle$ state, represented mathematically as: $$\alpha|0\rangle + \beta|1\rangle$$ where α and β are complex numbers representing the probability amplitudes of the qubit being in the $|0\rangle$ and $|1\rangle$ states, respectively, and $|\alpha|2+|\beta|2=1$.
- **Entanglement:** This is a peculiar quantum phenomenon where two or more qubits become linked together in such a way that they share the same fate, no matter how far apart they are. Measuring the state of one entangled qubit instantaneously determines the state of the other(s), even if they are light-years away.
    - **Example:** Imagine two of our spinning coins are entangled. If you observe one and find it to be heads, you instantly know the other one will be tails (or vice versa), regardless of the distance between them. In quantum computing, entangled qubits can be used to perform complex computations and transmit information in novel ways.
- **Quantum Tunneling:** This refers to the ability of a quantum particle to pass through a potential energy barrier even if it doesn't have enough energy to do so classically. While not directly used as a primary computational resource, it's a manifestation of the wave-like nature of quantum particles, which is fundamental to quantum mechanics.

2. Qubits: The Quantum Building Blocks

The fundamental unit of information in quantum computing is the **qubit** (quantum bit). Unlike classical bits that can only be 0 or 1, a qubit can exist in a **superposition** of these states.

- **Analogy Revisited:** As the initial example stated, a classical bit is like a light switch (on or off). A qubit is more like a dimmer switch that can be both on and off to varying degrees simultaneously.
- **Mathematical Representation:** The state of a qubit is represented as a vector in a two-dimensional complex vector space. The basis vectors of this space are the computational basis states, denoted as $|0\rangle$ and $|1\rangle$ (Dirac notation). A general state of a qubit $|\psi\rangle$ can be written as a linear combination of these basis states: $|\psi\rangle=\alpha|0\rangle+\beta|1\rangle$ where α and β are complex numbers such that $|\alpha|2$ represents the probability of measuring the qubit in the $|0\rangle$ state, and $|\beta|2$ represents the probability of measuring it in the $|1\rangle$ state, with $|\alpha|2+|\beta|2=1$.

3. Quantum Gates: Manipulating Qubits

Just as classical computers use logic gates (like AND, OR, NOT) to manipulate bits, quantum computers use **quantum gates** to manipulate the states of qubits. Quantum gates are unitary transformations that operate on one or more qubits.

- **Examples of Quantum Gates:**
  - **Pauli-X Gate (NOT Gate):** Flips the state of a qubit: $|0\rangle \to |1\rangle$ and $|1\rangle \to |0\rangle$.
  - **Pauli-Z Gate:** Introduces a phase shift: $|0\rangle \to |0\rangle$ and $|1\rangle \to -|1\rangle$.
  - **Hadamard Gate (H-Gate):** Creates a superposition: $|0\rangle \to 21(|0\rangle+|1\rangle)$ and $|1\rangle \to 2$ $1(|0\rangle-|1\rangle)$.
  - **CNOT Gate (Controlled-NOT Gate):** A two-qubit gate that flips the second qubit's state if the first qubit is in the $|1\rangle$ state. This gate is crucial for creating entanglement.

4. Quantum Algorithms: Harnessing Quantum Power

Quantum algorithms are sequences of quantum gates designed to solve specific computational problems. They leverage the principles of superposition and entanglement to achieve potential speedups over their classical counterparts for certain tasks.

- **Examples of Prominent Quantum Algorithms:**
  - **Shor's Algorithm:** Efficiently factorizes large integers, which has significant implications for cryptography (breaking widely used public-key encryption methods).
  - **Grover's Algorithm:** Provides a quadratic speedup for searching unsorted databases compared to classical algorithms.
  - **Quantum Simulation Algorithms:** Enable the efficient simulation of quantum systems (like molecules and materials), which is intractable for classical computers. This has potential applications in drug discovery, materials science, and fundamental physics research.

  - **Quantum Machine Learning Algorithms:** Explore the potential of quantum computing to accelerate and enhance machine learning tasks.

5. Measurement: Extracting Information

At the end of a quantum computation, the state of the qubits needs to be measured to obtain a classical output that we can understand. When a qubit in a superposition is measured, it collapses into one of the basis states (either $|0\rangle$ or $|1\rangle$) with a probability determined by the amplitudes α and β.

- **Example:** If a qubit is in the state $31|0\rangle+32|1\rangle$, then upon measurement, there is a (31)2=31 probability of observing $|0\rangle$ and a (32)2=32 probability of observing $|1\rangle$.

Why is Quantum Computing Revolutionary?

The ability of qubits to exist in superposition and become entangled allows quantum computers to perform certain computations in a fundamentally different and potentially much faster way than classical computers.

- **Parallelism:** Superposition allows a quantum computer with n qubits to potentially explore 2n states simultaneously. This exponential increase in the state space allows for massive parallel computation for certain problems.
  - **Example:** With just 50 qubits, a quantum computer can theoretically explore 250 states simultaneously, which is more than a quadrillion states. Simulating such a system classically would be practically impossible.
- **Solving Intractable Problems:** Quantum computers hold the promise of solving problems that are currently intractable for even the most powerful supercomputers, such as:
  - Factoring very large numbers (breaking modern encryption).
  - Simulating complex molecular interactions for drug discovery and materials science.
  - Optimizing complex logistical problems.
  - Developing new materials with specific properties.
  - Advancing artificial intelligence and machine learning.

Challenges and the Future of Quantum Computing:

Despite its immense potential, quantum computing is still in its early stages of development and faces significant challenges:

- **Qubit Stability (Decoherence):** Qubits are very sensitive to environmental noise, which can cause them to lose their quantum properties (superposition and entanglement) and behave like classical bits. Maintaining the delicate quantum states for long enough to perform complex computations is a major hurdle.

- **Scalability:** Building and controlling a large number of high-quality, stable qubits is a significant engineering challenge. Current quantum computers have a relatively small number of qubits.
- **Error Correction:** Due to the fragility of qubits, errors are inherent in quantum computations. Developing robust quantum error correction techniques is crucial for building fault-tolerant quantum computers.
- **Algorithm Development:** While some promising quantum algorithms exist, developing new algorithms that can effectively leverage the power of quantum computers for a wider range of problems is an ongoing area of research.

Evolution of Computing: Classical to Quantum

The history of computing is a fascinating journey of innovation, marked by increasingly powerful and efficient ways of processing information. From bulky, energy-intensive machines to sleek, portable devices, classical computing has undergone a remarkable transformation. However, as we push the boundaries of what classical computers can achieve, we are beginning to encounter fundamental physical limitations. This is where quantum computing emerges, representing a revolutionary paradigm shift in how we approach computation.

Let's delve into the evolution of computing, highlighting the key advancements that have led us to the cusp of the quantum era:

1. First Generation – Vacuum Tubes (1940s - 1950s)

- **Technology:** The earliest electronic digital computers relied on **vacuum tubes** as their primary switching components. These were glass tubes containing electrodes in a vacuum, controlling the flow of electrons.
- **Characteristics:**
  - **Large Size:** Computers of this era were enormous, often filling entire rooms. The ENIAC, for instance, occupied about 1800 square feet.
  - **Slow Speed:** Processing speeds were measured in milliseconds (thousandths of a second).
  - **High Power Consumption:** Vacuum tubes generated a significant amount of heat and consumed vast amounts of electricity. The ENIAC reportedly consumed around 150 kW of power.
  - **Low Reliability:** Vacuum tubes were prone to failure, requiring frequent maintenance.
  - **Limited Programming:** Programming was often done through manual wiring and plugboards, making it a laborious and time-consuming process.
- **Example: ENIAC (Electronic Numerical Integrator and Computer) - 1945**
  - Widely considered one of the first general-purpose electronic digital computers.
  - Developed for the U.S. Army to calculate artillery firing tables.
  - Contained approximately 17,468 vacuum tubes, weighed about 30 tons, and occupied a large room.

- Performed thousands of calculations per second, a significant leap over manual methods.

2. Second Generation – Transistors (1950s - 1960s)

- **Technology:** The invention of the **transistor** at Bell Labs in 1947 marked a pivotal moment in computing history. Transistors are semiconductor devices that can act as electronic switches and amplifiers.
- **Characteristics:**
  - **Smaller Size:** Transistors were significantly smaller than vacuum tubes, leading to smaller and more compact computers.
  - **Increased Reliability:** Transistors were much more durable and had a longer lifespan than vacuum tubes.
  - **Lower Power Consumption:** They required less power and generated less heat, making computers more energy-efficient.
  - **Faster Speed:** Transistor-based computers operated at faster speeds, with processing times measured in microseconds (millionths of a second).
  - **Easier Programming:** The development of high-level programming languages like FORTRAN and COBOL made programming more accessible.
- **Examples:**
  - **IBM 1401 (1959):** A popular mainframe computer used by businesses.
  - **DEC PDP-1 (1960):** Known for its use in early interactive computing and computer graphics.

3. Third Generation – Integrated Circuits (1960s - 1970s)

- **Technology:** The development of the **integrated circuit (IC)**, or microchip, revolutionized electronics. An IC contains numerous transistors and other electronic components miniaturized and fabricated on a single semiconductor chip (usually silicon).
- **Characteristics:**
  - **Further Miniaturization:** ICs allowed for the creation of even smaller and more powerful computers.
  - **Increased Speed:** Processing speeds increased to nanoseconds (billionths of a second).
  - **Lower Cost:** Mass production of ICs led to a significant decrease in the cost of computing.
  - **Increased Reliability:** With fewer interconnections, ICs were more reliable than systems built with discrete components.
- **Example:**
  - **IBM System/360 (1964):** A family of mainframe computers that could run the same software across different models.
  - **DEC PDP-8 (1965):** A commercially successful minicomputer.

4. Fourth Generation – Microprocessors (1970s onwards)

- **Technology:** The invention of the **microprocessor** in the early 1970s, which integrated an entire central processing unit (CPU) onto a single chip, was a landmark achievement.
- **Characteristics:**
  - **Personal Computers (PCs):** Microprocessors made it possible to develop affordable and compact personal computers for individual use.
  - **Exponential Growth:** This era witnessed an explosive growth in the computing industry, with the development of various types of computers, from desktops to laptops.
  - **Increased Processing Power:** Microprocessor performance has continued to increase exponentially over the decades, driven by Moore's Law (the observation that the number of transistors on a microchip doubles approximately every two years).
  - **Software Development:** The proliferation of PCs led to the development of a vast array of software applications.
  - **Networking and the Internet:** The fourth generation also saw the rise of computer networks and eventually the internet, transforming communication and information sharing.
- **Examples:**
  - **Intel 4004 (1971):** The first single-chip microprocessor.
  - **Apple II (1977):** One of the first highly successful personal computers.
  - **IBM PC (1981):** A pivotal machine that standardized the PC market.

5. Fifth Generation and Beyond – AI and Quantum

As we move into the fifth generation and beyond, classical computing is facing fundamental limitations:

- **Physical Limits:** The miniaturization of transistors is approaching the atomic scale. Quantum effects become significant at these levels, making it increasingly difficult to build and control traditional transistors.
- **Practical Limits (Moore's Law Slowing):** While transistor density continues to increase, the rate of improvement has slowed down due to physical constraints and increasing manufacturing complexity and costs.
- **Limitations in Solving Certain Problems:** Many computationally intensive problems, such as simulating large molecules, breaking modern encryption algorithms, and solving complex optimization problems, remain intractable for even the most powerful classical supercomputers due to their exponential scaling of computational resources with problem size.

Quantum Computing: A Paradigm Shift

Quantum computing emerges as a fundamentally different approach to computation, offering the potential to overcome some of these limitations. Instead of relying on classical bits that represent either 0 or 1, quantum computers utilize **qubits** (quantum bits) that leverage the principles of quantum mechanics:

- **Processes Information Using Quantum Principles:**
  - **Superposition:** As explained earlier, a qubit can exist in a superposition of both 0 and 1 simultaneously. This allows a quantum computer with n qubits to potentially explore 2n states concurrently, offering an exponential advantage in the amount of information it can represent and process compared to n classical bits.
    - **Example:** 3 classical bits can represent 23=8 distinct states (000, 001, 010, 011, 100, 101, 110, 111) at any given time. However, 3 qubits in superposition can exist in a combination of all 8 of these states simultaneously.
  - **Entanglement:** Entangled qubits are linked in such a way that their fates are intertwined. Measuring the state of one entangled qubit instantly determines the state of the others, regardless of the distance between them. This [1] allows for complex correlations and computations that are difficult to achieve classically.
    - **Example:** Imagine two entangled qubits. If one is measured to be $|0\rangle$, the other will instantaneously be $|1\rangle$ (or vice versa, depending on the entanglement). This correlation can be used to perform coordinated operations and computations.
- **Solves Problems in Exponentially Fewer Steps:** For certain types of problems, quantum algorithms can achieve a significant speedup compared to the best-known classical algorithms. This "quantum advantage" stems from the ability of quantum computers to explore a vast computational space in parallel due to superposition and to exploit quantum phenomena like interference to amplify the probability of finding the correct solution.
  - **Example (Conceptual):** Consider searching for a specific item in an unsorted database of N items. A classical computer would, on average, need to examine N/2 items. Grover's quantum algorithm can solve this problem in approximately N steps, offering a quadratic speedup. For a database with a trillion items, this translates to searching a million items instead of half a trillion.
  - **Example (Cryptography):** Shor's algorithm can factorize large integers exponentially faster than the best classical algorithms. This poses a threat to widely used public-key cryptography systems like RSA, which rely on the difficulty of factoring large numbers.

The Future:

Quantum computing is still in its nascent stages, facing significant technological hurdles in terms of qubit stability, scalability, and error correction. However, the potential impact of quantum computers on various fields, including medicine, materials science, finance, artificial intelligence, and cryptography, is immense. While they are not expected to replace classical computers entirely, quantum computers are poised to become powerful tools for tackling specific classes of computationally challenging problems that are currently beyond our reach. The evolution from classical to quantum computing represents not just an incremental improvement, but a fundamental shift in our approach to information processing and problem-solving.

Real-World Applications and Potential of Quantum Computing

Quantum computing, with its ability to tackle problems intractable for even the most powerful classical supercomputers, holds immense potential to revolutionize numerous industries and scientific fields. By leveraging the principles of superposition and entanglement, quantum computers can perform calculations with unprecedented speed and efficiency for specific types of problems. Let's explore some key real-world applications and their potential in detail, with illustrative examples:

❃□ Applications:

✓ 1. Cryptography:

- **The Threat:** Current widely used public-key encryption algorithms, such as RSA (Rivest–Shamir–Adleman) and ECC (Elliptic Curve Cryptography), rely on the computational difficulty of factoring large numbers and solving discrete logarithm problems for classical computers. **Shor's algorithm**, a quantum algorithm developed by Peter Shor in 1994, can theoretically solve these problems in polynomial time, which is exponentially faster than the best known classical algorithms.
    - **Example:** Imagine a secure communication protected by RSA encryption. The security hinges on the fact that factoring the large public key into its prime factors is computationally infeasible for classical computers within a reasonable timeframe. However, a sufficiently powerful quantum computer running Shor's algorithm could factor this key relatively quickly, allowing unauthorized access to the encrypted information.
- **The Response: Post-Quantum Cryptography (PQC):** Recognizing this threat, the field of **post-quantum cryptography** is a very active area of research. The goal is to develop new cryptographic algorithms that are resistant to attacks from both classical and quantum computers.
    - **Example:** Cryptographers are exploring various mathematical approaches for PQC, such as lattice-based cryptography, code-based cryptography, hash-based signatures, multivariate polynomial cryptography, and isogeny-based cryptography. These methods rely on different mathematical problems that are believed to be hard for both classical and quantum computers to solve efficiently. Organizations like NIST (National Institute of Standards and Technology) are actively involved in standardizing promising PQC algorithms for future use.
- **Potential Impact:** The advent of practical quantum computers could necessitate a complete overhaul of current cybersecurity infrastructure. The development and adoption of robust post-quantum cryptography are crucial to ensuring the security of sensitive data in the future.

✓ 2. Drug Discovery and Materials Science:

- **Simulating Molecular Interactions:** Understanding the behavior of molecules at the quantum level is fundamental to designing new drugs and materials. Classical computers struggle to accurately simulate the complex interactions of electrons in molecules, especially for larger systems, due to the exponential growth of the computational resources required.
    - **Example: Simulating Protein Folding Structure:** Predicting the three-dimensional structure of a protein from its amino acid sequence is a grand challenge in biology. The way a protein folds determines its function. Quantum computers can potentially simulate the quantum mechanical forces that govern protein folding with much higher accuracy and efficiency than classical methods. This could significantly accelerate the discovery of new drugs that target specific proteins by allowing researchers to simulate how drug candidates interact with their targets at a fundamental level.
    - **Example: Designing New Materials:** The properties of materials are determined by the quantum interactions of their constituent atoms and electrons. Quantum computers could enable the simulation of novel materials with desired properties, such as high-temperature superconductors, new catalysts, or more efficient energy storage materials. This could lead to breakthroughs in various fields, including energy, electronics, and manufacturing.
- **Potential Impact:** Quantum computing could dramatically accelerate the discovery of new medicines, reduce the cost and time associated with drug development, and enable the design of novel materials with revolutionary properties.

✅ **3. Optimization Problems:**

- **Finding the Best Solution:** Optimization problems involve finding the best solution from a vast number of possibilities, often under certain constraints. These problems are ubiquitous in various industries, including logistics, finance, manufacturing, and transportation. Classical algorithms can struggle with the exponential complexity of these problems as the number of variables increases.
    - **Example: Finding the Shortest Delivery Route:** Consider a logistics company that needs to find the most efficient delivery routes for a fleet of trucks visiting thousands of different locations. The number of possible routes grows factorially with the number of locations, making it computationally intractable for classical computers to find the absolute shortest route in a reasonable time. Quantum algorithms, such as quantum annealing and variational quantum eigensolvers (VQE), offer the potential to find near-optimal or even optimal solutions for such complex routing problems much faster. This could lead to significant cost savings in fuel consumption, delivery time, and resource allocation.
    - **Example: Supply Chain Optimization:** Optimizing complex supply chains involves managing inventory, production schedules, and transportation networks to minimize costs and maximize efficiency. Quantum computers could help in finding optimal strategies for these intricate systems, taking into account numerous variables and constraints simultaneously.
    - **Example: Traffic Flow Optimization:** In densely populated urban areas, optimizing traffic flow to reduce congestion is a significant challenge. Quantum

algorithms could potentially analyze real-time traffic data and devise optimal traffic light timings and routing strategies to improve overall traffic efficiency.

- **Potential Impact:** Quantum computing could lead to significant improvements in efficiency, cost reduction, and resource utilization across various industries by enabling the solution of complex optimization problems that are currently intractable.

✓ 4. Financial Modeling:

- **Analyzing Complex Financial Systems:** Financial markets are complex and influenced by numerous interconnected factors. Classical computers can struggle to accurately model and predict the behavior of these systems, especially when dealing with a large number of variables and uncertainties.
    - **Example: Risk Analysis:** Financial institutions need to assess and manage various types of risks, such as market risk, credit risk, and operational risk. Quantum algorithms could potentially simulate multiple market scenarios in parallel and provide more accurate and comprehensive risk assessments, leading to better decision-making and more resilient financial systems.
    - **Example: Fraud Detection:** Identifying fraudulent activities in financial transactions often involves analyzing vast datasets and detecting subtle patterns. Quantum machine learning algorithms could potentially enhance fraud detection capabilities by identifying complex anomalies more effectively than classical methods.
    - **Example: Option Pricing:** Pricing financial options accurately is a complex task that involves modeling future price movements. Quantum algorithms could potentially provide more accurate and faster option pricing models, leading to better trading strategies and risk management.
- **Potential Impact:** Quantum computing could revolutionize financial modeling by enabling more accurate risk analysis, enhanced fraud detection, improved algorithmic trading strategies, and more efficient portfolio optimization.

✓ 5. Artificial Intelligence and Machine Learning:

- **Boosting Training Speed and Model Complexity:** Training complex machine learning models on large datasets can be computationally very expensive and time-consuming for classical computers. Quantum Machine Learning (QML) explores the potential of using quantum algorithms to speed up the training process and enable the development of more powerful and complex AI models.
    - **Example: Quantum Feature Maps:** In machine learning, feature maps are used to transform input data into a higher-dimensional space where patterns can be more easily identified. Quantum computers can implement complex feature maps in a potentially more efficient way than classical computers, allowing for the development of more expressive and accurate machine learning models.
    - **Example: Quantum Optimization for Machine Learning:** Many machine learning algorithms involve optimization problems, such as finding the optimal weights for a neural network. Quantum optimization algorithms could potentially

speed up these optimization processes, leading to faster training times and better model performance.
    - **Example: Quantum Neural Networks:** Researchers are exploring the development of quantum analogs of classical neural networks that could potentially have enhanced capabilities for certain tasks, such as pattern recognition and classification.
- **Potential Impact:** Quantum computing could significantly accelerate the development and deployment of advanced AI and machine learning models, leading to breakthroughs in areas such as image recognition, natural language processing, drug discovery, and autonomous systems.

Beyond these core applications, quantum computing also holds promise in other areas, including:

- **Quantum Chemistry:** Simulating chemical reactions and molecular properties with unprecedented accuracy.
- **Fundamental Physics Research:** Exploring the mysteries of quantum mechanics and the universe.
- **Weather Forecasting and Climate Modeling:** Developing more accurate and long-term predictions.
- **Nuclear Fusion:** Simulating plasma behavior to advance fusion energy research.

Challenges and the Future:

While the potential of quantum computing is immense, it's important to note that the technology is still in its early stages of development. Building and controlling stable and scalable quantum computers is a significant engineering challenge. Error correction in quantum systems is also a crucial area of research.

Despite these challenges, the rapid progress in quantum computing hardware and software suggests a future where these powerful machines will play an increasingly important role in solving some of the world's most complex problems. As the technology matures, we can expect to see transformative applications emerge across various industries, ushering in a new era of computation and innovation.

Quantum Advantage & Limitations

Quantum computing has generated significant excitement due to its potential to outperform classical computers on certain types of problems. This superiority is often referred to as **quantum advantage** (sometimes historically called "quantum supremacy," though the latter term is increasingly avoided due to its connotations). However, it's crucial to understand that quantum computing is not a universal speedup for all computational tasks. It excels in specific domains while facing significant limitations in its current stage of development.

✸ Quantum Advantage

Quantum advantage refers to the demonstrated or potential ability of a quantum computer to solve a computational problem faster, more accurately, or with fewer resources (e.g., memory, energy) than the best-known classical algorithms running on the most powerful classical supercomputers. This advantage arises from the unique principles of quantum mechanics that qubits leverage.

Examples of Quantum Advantage (Demonstrated or Potential):

1. Google's Quantum Supremacy Experiment (2019):

- **The Problem:** Google's Sycamore processor, a 53-qubit superconducting quantum computer, was tasked with sampling the output of a pseudo-random quantum circuit. This specific problem was chosen for its difficulty for classical computers and its suitability for quantum processors.
- **The Achievement:** Google claimed that Sycamore could perform this sampling task in approximately **200 seconds**. They estimated that the most powerful classical supercomputer at the time would take around **10,000 years** to achieve a comparable result.
- **Significance:** This experiment was a significant milestone, providing the first experimental evidence that a quantum computer could indeed outperform the most powerful classical computers for a specific, albeit somewhat contrived, task. It demonstrated the potential for exponential speedups offered by quantum computation.
- **Nuances:** While groundbreaking, this experiment was met with some debate. IBM, a major player in classical and quantum computing, argued that with algorithmic improvements and more optimized classical simulations, the task could be performed on a classical supercomputer in significantly less time (though still substantial). Nevertheless, the experiment highlighted the growing computational capabilities of quantum processors.

2. Grover's Algorithm for Unstructured Search:

- **The Problem:** Imagine searching for a specific item in a large, unsorted database containing N elements. A classical algorithm would, on average, need to examine N/2 elements and in the worst case, all N elements to find the target. This results in a time complexity of O(N).
- **The Quantum Solution: Grover's algorithm** is a quantum algorithm that can solve this unstructured search problem in approximately O(N) time. This represents a **quadratic speedup** over classical search.
- **Example:** Consider a database with 1 million (106) entries. A classical search might require, on average, 500,000 steps. Grover's algorithm could potentially find the target in around 106=1000 steps. For even larger databases, this quadratic speedup becomes increasingly significant.
- **Real-World Relevance:** While searching a truly unstructured database is rare, Grover's algorithm and its variations have applications in areas like:

- **Database Searching:** Speeding up searches in large, complex datasets.
- **Optimization Problems:** Providing a quadratic speedup for certain types of optimization problems by searching the solution space more efficiently.
- **Machine Learning:** Enhancing certain machine learning algorithms.

3. Quantum Algorithms for Factoring (Shor's Algorithm):

- **The Problem:** Factoring large composite numbers into their prime factors is a computationally difficult problem for classical computers. The difficulty of this problem underpins the security of widely used public-key cryptography systems like RSA.
- **The Quantum Solution: Shor's algorithm** provides an exponential speedup for integer factorization compared to the best-known classical algorithms. For a number N, the best classical algorithms take roughly sub-exponential time, while Shor's algorithm can factor N in polynomial time.
- **Example:** Factoring a 2048-bit number, which is commonly used in RSA, would take classical supercomputers an astronomically long time (potentially billions of years). A sufficiently powerful quantum computer running Shor's algorithm could theoretically perform this factorization in a matter of hours or days.
- **Real-World Implications:** The development of fault-tolerant quantum computers capable of running Shor's algorithm would have profound implications for cybersecurity, potentially rendering current public-key encryption methods obsolete. This is a major driver for research in post-quantum cryptography.

4. Quantum Simulation:

- **The Problem:** Simulating complex quantum systems, such as molecules, materials, and fundamental particles, is extremely challenging for classical computers. The number of classical bits required to represent the state of a quantum system grows exponentially with the number of particles.
- **The Quantum Solution:** Quantum computers, being inherently quantum systems themselves, are naturally well-suited for simulating other quantum systems. They can represent the quantum states directly and evolve them according to the laws of quantum mechanics.
- **Example:** Simulating the behavior of a complex molecule to understand its properties or predict its reactivity is crucial for drug discovery and materials science. Classical computers can only handle relatively small molecules. Quantum computers hold the potential to simulate much larger and more intricate molecular systems with high accuracy.
- **Real-World Applications:** This capability has vast potential in:
  - **Drug Discovery:** Designing new drugs by simulating molecular interactions.
  - **Materials Science:** Discovering new materials with desired properties (e.g., superconductors, catalysts).
  - **Fundamental Physics:** Studying the behavior of quantum particles and fields.

⚠□ Limitations of Quantum Computing

Despite the exciting potential of quantum advantage, quantum computing currently faces significant limitations that need to be addressed for it to become a widely applicable technology.

1. Error Rates and Noise (Decoherence):

- **The Challenge:** Qubits are extremely delicate and highly susceptible to environmental noise, such as vibrations, temperature fluctuations, and electromagnetic interference. These disturbances can cause qubits to lose their quantum properties (superposition and entanglement) and collapse into classical states, leading to errors in computation. This phenomenon is called **decoherence**.
- **Impact:** High error rates make it difficult to perform long and complex quantum computations reliably. Current quantum computers are often referred to as **Noisy Intermediate-Scale Quantum (NISQ)** devices, characterized by a limited number of qubits and high error rates.
- **Example:** Imagine trying to perform a complex calculation with a series of entangled spinning coins. If even a slight breeze disturbs the coins during the process, they might randomly fall heads or tails, corrupting the computation. Similarly, noise in a quantum computer can randomly flip qubit states or destroy their superposition, leading to incorrect results.

2. Scalability (Limited Number of Qubits):

- **The Challenge:** Building quantum computers with a large number of high-quality, stable, and well-connected qubits is a significant engineering and scientific challenge. While the number of qubits in quantum processors has been increasing, current systems are still far from the number required to tackle many real-world problems that promise significant quantum advantage, especially those requiring fault tolerance.
- **Impact:** The limited number of qubits restricts the size and complexity of the quantum algorithms that can be implemented. Many promising quantum algorithms require a significantly larger number of qubits with high fidelity to demonstrate a practical advantage over classical methods.
- **Example:** Shor's algorithm for factoring large numbers requires a substantial number of logical (error-corrected) qubits to break modern encryption. Current NISQ devices do not yet have the required qubit count and quality to perform such a feat.

3. Programming Complexity:

- **The Challenge:** Programming quantum computers is fundamentally different from classical programming. It requires a deep understanding of linear algebra, complex numbers, and the principles of quantum mechanics. Quantum algorithms are designed using quantum gates that manipulate the probabilistic amplitudes of qubit states.
- **Impact:** The specialized knowledge required makes quantum programming challenging for traditional software developers. Furthermore, quantum programs behave **probabilistically**, meaning that running the same quantum algorithm multiple times on the same input may yield different outcomes. The desired result is obtained by analyzing the probabilities of the different measurement outcomes.

- **Example:** A classical program for adding two numbers will always produce the same deterministic output. In contrast, a quantum algorithm might produce a probability distribution over different possible answers. The programmer needs to design the algorithm such that the desired answer has a high probability of being measured.

4. Limited Hardware Access:

- **The Challenge:** Quantum hardware is currently rare, expensive to build and maintain, and not widely accessible. Building and operating quantum computers requires specialized infrastructure and expertise.
- **Impact:** Most researchers and developers currently access quantum hardware through cloud platforms offered by companies like IBM (IBM Quantum Experience), Google (Google AI Quantum), Amazon (AWS Braket), and others. While these platforms provide valuable access, they can have limitations in terms of availability, queue times, and the specific hardware features offered.
- **Example:** A researcher in a university might have a brilliant idea for a new quantum algorithm but may need to wait in a queue to run their experiment on a cloud-based quantum computer due to limited availability.

🔚 Summary

Quantum computing isn't just a faster computer—it's a **different kind of computer**, based on principles from quantum physics. By understanding its evolution, real-world impact, and limitations, students can appreciate both its **promise and its complexity**.

30 multiple-choice questions (MCQs) on Quantum Computing, covering the topics you requested:

What is Quantum Computing?

1. What is the fundamental unit of information in quantum computing?
    - a) Bit
    - b) Byte
    - c) Qubit
    - d) Quantum Byte
    - Answer: c) Qubit
2. Which principle allows a qubit to exist in a combination of 0 and 1 states?
    - a) Entanglement
    - b) Superposition
    - c) Interference
    - d) Decoherence

- Answer: b) Superposition

3. What is the phenomenon where two or more qubits become linked, sharing the same fate?
   - a) Superposition
   - b) Interference
   - c) Entanglement
   - d) Decoherence
   - Answer: c) Entanglement
4. What does the term "quantum" in quantum computing refer to?
   - a) The size of the computer
   - b) The speed of computation
   - c) Principles of quantum mechanics
   - d) The type of programming language used
   - Answer: c) Principles of quantum mechanics
5. In quantum computing, what are used to manipulate the state of qubits?
   - a) Logic gates
   - b) Quantum gates
   - c) Classical circuits
   - d) Integrated circuits
   - Answer: b) Quantum gates

Evolution of Computing: Classical to Quantum

6. What were the primary switching components in first-generation computers?
   - a) Transistors
   - b) Integrated circuits
   - c) Vacuum tubes
   - d) Microprocessors
   - Answer: c) Vacuum tubes
7. Which technology replaced vacuum tubes in second-generation computers?
   - a) Integrated circuits
   - b) Transistors
   - c) Microprocessors
   - d) Quantum gates
   - Answer: b) Transistors
8. Integrated circuits, containing millions of transistors on a single chip, characterize which generation of computers?
   - a) First
   - b) Second
   - c) Third
   - d) Fourth
   - Answer: c) Third
9. The invention of the microprocessor led to the development of:
   - a) Mainframe computers
   - b) Minicomputers
   - c) Personal computers

- d) Supercomputers
- Answer: c) Personal computers

10. Which of the following is a key characteristic of fifth-generation computing?
    - a) Vacuum tubes
    - b) Transistors
    - c) Integrated circuits
    - d) Quantum computing
    - Answer: d) Quantum computing
11. Moore's Law, which states that the number of transistors on a chip doubles approximately every two years, is most closely associated with which generation of computing?
    - a) Second Generation
    - b) Third Generation
    - c) Fourth Generation
    - d) Fifth Generation
    - Answer: c) Fourth Generation
12. Which of these was one of the first general-purpose electronic digital computers?
    - a) UNIVAC
    - b) ENIAC
    - c) IBM 701
    - d) EDSAC
    - Answer: b) ENIAC
13. Which programming language was developed during the second generation of computers?
    - a) Machine Language
    - b) Assembly Language
    - c) FORTRAN
    - d) BASIC
    - Answer: c) FORTRAN
14. What technological advancement enabled the development of personal computers?
    - a) Vacuum Tubes
    - b) Transistors
    - c) Integrated Circuits
    - d) Microprocessors
    - Answer: d) Microprocessors
15. The development of the Internet occurred during which generation of computers?
    - a) Second Generation
    - b) Third Generation
    - c) Fourth Generation
    - d) Fifth Generation
    - Answer: c) Fourth Generation

Real-World Applications and Potential

16. Which quantum algorithm has the potential to break widely used encryption methods like RSA?
    - a) Grover's algorithm

- b) Shor's algorithm
- c) Deutsch-Jozsa algorithm
- d) Quantum Fourier Transform
- Answer: b) Shor's algorithm

17. Quantum computers can potentially revolutionize drug discovery by:
    - a) Simulating molecular interactions
    - b) Replacing clinical trials
    - c) Directly synthesizing drugs
    - d) Analyzing patient data
    - Answer: a) Simulating molecular interactions
18. In which of the following areas can quantum computing be applied to find optimal solutions?
    - a) Cryptography
    - b) Drug discovery
    - c) Optimization problems
    - d) All of the above
    - Answer: d) All of the above
19. Quantum computing can enhance financial modeling through applications like:
    - a) Risk analysis
    - b) Fraud detection
    - c) Option pricing
    - d) All of the above
    - Answer: d) All of the above
20. What is the term for quantum computing's potential to speed up the training of complex AI models?
    - a) Quantum supremacy
    - b) Quantum advantage
    - c) Quantum machine learning (QML)
    - d) Quantum optimization
    - Answer: c) Quantum machine learning (QML)
21. Which industry could use quantum computers to design new catalysts?
    - a) Finance
    - b) Pharmaceuticals
    - c) Materials Science
    - d) Logistics
    - Answer: c) Materials Science
22. Quantum computing can help in logistics by:
    - a) Finding shortest delivery routes
    - b) Optimizing supply chains
    - c) Improving traffic flow
    - d) All of the above
    - Answer: d) All of the above
23. What is a potential application of quantum computing in the financial industry?
    - a) Predicting stock market crashes
    - b) Optimizing investment portfolios
    - c) Detecting fraudulent transactions

- d) All of the above
- Answer: d) All of the above

24. Quantum computers could accelerate the development of new materials with specific properties for use in:
    - a) Energy storage
    - b) Electronics
    - c) Manufacturing
    - d) All of the above
    - Answer: d) All of the above
25. In drug discovery, quantum computers can assist in:
    - a) Simulating protein folding
    - b) Designing better medicines
    - c) Understanding molecular interactions
    - d) All of the above
    - Answer: d) All of the above

Quantum Advantage & Limitations

26. What does "quantum advantage" refer to?
    - a) The ability of quantum computers to solve all problems faster than classical computers
    - b) The ability of quantum computers to perform certain tasks more efficiently than classical computers
    - c) The ability of quantum computers to replace classical computers
    - d) The theoretical limit of quantum computation
    - Answer: b) The ability of quantum computers to perform certain tasks more efficiently than classical computers
27. Which quantum algorithm provides a quadratic speedup for searching an unsorted database?
    - a) Shor's algorithm
    - b) Grover's algorithm
    - c) Quantum Fourier Transform
    - d) Deutsch-Jozsa algorithm
    - Answer: b) Grover's algorithm
28. What is a major factor that causes errors in quantum computations?
    - a) Scalability
    - b) Decoherence
    - c) Programming complexity
    - d) Limited hardware access
    - Answer: b) Decoherence
29. What does NISQ stand for in the context of quantum computing?
    - a) Noisy Integrated Superconducting Qubits
    - b) Noisy Intermediate-Scale Quantum
    - c) Near Ideal Superconducting Qubits
    - d) Non-Ideal Small Quantum
    - Answer: b) Noisy Intermediate-Scale Quantum

30. Which of the following is a limitation of current quantum computers?
    - a) High error rates
    - b) Limited scalability
    - c) Programming complexity
    - d) All of the above
    - Answer: d) All of the above

20 short questions and answers on Quantum Computing:

What is Quantum Computing?

1. **Q: What is the primary difference between a classical bit and a qubit?**
    - **A:** A classical bit is either 0 or 1, while a qubit can be 0, 1, or a superposition of both.
2. **Q: What is superposition in quantum computing?**
    - **A:** The ability of a qubit to exist in multiple states (0 and 1) simultaneously.
3. **Q: What is entanglement?**
    - **A:** A phenomenon where two or more qubits are linked, and their states are correlated.
4. **Q: What are quantum gates?**
    - **A:** Operations that manipulate the states of qubits in a quantum computer.
5. **Q: What is decoherence?**
    - **A:** The loss of quantum properties (like superposition and entanglement) due to environmental noise.

Evolution of Computing: Classical to Quantum

6. **Q: What were the main components of first-generation computers?**
    - **A:** Vacuum tubes.
7. **Q: What device replaced vacuum tubes in second-generation computers?**
    - **A:** Transistors.
8. **Q: What technology characterized third-generation computers?**
    - **A:** Integrated circuits.
9. **Q: What key development enabled the creation of personal computers?**
    - **A:** Microprocessors.
10. **Q: What is the major shift in computing in the fifth generation?**
    - **A:** The emergence of quantum computing and AI.

Real-World Applications and Potential

11. **Q: Which quantum algorithm threatens current encryption methods?**
    - **A:** Shor's algorithm.
12. **Q: How can quantum computing aid in drug discovery?**
    - **A:** By simulating molecular interactions.
13. **Q: What types of problems in logistics can quantum computing optimize?**
    - **A:** Delivery routes, supply chains, traffic flow.

14. **Q: How can quantum computers improve financial modeling?**
    - **A:** Through better risk analysis, fraud detection, and option pricing.
15. **Q: What is QML?**
    - **A:** Quantum Machine Learning.

Quantum Advantage & Limitations

16. **Q: What is quantum advantage?**
    - **A:** The ability of a quantum computer to outperform classical computers on specific tasks.
17. **Q: Which quantum algorithm offers a quadratic speedup for searching unsorted lists?**
    - **A:** Grover's algorithm.
18. **Q: What is a major factor limiting the stability of qubits?**
    - **A:** Error rates and noise (decoherence).
19. **Q: What does "NISQ" stand for?**
    - **A:** Noisy Intermediate-Scale Quantum.
20. **Q: What is a significant challenge in scaling up quantum computers?**
    - **A:** Limited scalability (building more stable and connected qubits).

10 medium-length questions and answers on Quantum Computing:

What is Quantum Computing?

1. **Q: Explain the concept of superposition in quantum computing and how it differs from classical computing.**
    - **A:** In classical computing, a bit can represent either 0 or 1. In quantum computing, a qubit can exist in a superposition, meaning it can be in a combination of both 0 and 1 states simultaneously. This is a fundamental difference. Superposition allows quantum computers to explore many possibilities concurrently, offering a potential speedup for certain computations.
2. **Q: How does entanglement contribute to the power of quantum computers?**
    - **A:** Entanglement is a phenomenon where two or more qubits become interconnected in such a way that the quantum state of each qubit depends on the others, regardless of the distance separating them. Entangled qubits act as a single system, and this correlation can be harnessed to perform complex calculations that are impossible for classical computers. It allows for the creation of complex quantum circuits and algorithms.

Evolution of Computing: Classical to Quantum

3. **Q: Briefly describe the evolution of computing from vacuum tubes to microprocessors, highlighting the key advancements in each stage.**
    - **A:** The evolution began with vacuum tubes in the first generation, which were large, unreliable, and generated much heat. Transistors replaced them in the second generation, leading to smaller, more reliable computers. Integrated circuits

in the third generation allowed for further miniaturization and increased speed. The invention of the microprocessor in the fourth generation revolutionized computing, leading to personal computers and the rise of the internet.

4. **Q: What are some of the limitations of classical computers that quantum computing aims to address?**
   - **A:** Classical computers struggle with problems that involve vast numbers of possibilities, such as factoring large numbers, simulating quantum systems, and solving complex optimization problems. These problems often have exponential complexity, meaning the computational time increases exponentially with the size of the problem. Quantum computing leverages quantum phenomena to potentially solve these problems more efficiently.

Real-World Applications and Potential

5. **Q: Explain how quantum computing could revolutionize the field of drug discovery.**
   - **A:** Quantum computers can simulate molecular interactions at the quantum level with much higher accuracy than classical computers. This capability can help in understanding protein folding, designing new drugs, and predicting how drug candidates will interact with biological systems. This could significantly accelerate the drug discovery process and lead to the development of more effective treatments.
6. **Q: Discuss the potential applications of quantum computing in the financial industry.**
   - **A:** Quantum computing has the potential to transform finance by improving risk analysis, detecting fraud more effectively, optimizing investment portfolios, and enhancing algorithmic trading. Quantum computers could simulate complex market scenarios, analyze vast amounts of financial data, and identify patterns that classical computers cannot, leading to better decision-making and more efficient financial systems.

Quantum Advantage & Limitations

7. **Q: What is quantum advantage, and what are some examples of problems where it might be achieved?**
   - **A:** Quantum advantage refers to the ability of a quantum computer to solve a computational problem faster, more accurately, or more efficiently than any known classical algorithm. Examples include Shor's algorithm for factoring large numbers, Grover's algorithm for database searching, and quantum simulations of quantum systems.
8. **Q: Describe the challenges posed by decoherence in quantum computing and how researchers are trying to overcome them.**
   - **A:** Decoherence is the loss of quantum information due to interactions with the environment, causing qubits to lose their superposition and entanglement. This leads to errors in quantum computations. Researchers are working on quantum error correction techniques, developing more stable qubits, and isolating quantum systems from external noise to mitigate decoherence.

9. **Q: What are the main obstacles in scaling up quantum computers to handle more complex problems?**
    - **A:** Scaling up quantum computers involves increasing the number of qubits while maintaining their quality and connectivity. Key obstacles include:
        - Maintaining low error rates as the number of qubits increases.
        - Developing effective quantum error correction methods.
        - Engineering the complex hardware required to control and connect many qubits.
        - Improving qubit coherence times.
10. **Q: Explain why quantum computing is not expected to replace classical computing entirely.**
    - **A:** Quantum computers are best suited for specific types of problems that exploit quantum phenomena to offer a speedup. Classical computers excel at a wide range of tasks and are more practical and cost-effective for everyday computing. Quantum computing is expected to work alongside classical computing, tackling specialized computational challenges while classical computers handle general-purpose computing.

CHAPTER 2: MATHEMATICAL FOUNDATIONS

Linear Algebra Essentials for Quantum Computing

Linear algebra provides the mathematical framework for understanding quantum computing. Here's a breakdown of the key concepts with examples:

📌 Vectors

- **Definition:** A vector is an ordered set of numbers, often written as a column. In quantum computing, vectors are used to represent quantum states.
- **Classical Bits as Vectors:**
    - A classical bit can be either 0 or 1. We can represent these states as vectors:
        - |0\rangle is represented as \begin{bmatrix} 1 \ 0 \end{bmatrix}
        - |1\rangle is represented as \begin{bmatrix} 0 \ 1 \end{bmatrix}
    - In this representation, the state |0\rangle corresponds to a vector where the first element is 1 and the second is 0, while the state |1\rangle corresponds to a vector where the first element is 0 and the second is 1.
- **Qubits and Superposition:**
    - A qubit, unlike a classical bit, can exist in a superposition of both |0\rangle and |1\rangle. This is a fundamental concept in quantum computing.
    - The general state of a qubit, denoted as |\psi\rangle, can be expressed as a linear combination of the basis states:
        - |\psi\rangle = \alpha|0\rangle + \beta|1\rangle
    - Where \alpha and \beta are complex numbers called amplitudes.
    - Using the vector representation, this becomes:
        - |\psi\rangle = \alpha \begin{bmatrix} 1 \ 0 \end{bmatrix} + \beta \begin{bmatrix} 0 \ 1 \end{bmatrix} = \begin{bmatrix} \alpha \ \beta \end{bmatrix}
- **Example:**
    - Consider a qubit in the state: |\psi\rangle = \frac{1}{\sqrt{2}}|0\rangle + \frac{i}{\sqrt{2}}|1\rangle
    - Here, \alpha = \frac{1}{\sqrt{2}} and \beta = \frac{i}{\sqrt{2}} are complex numbers.
    - The vector representation of this state is: |\psi\rangle = \begin{bmatrix} \frac{1}{\sqrt{2}} \ \frac{i}{\sqrt{2}} \end{bmatrix}
    - The coefficients \alpha and \beta determine the probability of measuring the qubit in the states |0\rangle or |1\rangle, respectively.

📌 Matrices

- **Definition:** A matrix is a rectangular array of numbers arranged in rows and columns.
- **Quantum Gates as Matrices:**
    - In quantum computing, quantum gates, which perform operations on qubits, are represented by matrices.

- When a quantum gate acts on a qubit, the corresponding matrix is multiplied by the state vector of the qubit.

- **Unitary Matrices:**
    - Quantum gates are represented by unitary matrices. A matrix U is unitary if its conjugate transpose ($U^\dagger$) is also its inverse (U^{-1}), i.e., $UU^\dagger = U^\dagger U = I$, where I is the identity matrix.
    - Unitary matrices are crucial because they preserve the norm (length) of the quantum state vector. This preservation is essential for the probabilities to remain valid (i.e., the probabilities must sum to 1).
- **Example: Hadamard Gate**
    - The Hadamard gate (H) is a fundamental quantum gate that puts a qubit into an equal superposition of $|0\rangle$ and $|1\rangle$.
    - The matrix representation of the Hadamard gate is:
        - $H = \frac{1}{\sqrt{2}} \begin{bmatrix} 1 & 1 \\ 1 & -1 \end{bmatrix}$
    - Applying the Hadamard gate to the qubit in the state $|0\rangle$:
        - $H|0\rangle = \frac{1}{\sqrt{2}} \begin{bmatrix} 1 & 1 \\ 1 & -1 \end{bmatrix} \begin{bmatrix} 1 \\ 0 \end{bmatrix} = \frac{1}{\sqrt{2}} \begin{bmatrix} 1 \\ 1 \end{bmatrix} = \frac{|0\rangle + |1\rangle}{\sqrt{2}}$
    - This shows that the Hadamard gate transforms the $|0\rangle$ state into an equal superposition of $|0\rangle$ and $|1\rangle$.

📌 Complex Numbers

- **Definition:** Complex numbers are numbers of the form $z = a + bi$, where a and b are real numbers, and i is the imaginary unit, defined as $i^2 = -1$.
- **Importance in Quantum Computing:**
    - Quantum states and quantum operations involve complex numbers. The amplitudes α and β in the qubit state $|\psi\rangle = \alpha|0\rangle + \beta|1\rangle$ can be complex numbers.
    - This is essential because quantum mechanics operates in a complex vector space. The complex nature of these amplitudes is what gives quantum systems their unique properties.
- **Probability Calculation:**
    - While the amplitudes can be complex, the probabilities of measuring a qubit in a particular state are always real numbers.
    - To calculate the probability of measuring a qubit in the state $|0\rangle$ (or $|1\rangle$), we take the magnitude squared of the corresponding amplitude:
        - Probability of measuring $|0\rangle$ is $|\alpha|^2$
        - Probability of measuring $|1\rangle$ is $|\beta|^2$
    - For a complex number $z = a + bi$, the magnitude squared is calculated as $|z|^2 = a^2 + b^2$.
- **Example:**
    - Consider a qubit in the state: $|\psi\rangle = \frac{1}{2}|0\rangle + \frac{\sqrt{3}}{2}i|1\rangle$
    - Here, $\alpha = \frac{1}{2}$ and $\beta = \frac{\sqrt{3}}{2}i$

- The probability of measuring the qubit in the state $|0\rangle$ is:
    - $|\alpha|^2 = \left| \frac{1}{2} \right|^2 = \left(\frac{1}{2} \right)^2 = \frac{1}{4} = 0.25$
- The probability of measuring the qubit in the state $|1\rangle$ is:
    - $|\beta|^2 = \left| \frac{\sqrt{3}}{2}i \right|^2 = \left(\frac{\sqrt{3}}{2} \right)^2 = \frac{3}{4} = 0.75$
- As expected, the sum of the probabilities is $0.25 + 0.75 = 1$.

Probability and Complex Probability Amplitudes in Quantum Mechanics

In quantum mechanics, the concept of probability takes on a slightly different form than in classical probability. Here's a detailed explanation:

📌 Probability Amplitude

- **The Nature of Quantum Measurement:** In quantum mechanics, the outcome of a measurement on a quantum system is not deterministic until the moment of measurement. Before measurement, the system exists in a superposition of possible states.
- **Probability Amplitudes:** Instead of dealing directly with probabilities, we work with complex numbers called probability amplitudes. These amplitudes are associated with each possible outcome of a measurement.
- **Complex Coefficients:** In the expression for a quantum state, such as:

  $|\psi\rangle = \alpha|0\rangle + \beta|1\rangle$

  The coefficients α and β are the probability amplitudes. They are complex numbers that encode information about the likelihood of finding the system in the states $|0\rangle$ or $|1\rangle$, respectively.

- **Calculating Probabilities:** To obtain the actual probability of measuring a specific outcome, we take the magnitude squared of the corresponding probability amplitude.
    - If the amplitude for measuring the state $|0\rangle$ is α, then the probability of measuring $|0\rangle$ is given by:

      $P(0) = |\alpha|^2$

    - Similarly, if the amplitude for measuring the state $|1\rangle$ is β, then the probability of measuring $|1\rangle$ is:

      $P(1) = |\beta|^2$

- **Example:**

Let's say we have a qubit in the state:

$$|\psi\rangle = \frac{1}{\sqrt{2}}|0\rangle + \frac{i}{\sqrt{2}}|1\rangle$$

Here, the probability amplitude for measuring $|0\rangle$ is $\alpha = \frac{1}{\sqrt{2}}$, and the probability amplitude for measuring $|1\rangle$ is $\beta = \frac{i}{\sqrt{2}}$.

To find the probabilities:

- Probability of measuring $|0\rangle$:

  $$P(0) = |\alpha|^2 = \left| \frac{1}{\sqrt{2}} \right|^2 = \left(\frac{1}{\sqrt{2}} \right)^2 = \frac{1}{2}$$

- Probability of measuring $|1\rangle$:

  $$P(1) = |\beta|^2 = \left| \frac{i}{\sqrt{2}} \right|^2 = \left(\frac{1}{\sqrt{2}} \right)^2 = \frac{1}{2}$$

This means that there is a 50% chance of measuring the qubit in the state $|0\rangle$ and a 50% chance of measuring it in the state $|1\rangle$.

- **Born Rule:** The rule for calculating probabilities from probability amplitudes is known as the Born rule. It's a fundamental principle in quantum mechanics.
- **Why Complex Numbers?** Probability amplitudes are complex numbers because quantum mechanics describes the evolution of a system using the Schrödinger equation, which involves complex quantities. These complex amplitudes allow for phenomena like quantum interference, which are essential to quantum computing.

📌 Normalization

- **Total Probability:** A fundamental requirement in probability theory is that the sum of the probabilities of all possible outcomes must equal 1. This is also true in quantum mechanics.
- **Normalization Condition:** For the qubit state $|\psi\rangle = \alpha|0\rangle + \beta|1\rangle$, this means:

  $$|\alpha|^2 + |\beta|^2 = 1$$

- **Ensuring Valid Probabilities:** This condition ensures that when we perform a measurement, we will obtain one of the possible outcomes with certainty. In other words, the qubit must be in *some* state.
- **Normalized State:** A quantum state that satisfies this condition is said to be normalized.
- **Example:** In the previous example, we had: $|\psi\rangle = \frac{1}{\sqrt{2}}|0\rangle + \frac{i}{\sqrt{2}}|1\rangle$ We calculated: $P(0) = |\alpha|^2 = \frac{1}{2}$ $P(1) = |\beta|^2$

$= \frac{1}{2}$ The total probability is: $P(0) + P(1) = \frac{1}{2} + \frac{1}{2} = 1$ Since the total probability is 1, the state is normalized.

- **Non-Normalized Example:** Consider a state: $|\phi\rangle = 2|0\rangle + 3|1\rangle$ Here, $\alpha = 2$ and $\beta = 3$. $|\alpha|^2 = 4$ and $|\beta|^2 = 9$ $|\alpha|^2 + |\beta|^2 = 4 + 9 = 13 \neq 1$ This state is not normalized.
- **Importance of Normalization:** Quantum states must be normalized to ensure that the probabilities calculated from the amplitudes are physically meaningful. If a state is not normalized, the calculated probabilities will not sum to 1, violating a basic principle of probability.

Basics of Quantum Mechanics for Computing

Quantum computing leverages several key principles from quantum mechanics. Here's a breakdown of the essential concepts:

📌 Superposition

- **Description:** In classical computing, a bit can only be in one of two states: 0 or 1. However, a qubit, the quantum counterpart of a bit, can exist in a superposition of both states simultaneously. This means that a qubit can be in a combination of 0 and 1.
- **Mathematical Representation:** The state of a qubit in superposition is described as a linear combination of the basis states $|0\rangle$ and $|1\rangle$:

  $$|\psi\rangle = \alpha|0\rangle + \beta|1\rangle$$

  Where α and β are complex numbers representing the probability amplitudes of the states $|0\rangle$ and $|1\rangle$, respectively.

- **Example:**

  $$|\psi\rangle = \frac{|0\rangle + |1\rangle}{\sqrt{2}}$$

  In this example:

  - $\alpha = \frac{1}{\sqrt{2}}$ and $\beta = \frac{1}{\sqrt{2}}$
  - $|\alpha|^2 = \left(\frac{1}{\sqrt{2}}\right)^2 = \frac{1}{2}$
  - $|\beta|^2 = \left(\frac{1}{\sqrt{2}}\right)^2 = \frac{1}{2}$

  This means that the qubit is in an equal superposition of $|0\rangle$ and $|1\rangle$. When measured, there is a 50% probability of finding it in the state $|0\rangle$ and a 50% probability of finding it in the state $|1\rangle$.

- **Key Idea:** Superposition allows quantum computers to explore multiple possibilities simultaneously, giving them a potential advantage over classical computers for certain tasks.

📌 Entanglement

- **Description:** Entanglement is a phenomenon where two or more qubits become linked in such a way that their fates are intertwined. The state of one qubit is correlated with the state of the other(s), regardless of the distance separating them.
- **Entangled States:** Entangled states cannot be described as independent states of individual qubits. They must be described as a joint state of the combined system.
- **Example:**

  $$|\Phi^+\rangle = \frac{|00\rangle + |11\rangle}{\sqrt{2}}$$

  This is known as a Bell state. In this state:

  - If the first qubit is measured to be $|0\rangle$, the second qubit is also guaranteed to be $|0\rangle$.
  - If the first qubit is measured to be $|1\rangle$, the second qubit is also guaranteed to be $|1\rangle$.

  The outcomes of measurements on the two qubits are perfectly correlated.

- **Spooky Action at a Distance:** Entanglement exhibits what Einstein called "spooky action at a distance" because the correlation between the qubits is instantaneous, even if they are far apart.
- **Usefulness:** Entanglement is a crucial resource in quantum computing. It enables the creation of quantum circuits and algorithms that can perform tasks that are impossible for classical computers.

📌 Measurement

- **Description:** Measurement is the process of obtaining information about a quantum state. When a quantum state is measured, it collapses from a superposition of states to one of the basis states.
- **Wave Function Collapse:** This collapse is a fundamental aspect of quantum mechanics and is often referred to as wave function collapse. The act of measurement changes the state of the qubit.
- **Probabilistic Outcome:** The outcome of a measurement is probabilistic. The probability of collapsing to a particular basis state is determined by the square of the corresponding probability amplitude.
- **Example:**

  $$|\psi\rangle = \frac{\sqrt{3}}{2}|0\rangle + \frac{1}{2}|1\rangle$$

In this example:

- \alpha = \frac{\sqrt{3}}{2} and \beta = \frac{1}{2}
- P(0) = |\alpha|^2 = \left(\frac{\sqrt{3}}{2}\right)^2 = \frac{3}{4} = 0.75
- P(1) = |\beta|^2 = \left(\frac{1}{2}\right)^2 = \frac{1}{4} = 0.25

When this qubit is measured:

- There is a 75% chance that the state will collapse to |0\rangle.
- There is a 25% chance that the state will collapse to |1\rangle.

After the measurement, the qubit is no longer in a superposition. It is definitively in either the state |0\rangle or the state |1\rangle.

- **Key Points:**
  - Measurement is irreversible. The information about the superposition is lost.
  - The probabilities of the measurement outcomes are determined by the Born rule.

✅ Summary and Learning Outcomes

By the end of this chapter, students will:

- Understand how vectors and matrices represent quantum states and operations.
- Grasp the role of **complex numbers** in quantum amplitude.
- Be able to calculate **probabilities** from amplitudes.
- Recognize key **quantum principles** like superposition and entanglement.
- Build the mathematical foundation needed to explore **quantum gates and algorithms** in later chapters.

10 practical questions and answers covering the essentials:

Linear Algebra Essentials

1. **Q: Represent the following qubit state as a vector: |\psi\rangle = \frac{1}{\sqrt{3}}|0\rangle - \frac{\sqrt{2}}{\sqrt{3}}i|1\rangle**
   - **A:** The vector representation is: \begin{bmatrix} \frac{1}{\sqrt{3}} \ - \frac{\sqrt{2}}{\sqrt{3}}i \end{bmatrix}
2. **Q: The Hadamard gate is represented by the matrix: H = \frac{1}{\sqrt{2}}\begin{bmatrix} 1 & 1 \ 1 & -1 \end{bmatrix}. Apply the Hadamard gate to the qubit state |1\rangle (represented as \begin{bmatrix} 0 \ 1**

$\end{bmatrix}$) and express the resulting state as a linear combination of $|0\rangle$ and $|1\rangle$.

- **A:**
  - $H|1\rangle = \frac{1}{\sqrt{2}}\begin{bmatrix} 1 & 1 \\ 1 & -1 \end{bmatrix}\begin{bmatrix} 0 \\ 1 \end{bmatrix} = \frac{1}{\sqrt{2}}\begin{bmatrix} 1 \\ -1 \end{bmatrix}$
  - Resulting state: $\frac{1}{\sqrt{2}}|0\rangle - \frac{1}{\sqrt{2}}|1\rangle$

3. **Q: Calculate the magnitude squared of the complex number $z = 2 - 3i$.**
   - **A:** $|z|^2 = (2)^2 + (-3)^2 = 4 + 9 = 13$

Probability and Complex Probability Amplitudes

4. **Q: A qubit is in the state $|\psi\rangle = \frac{1}{2}|0\rangle + \frac{\sqrt{3}}{2}i|1\rangle$. What is the probability of measuring the qubit in the state $|1\rangle$?**
   - **A:** The probability of measuring $|1\rangle$ is $|\beta|^2 = \left| \frac{\sqrt{3}}{2}i \right|^2 = \left(\frac{\sqrt{3}}{2} \right)^2 = \frac{3}{4} = 0.75$
5. **Q: A qubit has a probability amplitude of $\frac{1}{\sqrt{5}}$ for being in the state $|0\rangle$. If the qubit is normalized, what is the magnitude squared of the probability amplitude for being in the state $|1\rangle$?**
   - **A:**
     - Let $\alpha = \frac{1}{\sqrt{5}}$, then $|\alpha|^2 = \frac{1}{5}$.
     - Since the qubit is normalized, $|\alpha|^2 + |\beta|^2 = 1$.
     - Therefore, $|\beta|^2 = 1 - |\alpha|^2 = 1 - \frac{1}{5} = \frac{4}{5}$.

Basics of Quantum Mechanics for Computing

6. **Q: A qubit is in the superposition state $|\psi\rangle = \frac{1}{\sqrt{3}}|0\rangle + \frac{\sqrt{2}}{\sqrt{3}}|1\rangle$. What are the probabilities of measuring $|0\rangle$ and $|1\rangle$?**
   - **A:**
     - $P(0) = \left| \frac{1}{\sqrt{3}} \right|^2 = \frac{1}{3}$
     - $P(1) = \left| \frac{\sqrt{2}}{\sqrt{3}} \right|^2 = \frac{2}{3}$
7. **Q: In the context of quantum computing, explain what happens to a qubit in superposition when it is measured.**
   - **A:** When a qubit in superposition is measured, it collapses to one of the basis states, either $|0\rangle$ or $|1\rangle$. The outcome of the measurement is probabilistic, with the probability of collapsing to each state determined by the square of the corresponding probability amplitude.
8. **Q: Two qubits are in the entangled state $\frac{|01\rangle - |10\rangle}{\sqrt{2}}$. If the first qubit is measured to be $|1\rangle$, what is the state of the second qubit immediately after the measurement?**
   - **A:** If the first qubit is measured to be $|1\rangle$, the second qubit is guaranteed to be in the state $|0\rangle$. The entangled state collapses such that the second qubit is in state $|0\rangle$.

9. **Q: A quantum gate is represented by a matrix. What property must this matrix satisfy to ensure that the quantum state remains normalized after the gate is applied?**
    - **A:** The matrix representing the quantum gate must be a unitary matrix.
10. **Q: Explain why complex numbers are necessary to describe quantum states, even though probabilities are always real numbers.**
    - **A:** Complex numbers are necessary because the probability amplitudes that describe quantum states are complex. Quantum mechanics uses the Schrödinger equation, which operates in a complex vector space. While probabilities, calculated from the magnitude squared of these amplitudes, are real, the underlying quantum state and its evolution are fundamentally described using complex numbers.

30 multiple-choice questions with answers, covering the essentials:

Linear Algebra Essentials

1. **Q: Which of the following is a correct representation of the qubit state $|\psi\rangle = \alpha|0\rangle + \beta|1\rangle$ as a vector?**
    - A) \begin{bmatrix} \alpha \ \beta \end{bmatrix}
    - B) \begin{bmatrix} \beta \ \alpha \end{bmatrix}
    - C) \begin{bmatrix} \alpha \ -\beta \end{bmatrix}
    - D) \begin{bmatrix} 1 \ 1 \end{bmatrix}
    - **A:** A
2. **Q: A classical bit can be represented as a vector. Which vector represents the state $|0\rangle$?**
    - A) \begin{bmatrix} 0 \ 1 \end{bmatrix}
    - B) \begin{bmatrix} 1 \ 0 \end{bmatrix}
    - C) \begin{bmatrix} 1 \ 1 \end{bmatrix}
    - D) \begin{bmatrix} 0 \ 0 \end{bmatrix}
    - **A:** B
3. **Q: What type of matrix represents a quantum gate?**
    - A) Rectangular matrix
    - B) Diagonal matrix
    - C) Unitary matrix
    - D) Symmetric matrix
    - **A:** C
4. **Q: The Hadamard gate is given by H = \frac{1}{\sqrt{2}}\begin{bmatrix} 1 & 1 \ 1 & -1 \end{bmatrix}. If you apply this gate to the state $|0\rangle$, what is the resulting vector?**
    - A) \begin{bmatrix} 1 \ 0 \end{bmatrix}
    - B) \begin{bmatrix} 0 \ 1 \end{bmatrix}
    - C) \frac{1}{\sqrt{2}}\begin{bmatrix} 1 \ 1 \end{bmatrix}
    - D) \frac{1}{\sqrt{2}}\begin{bmatrix} 1 \ -1 \end{bmatrix}
    - **A:** C
5. **Q: What is the magnitude squared of the complex number z = a + bi?**
    - A) a^2 - b^2

- B) a^2 + b^2
- C) (a + b)^2
- D) (a - b)^2
- **A:** B

6. **Q: Calculate the magnitude squared of the complex number z = 3 - 4i.**
   - A) 25
   - B) 7
   - C) 5
   - D) -5
   - **A:** A
7. **Q: Which of the following is a property of a unitary matrix U?**
   - A) UU† = 0
   - B) UU† = I
   - C) U = U†
   - D) U† = -U
   - **A:** B
8. **Q: If a quantum gate is represented by a matrix, what kind of matrix must it be?**
   - A) Hermitian
   - B) Symmetric
   - C) Unitary
   - D) Anti-symmetric
   - **A:** C

Probability and Complex Probability Amplitudes

9. **Q: In quantum mechanics, what does the magnitude squared of a probability amplitude represent?**
   - A) The complex phase
   - B) The probability of measuring a specific outcome
   - C) The energy of the system
   - D) The uncertainty in measurement
   - **A:** B
10. **Q: For a qubit in the state $|\psi\rangle = \alpha|0\rangle + \beta|1\rangle$, what is the probability of measuring the state $|0\rangle$?**
    - A) |β|^2
    - B) |α|^2
    - C) α + β
    - D) α - β
    - **A:** B
11. **Q: A qubit is in the state $|\psi\rangle$ = \frac{1}{\sqrt{2}}|0\rangle + \frac{1}{\sqrt{2}}|1\rangle. What is the probability of measuring the state $|1\rangle$?**
    - A) 1
    - B) 0
    - C) \frac{1}{2}
    - D) \frac{1}{\sqrt{2}}
    - **A:** C

12. **Q: If a qubit is in the state $|\psi\rangle = \alpha|0\rangle + \beta|1\rangle$, what equation must be satisfied for the state to be normalized?**
    - A) $\alpha + \beta = 1$
    - B) α^2 + β^2 = 1
    - C) |α|^2 + |β|^2 = 1
    - D) $|\alpha| + |\beta| = 1$
    - **A:** C
13. **Q: A qubit has a probability amplitude of \frac{i}{\sqrt{3}} for being in the state $|1\rangle$. What is the probability of measuring the qubit in the state $|1\rangle$?**
    - A) \frac{1}{9}
    - B) \frac{1}{3}
    - C) \frac{2}{3}
    - D) 1
    - **A:** B
14. **Q: The total probability of all possible outcomes in a quantum measurement must equal:** * A) 0 * B) -1 * C) 1 * D) Infinity * **A:** C
15. **Q: Which rule is used to calculate probabilities from probability amplitudes?** * A) Pauli Exclusion Principle * B) Heisenberg Uncertainty Principle * C) Born Rule * D) Superposition Principle * **A:** C

Basics of Quantum Mechanics for Computing

16. **Q: What is the term for the ability of a qubit to be in multiple states simultaneously?** * A) Entanglement * B) Superposition * C) Measurement * D) Decoherence * **A:** B
17. **Q: In the state |\psi\rangle = \frac{|0\rangle + |1\rangle}{\sqrt{2}}, what is the probability of measuring $|0\rangle$?** * A) 0 * B) 1 * C) \frac{1}{\sqrt{2}} * D) \frac{1}{2} * **A:** D
18. **Q: What happens to a qubit in superposition when it is measured?** * A) It remains in superposition * B) It collapses to one of the basis states * C) It becomes entangled * D) It loses its quantum properties * **A:** B
19. **Q: What is the phenomenon where two qubits become linked such that the state of one instantly affects the other, regardless of the distance between them?** * A) Superposition * B) Entanglement * C) Measurement * D) Decoherence * **A:** B
20. **Q: Two qubits are in the entangled state \frac{|00\rangle + |11\rangle}{\sqrt{2}}. If the first qubit is measured to be $|0\rangle$, what is the state of the second qubit immediately after the measurement?** * A) $|0\rangle$ * B) $|1\rangle$ * C) A superposition of $|0\rangle$ and $|1\rangle$ * D) Unknown * **A:** A
21. **Q: In quantum measurement, the outcome is:** * A) Deterministic * B) Probabilistic * C) Always $|0\rangle$ * D) Always $|1\rangle$ * **A:** B
22. **Q: Which of the following is a fundamental principle of quantum mechanics?** * A) Classical determinism * B) Quantum superposition * C) Absolute certainty in measurement * D) Locality of quantum states * **A:** B
23. **Q: What is the process called when a quantum state collapses to a basis state upon measurement?** * A) Quantum entanglement * B) Quantum superposition * C) Wave function collapse * D) Quantum coherence * **A:** C

24. **Q: The state of a qubit in superposition is described by:** * A) A single binary value (0 or 1) * B) A linear combination of |0⟩ and |1⟩ * C) A classical probability distribution * D) A vector with only real number components * **A:** B
25. **Q: What is a key difference between a classical bit and a qubit?** * A) A qubit can store more information than a bit * B) A bit can be in superposition, but a qubit cannot * C) A qubit can be in superposition, but a bit cannot * D) There is no difference * **A:** C

More Challenging Questions

26. **Q: A quantum system is in the state |\psi\rangle = \frac{1}{\sqrt{3}}|0\rangle + \frac{\sqrt{2}}{\sqrt{3}}e^{i\frac{\pi}{4}}|1\rangle. What is the probability of measuring the state |1⟩?** * A) \frac{1}{3} * B) \frac{2}{3} * C) \frac{\sqrt{2}}{3} * D) \frac{2}{9} * **A:** B
27. **Q: Which gate, when applied to the |0⟩ state, creates an equal superposition of |0⟩ and |1⟩?** * A) Pauli-X gate * B) Pauli-Z gate * C) Hadamard gate * D) CNOT gate * **A:** C
28. **Q: What is the significance of unitary matrices in quantum computing?** * A) They represent irreversible operations * B) They preserve the norm of quantum state vectors * C) They introduce errors into the system * D) They are easy to implement physically * **A:** B
29. **Q: If two qubits are entangled, and one is measured to be in the state |0⟩, what does this imply about the other qubit?** * A) The other qubit must be in the state |1⟩ * B) The other qubit is also in the state |0⟩ * C) The other qubit is in a random state * D) The other qubit is destroyed * **A:** B
30. **Q: Why are complex numbers essential in quantum computing?** * A) Because they simplify probability calculations * B) Because they are required to represent the superposition of states * C) Because they make quantum computers faster * D) Because they are easier to store in a computer * **A:** B

20 short questions and answers on the essentials:

Linear Algebra Essentials

1. **Q: What is a vector?**
   - **A:** An ordered set of numbers.
2. **Q: What do vectors represent in quantum computing?**
   - **A:** Quantum states.
3. **Q: How is the classical bit |0⟩ represented as a vector?**
   - **A:** \begin{bmatrix} 1 \ 0 \end{bmatrix}
4. **Q: What is a matrix?**
   - **A:** A rectangular array of numbers.
5. **Q: What do matrices represent in quantum computing?**
   - **A:** Quantum gates.
6. **Q: What type of matrices are quantum gates?**

- **A:** Unitary matrices.

7. **Q: What is a unitary matrix?**
   - **A:** A matrix whose conjugate transpose is also its inverse.
8. **Q: What is a complex number?**
   - **A:** A number of the form a + bi, where $i^2 = -1$.

Probability and Complex Probability Amplitudes

9. **Q: What are probability amplitudes?**
   - **A:** Complex coefficients of quantum states.
10. **Q: How do you calculate probability from probability amplitude?**
    - **A:** By taking the magnitude squared.
11. **Q: If a qubit is in the state $\alpha|0\rangle + \beta|1\rangle$, what is the probability of measuring $|0\rangle$?**
    - **A:** $|\alpha|^2$
12. **Q: What must the total probability of all possible outcomes equal?**
    - **A:** 1
13. **Q: What does it mean for a quantum state to be normalized?**
    - **A:** The sum of the squares of the magnitudes of the amplitudes equals 1.

Basics of Quantum Mechanics for Computing

14. **Q: What is superposition?**
    - **A:** The ability of a qubit to be in multiple states simultaneously.
15. **Q: Can a classical bit be in superposition?**
    - **A:** No.
16. **Q: What is entanglement?**
    - **A:** The linking of two or more qubits, such that the state of one affects the others.
17. **Q: What happens when you measure a quantum state?**
    - **A:** It collapses to one of the basis states.
18. **Q: Is the outcome of a quantum measurement deterministic or probabilistic?**
    - **A:** Probabilistic.
19. **Q: If a qubit is in the state $\alpha|0\rangle + \beta|1\rangle$, and $|\alpha|^2 = 0.6$, what is the probability of measuring $|1\rangle$?**
    - **A:** 0.4
20. **Q: What are the three core principles of quantum mechanics used in quantum computing?**
    - **A:** Superposition, entanglement, and measurement.

10 medium-length questions and answers:

Linear Algebra Essentials

1. **Q: Explain how vectors are used to represent quantum states, and provide an example of how a qubit's superposition state is represented as a vector.**

- **A:** In quantum computing, vectors are used to represent the state of a quantum system. For example, a qubit's state can be represented as a linear combination of the basis states $|0\rangle$ and $|1\rangle$. If a qubit is in the state |\psi\rangle = \alpha|0\rangle + \beta|1\rangle, this state is represented by the vector \begin{bmatrix} \alpha \ \beta \end{bmatrix}. The coefficients α and β are complex numbers that define the probability amplitudes of the states $|0\rangle$ and $|1\rangle$, respectively.

2. **Q: Describe how matrices are used to represent quantum gates, and why are these matrices required to be unitary?**
   - **A:** Quantum gates, which perform operations on qubits, are represented by matrices. These matrices must be unitary because quantum operations must preserve the normalization of quantum states. A unitary matrix ensures that the total probability of all possible outcomes remains 1 after the gate is applied. This is crucial for the consistency of quantum mechanics.

Probability and Complex Probability Amplitudes

3. **Q: Explain the concept of probability amplitudes in quantum mechanics and how they differ from classical probabilities. Also, state how probabilities are calculated from probability amplitudes.**
   - **A:** In quantum mechanics, we use complex numbers called probability amplitudes to describe the likelihood of measuring a quantum system in a particular state. Unlike classical probabilities, which are real numbers between 0 and 1, probability amplitudes can be complex. The probability of measuring a state is calculated by taking the magnitude squared of its corresponding probability amplitude.
4. **Q: A qubit is in the state |\psi\rangle = \frac{1}{\sqrt{3}}|0\rangle + \frac{\sqrt{2}}{\sqrt{3}}i|1\rangle. Calculate the probability of measuring the qubit in each of the states, $|0\rangle$ and $|1\rangle$.**
   - **A:**
     - Probability of measuring $|0\rangle$: |\frac{1}{\sqrt{3}}|^2 = \frac{1}{3}
     - Probability of measuring $|1\rangle$: |\frac{\sqrt{2}}{\sqrt{3}}i|^2 = \frac{2}{3}

Basics of Quantum Mechanics for Computing

5. **Q: Describe the principle of superposition in quantum computing, and give an example of a qubit in a superposition state.**
   - **A:** Superposition is the principle that a qubit can exist in a combination of both the $|0\rangle$ and $|1\rangle$ states simultaneously. For example, a qubit in the state \frac{|0\rangle + |1\rangle}{\sqrt{2}} is in an equal superposition of $|0\rangle$ and $|1\rangle$, meaning that there is a 50% chance of measuring it in either state.
6. **Q: Explain the phenomenon of quantum entanglement, and why is it important in quantum computing?**
   - **A:** Quantum entanglement occurs when two or more qubits become linked in such a way that their states are correlated, regardless of the distance between them. This is important in quantum computing because it allows for the creation of

complex quantum states and enables quantum algorithms to perform tasks that are impossible for classical computers.

7. **Q: What happens when a measurement is performed on a qubit in superposition, and how is the outcome determined?**
    - **A:** When a measurement is performed on a qubit in superposition, the qubit collapses to one of the basis states, either $|0\rangle$ or $|1\rangle$. The outcome is probabilistic, and the probability of collapsing to a particular state is determined by the square of the magnitude of the corresponding probability amplitude.

More Challenging Questions

8. **Q: Explain how complex numbers are fundamental to quantum mechanics, even though measurement outcomes are always real numbers.**
    - **A:** Complex numbers are essential in quantum mechanics because the equations that govern the evolution of quantum systems, suchs as the Schrödinger equation, involve complex quantities. Probability amplitudes, which are the coefficients that define quantum states, are complex numbers. While the probabilities of measurement outcomes are real numbers (calculated as the magnitude squared of the amplitudes), the underlying quantum framework relies on complex numbers to describe the behavior of quantum systems.
9. **Q: Describe the process of normalization in quantum computing and why it is necessary for quantum states. Give an example of a non-normalized state and explain how to normalize it.**
    - **A:** Normalization is the process of ensuring that the total probability of all possible outcomes of a quantum state is equal to 1. This is necessary because probabilities must sum to 1. A non-normalized state is one where the sum of the squares of the magnitudes of the amplitudes is not equal to 1. For example, the state $2|0\rangle + 3|1\rangle$ is not normalized. To normalize it, divide each amplitude by the square root of the sum of the squares of the magnitudes:
        - $\sqrt{(2^2 + 3^2)} = \sqrt{13}$.
        - Normalized state: \frac{2}{\sqrt{13}}|0\rangle + \frac{3}{\sqrt{13}}|1\rangle
10. **Q: Explain how quantum gates are represented mathematically and what properties they must possess. Give an example of a quantum gate and how it operates on a single qubit.**
    - **A:** Quantum gates are represented mathematically by unitary matrices. These matrices operate on quantum state vectors to transform them from one state to another. They must be unitary to preserve the normalization of the quantum state.
        - For example, the Hadamard gate: H = \frac{1}{\sqrt{2}}\begin{bmatrix} 1 & 1 \ 1 & -1 \end{bmatrix}
        - When applied to the state $|0\rangle$:
            - H|0\rangle = \frac{1}{\sqrt{2}}\begin{bmatrix} 1 & 1 \ 1 & -1 \end{bmatrix} \begin{bmatrix} 1 \ 0 \end{bmatrix} = \frac{1}{\sqrt{2}} \begin{bmatrix} 1 \ 1 \end{bmatrix} = \frac{|0\rangle + |1\rangle}{\sqrt{2}}

CHAPTER 3: QUBITS AND QUANTUM STATES

Classical Bits vs. Quantum Bits (Qubits)

Here's a detailed explanation of the key differences between classical bits and qubits:

📌 Classical Bit

- **Definition:** A classical bit is the fundamental unit of information in classical computing. It can exist in one of two definite states, representing either a 0 or a 1.
- **States:** A classical bit can only be in one state at a time. It's either 0 or 1, with no intermediate states.
- **Representation:**
    - 0 is typically represented as 0.
    - 1 is typically represented as 1.
- **Example:**
    - A light switch is a good analogy. It can be either off (0) or on (1). There's no state in between.
    - A single binary digit in a computer's memory can store either 0 or 1.
    - The voltage in an electrical circuit can represent a bit, where a low voltage might be 0, and a high voltage might be 1.
- **Operations:** Classical computers operate on these bits using logic gates (like AND, OR, NOT), which manipulate the bits according to Boolean algebra.

📌 Quantum Bit (Qubit)

- **Definition:** A qubit is the quantum counterpart of the classical bit and the fundamental unit of information in quantum computing.
- **Superposition:** Unlike a classical bit, a qubit can exist in a superposition of both states, 0 and 1, simultaneously. This is a crucial concept in quantum mechanics.
- **State Representation:** The state of a qubit is represented using the Dirac notation (or bra-ket notation) as:
    - $|\psi\rangle = \alpha|0\rangle + \beta|1\rangle$
    - Where:
        - $|\psi\rangle$ represents the quantum state of the qubit.
        - $|0\rangle$ and $|1\rangle$ are the basis states, analogous to 0 and 1 in classical bits.
        - α and β are complex numbers called probability amplitudes.
- **Probability Amplitudes:**
    - α and β are complex numbers that determine the probabilities of measuring the qubit in the states $|0\rangle$ or $|1\rangle$.
    - The probability of measuring the qubit in the state $|0\rangle$ is given by $|\alpha|^2$.
    - The probability of measuring the qubit in the state $|1\rangle$ is given by $|\beta|^2$.
- **Normalization Condition:** The sum of the probabilities must equal 1:

    - $|\alpha|^2 + |\beta|^2 = 1$
    - This condition ensures that when you measure the qubit, you will get either 0 or 1 with certainty.
- **Example:**
    - Consider a qubit in the state: $|\psi\rangle = \frac{1}{\sqrt{2}}|0\rangle + \frac{i}{\sqrt{2}}|1\rangle$
    - Here, $\alpha = \frac{1}{\sqrt{2}}$ and $\beta = \frac{i}{\sqrt{2}}$.
    - Probability of measuring $|0\rangle$: $|\alpha|^2 = \left| \frac{1}{\sqrt{2}} \right|^2 = \frac{1}{2}$
    - Probability of measuring $|1\rangle$: $|\beta|^2 = \left| \frac{i}{\sqrt{2}} \right|^2 = \frac{1}{2}$
    - This qubit has a 50% chance of being measured as 0 and a 50% chance of being measured as 1.
- **Real-World Analogy:**
    - A classical bit is like a light switch: it's either on or off.
    - A qubit is like a spinning coin: before you observe it, it's in a combination of heads and tails. The amplitudes α and β describe how much of each state is present. When you measure the coin, it collapses to either heads or tails.

Superposition and Measurement

Here's a detailed explanation of superposition and measurement in quantum computing:

📌 Superposition

- **Description:**
    - In classical computing, a bit can only be in one of two states: 0 or 1.
    - In quantum computing, a qubit can exist in a superposition of both states simultaneously. This means that a qubit can be in a combination of both $|0\rangle$ and $|1\rangle$.
- **Mathematical Representation:**
    - The state of a qubit in superposition is described as a linear combination of the basis states $|0\rangle$ and $|1\rangle$: $|\psi\rangle = \alpha|0\rangle + \beta|1\rangle$
    - Where:
        - $|\psi\rangle$ represents the quantum state of the qubit.
        - $|0\rangle$ and $|1\rangle$ are the basis states.
        - α and β are complex numbers called probability amplitudes.
- **Example:**
    - Consider the state: $|\psi\rangle = \frac{1}{\sqrt{2}}(|0\rangle + |1\rangle)$
    - In this case:
        - $\alpha = \frac{1}{\sqrt{2}}$ and $\beta = \frac{1}{\sqrt{2}}$
        - The probability of measuring $|0\rangle$ is $|\alpha|^2 = \left(\frac{1}{\sqrt{2}}\right)^2 = \frac{1}{2} = 50\%$

        - The probability of measuring $|1\rangle$ is $|\beta|^2 = \left(\frac{1}{\sqrt{2}}\right)^2 = \frac{1}{2}$ = 50%
    - This means the qubit is in an equal superposition of $|0\rangle$ and $|1\rangle$.
- **Key Points:**
    - Superposition allows quantum computers to explore multiple possibilities simultaneously.
    - A qubit in superposition is not either 0 or 1, but rather a probabilistic combination of both.

📌 Measurement

- **Description:**
    - Measurement is the process of obtaining information about a quantum state.
    - When a qubit in superposition is measured, it collapses to one of the basis states: either $|0\rangle$ or $|1\rangle$.
    - This collapse is known as wave function collapse.
- **Probabilistic Outcome:**
    - The outcome of the measurement is probabilistic.
    - The probability of collapsing to a particular basis state is determined by the square of the magnitude of the corresponding probability amplitude.
- **Example:**
    - Consider the qubit in the state: $|\psi\rangle = \frac{\sqrt{3}}{2}|0\rangle + \frac{1}{2}|1\rangle$
    - In this case:
        - $\alpha = \frac{\sqrt{3}}{2}$ and $\beta = \frac{1}{2}$
        - The probability of measuring $|0\rangle$ is $P(0) = |\alpha|^2 = \left(\frac{\sqrt{3}}{2}\right)^2 = \frac{3}{4}$ = 75%
        - The probability of measuring $|1\rangle$ is $P(1) = |\beta|^2 = \left(\frac{1}{2}\right)^2 = \frac{1}{4}$ = 25%
    - When this qubit is measured:
        - There is a 75% chance that the state will collapse to $|0\rangle$.
        - There is a 25% chance that the state will collapse to $|1\rangle$.
    - After the measurement, the qubit is no longer in a superposition; it is definitively in either the state $|0\rangle$ or the state $|1\rangle$.
- **Key Points:**
    - Measurement is irreversible. The information about the superposition is lost.
    - The act of measurement causes the quantum state to collapse.
    - The probabilities of the measurement outcomes are determined by the Born rule.

Multiple Qubits and Tensor Products

To represent multiple qubits, we use the tensor product (denoted by $\otimes$) to combine the states of individual qubits. This allows us to describe the joint state of the multi-qubit system.

Two-Qubit Example

- **Individual Qubit States:**
  - Let's say we have two qubits, A and B, with their states defined as:
    - Qubit A: |\psi_1\rangle = |0\rangle = \begin{bmatrix} 1 \ 0 \end{bmatrix}
    - Qubit B: |\psi_2\rangle = |1\rangle = \begin{bmatrix} 0 \ 1 \end{bmatrix}
- **Combining Qubit States with Tensor Product:**
  - To find the joint state of qubits A and B, we take the tensor product of their individual state vectors:
    - |\psi\rangle = |\psi_1\rangle \otimes |\psi_2\rangle = |0\rangle \otimes |1\rangle = |01\rangle
- **Tensor Product Calculation:**
  - The tensor product of the two vectors is calculated as follows:
    - \begin{bmatrix} 1 \ 0 \end{bmatrix} \otimes \begin{bmatrix} 0 \ 1 \end{bmatrix} = \begin{bmatrix} 1 \cdot \begin{bmatrix} 0 \ 1 \end{bmatrix} \ 0 \cdot \begin{bmatrix} 0 \ 1 \end{bmatrix} \end{bmatrix} = \begin{bmatrix} 0 \ 1 \ 0 \ 0 \end{bmatrix}
- **Interpretation of the Result:**
  - The resulting vector represents the combined state of the two-qubit system. In this case, |01\rangle means that qubit A is in the state |0\rangle and qubit B is in the state |1\rangle.
  - The basis states for a two-qubit system are: |00\rangle, |01\rangle, |10\rangle, and |11\rangle. The vector \begin{bmatrix} 0 \ 1 \ 0 \ 0 \end{bmatrix} corresponds to the state |01\rangle.

Superposition with Multiple Qubits

- **Example of a Two-Qubit Superposition:**
  - Consider the following state:
    - |\psi\rangle = \frac{1}{2}(|00\rangle + |01\rangle + |10\rangle + |11\rangle)
- **Interpretation:**
  - This state represents a two-qubit system where each qubit is in a superposition. The system is in an equal superposition of all four possible two-qubit states:
    - |00\rangle: Both qubits are in the state |0\rangle.
    - |01\rangle: Qubit A is in the state |0\rangle, and qubit B is in the state |1\rangle.
    - |10\rangle: Qubit A is in the state |1\rangle, and qubit B is in the state |0\rangle.
    - |11\rangle: Both qubits are in the state |1\rangle.
  - The coefficient \frac{1}{2} ensures that the state is normalized (the sum of the squares of the amplitudes is 1).

Quantum Parallelism

- **Scaling of Quantum States:**
  - A single qubit can represent a superposition of $2^1 = 2$ states ($|0\rangle$ and $|1\rangle$).
  - Two qubits can represent a superposition of $2^2 = 4$ states ($|00\rangle$, $|01\rangle$, $|10\rangle$, and $|11\rangle$).
  - In general, *n* qubits can represent a superposition of 2^n states simultaneously.
- **Quantum Parallelism:**
  - This exponential scaling is the basis of quantum parallelism. Quantum computers can perform operations on all these 2^n states at once, allowing them to potentially solve certain problems much faster than classical computers.
- **Example:**
  - A quantum computer with 300 qubits can represent 2^{300} states simultaneously. This is a massive number, far exceeding the number of atoms in the observable universe.
- **Significance:**
  - Quantum parallelism is a key reason why quantum computers have the potential to revolutionize computing. By exploiting superposition and entanglement, they can explore a vast number of possibilities simultaneously, offering a significant speedup for certain types of calculations.

Bloch Sphere Visualization

The Bloch Sphere is a powerful tool in quantum computing that provides a geometric representation of a single qubit's state. It allows us to visualize the abstract concept of superposition and understand how quantum gates manipulate qubit states.

📌 Representation of a Qubit on the Bloch Sphere

- **Unit Sphere:** Any pure state of a single qubit can be represented as a point on the surface of a unit sphere (a sphere with radius 1).
- **Coordinates:** The position of a qubit on the Bloch Sphere is defined by two angles:
  - **θ (theta):** The angle from the vertical axis, also known as the z-axis. It ranges from 0° to 180°.
  - **φ (phi):** The angle around the z-axis, in the xy-plane. It ranges from 0° to 360°.

📌 Mathematical Representation

- The general formula for representing a qubit state using the angles θ and φ is:

  $$|\psi\rangle = \cos\left(\frac{\theta}{2}\right)|0\rangle + e^{i\varphi} \sin\left(\frac{\theta}{2}\right)|1\rangle$$

- Let's break down this equation:

   - The term $\cos(\frac{\theta}{2})$ gives the amplitude for the state $|0\rangle$.
   - The term $e^{i\varphi} \sin(\frac{\theta}{2})$ gives the amplitude for the state $|1\rangle$.
   - The factor $e^{i\varphi}$ encodes the relative phase between the states $|0\rangle$ and $|1\rangle$.

📌 Examples of Qubit States on the Bloch Sphere

- **$|0\rangle$ State:**
   - The state $|0\rangle$ is located at the North Pole of the Bloch Sphere.
   - This corresponds to $\theta = 0°$.
   - Using the formula:
      - $|\psi\rangle = \cos(0)|0\rangle + e^{i\varphi} \sin(0)|1\rangle = 1|0\rangle + 0|1\rangle = |0\rangle$
- **$|1\rangle$ State:**
   - The state $|1\rangle$ is located at the South Pole of the Bloch Sphere.
   - This corresponds to $\theta = 180°$.
   - Using the formula:
      - $|\psi\rangle = \cos(90°)|0\rangle + e^{i\varphi} \sin(90°)|1\rangle = 0|0\rangle + e^{i\varphi}1|1\rangle = e^{i\varphi}|1\rangle$
      - Since the global phase factor doesn't affect the state, we can say it's equivalent to $|1\rangle$
- **Equal Superposition State:**
   - An equal superposition state, such as $\frac{|0\rangle + |1\rangle}{\sqrt{2}}$, is located on the equator of the Bloch Sphere.
   - This corresponds to $\theta = 90°$.
   - The value of φ determines the specific superposition state. For example:
      - If $|\psi\rangle = \frac{|0\rangle + |1\rangle}{\sqrt{2}}$, then $\varphi = 0$
      - If $|\psi\rangle = \frac{|0\rangle + i|1\rangle}{\sqrt{2}}$, then $\varphi = \pi/2$

📌 Uses of the Bloch Sphere Visualization

- **Visualizing Qubit Transformations:** The Bloch Sphere provides an intuitive way to visualize how quantum gates rotate the state of a qubit. Quantum gates correspond to rotations around different axes of the sphere.
   - For example, the Pauli-X gate rotates a qubit by 180° around the x-axis.
   - The Hadamard gate rotates the qubit to an equal superposition state.
- **Understanding Phase Shifts:** The angle φ represents the phase of the qubit state. The Bloch Sphere helps visualize how quantum gates introduce phase shifts, which are crucial for quantum interference.
- **Conceptual Clarity:** The Bloch Sphere simplifies the understanding of abstract quantum states and their evolution, making it easier to grasp concepts like superposition and quantum operations.

- .

✓ Summary and Key Takeaways:

Concept	Classical Bit	Quantum Qubit
Possible States	0 or 1	Superposition of 0 and 1
Representation	1 bit	Vector in 2D complex space
Combined States	Binary sequence	Tensor product of qubit vectors
Visualization	Not Applicable	Bloch Sphere
Computation Speedup	Linear	Exponential (in certain problems)

---

10 practical questions and answers:

Classical Bits vs. Quantum Bits

1. **Q: If you have 3 classical bits, how many different states can they represent simultaneously? If you have 3 qubits, how many states can they represent simultaneously?**
   - **A:** 3 classical bits can represent only 1 state at a time. Each bit is either 0 or 1, so the 3 bits together form one specific combination (e.g., 000, 010, 111). 3 qubits, due to the principle of superposition, can exist in a combination of all possible states simultaneously. Each qubit can be in a superposition of 0 and 1, so the total number of simultaneous states is $2^3 = 8$ (000, 001, 010, 011, 100, 101, 110, 111).
2. **Q: A classical bit is like a switch. Give an example of a real-world analogy for a qubit.**
   - **A:** A classical bit is like a switch that is either on (1) or off (0). A qubit is more analogous to a spinning coin before it lands. While spinning, the coin is neither definitively heads nor tails but exists in a combination of both possibilities. Only when the coin lands (is observed) does it resolve to a definite state (heads or tails).

Superposition and Measurement

3. **Q: A qubit is in the state $|\psi\rangle = (1/\sqrt{3})|0\rangle + (\sqrt{2}/\sqrt{3})|1\rangle$. What is the probability of measuring it in the state $|1\rangle$?**
   - **A:** The probability of measuring the qubit in the state $|1\rangle$ is given by the square of the magnitude of its corresponding amplitude. The amplitude for $|1\rangle$ is $\sqrt{2}/\sqrt{3}$. Therefore, the probability is $|\sqrt{2}/\sqrt{3}|^2 = (\sqrt{2}/\sqrt{3}) * (\sqrt{2}/\sqrt{3}) = 2/3$.
4. **Q: What happens to a qubit in superposition when it is measured?**

- **A:** When a qubit in superposition is measured, it collapses to one of the basis states, either |0⟩ or |1⟩. This means that the act of measurement forces the qubit to "choose" a definite state. The outcome of the measurement is probabilistic, and the probability of collapsing to each state is determined by the square of the magnitude of the corresponding probability amplitude in the superposition.

Multiple Qubits and Tensor Products

5. **Q: Two qubits are in the states |0⟩ and |1⟩ respectively. What is the combined state of the two-qubit system?**
   - **A:** To represent the combined state of two qubits, we use the tensor product (denoted by ⊗). If the first qubit is in the state |0⟩ and the second qubit is in the state |1⟩, the combined state of the two-qubit system is |0⟩ ⊗ |1⟩, which is written as |01⟩.
6. **Q: How many states can 4 qubits represent simultaneously?**
   - **A:** Each qubit can be in a superposition of 2 states. With 4 qubits, the number of simultaneous states is 2 multiplied by itself 4 times: $2^4 = 2 * 2 * 2 * 2 = 16$ states. This exponential growth in the number of states is a key feature of quantum computing.

Bloch Sphere Visualization

7. **Q: On the Bloch sphere, where is the state |0⟩ located?**
   - **A:** The state |0⟩ is located at the North Pole of the Bloch sphere.
8. **Q: A qubit is at the South Pole of the Bloch sphere. What state does it represent?**
   - **A:** A qubit located at the South Pole of the Bloch sphere represents the state |1⟩.
9. **Q: What angles are used to define the position of a qubit on the Bloch sphere?**
   - **A:** The position of a qubit on the Bloch sphere is defined by two angles:
     - θ (theta): The angle from the vertical axis (z-axis).
     - φ (phi): The angle around the z-axis.
10. **Q: What does the Bloch sphere help us visualize?**
    - **A:** The Bloch sphere is a geometrical representation that helps us visualize single-qubit states. It provides a way to understand the abstract concept of superposition and how quantum gates (represented by rotations on the sphere) affect these states. It allows us to see how quantum gates rotate the qubit state.

30 multiple-choice questions with answers:

Classical Bits vs. Quantum Bits

1. **Q: How many states can a classical bit represent at any given time?**
   - A) 1
   - B) 2
   - C) Infinite

- D) 0 or 1
- **A:** B

2. **Q: Which of the following is true about a qubit?**
   - A) It can only be 0 or 1.
   - B) It can be in a superposition of 0 and 1.
   - C) It is always either 0 or 1.
   - D) It cannot represent any information.
   - **A:** B
3. **Q: A classical bit is analogous to:**
   - A) A spinning coin
   - B) A dimmer switch
   - C) A light switch
   - D) A wave
   - **A:** C
4. **Q: In contrast to a classical bit, a qubit can exist in a:**
   - A) Single state
   - B) Superposition of states
   - C) Definite state
   - D) Binary state
   - **A:** B
5. **Q: If a classical computer uses 'n' bits, how many states can it represent at a time?**
   - A) n
   - B) 2n
   - C) n^2
   - D) 2^n
   - **A:** A
6. **Q: If a quantum computer uses 'n' qubits, how many states can it represent simultaneously?**
   - A) n
   - B) 2n
   - C) n^2
   - D) 2^n
   - **A:** D
7. **Q: The state of a classical bit is definite, while the state of a qubit is:**
   - A) Always zero
   - B) Always one
   - C) A superposition until measured
   - D) Undefined
   - **A:** C
8. **Q: Which of the following is a fundamental difference between a bit and a qubit?**
   - A) A bit can store more information
   - B) A qubit can store more information
   - C) A bit can be in superposition
   - D) A qubit cannot be measured
   - **A:** B

Superposition and Measurement

9. **Q: What does it mean for a qubit to be in superposition?**
   - A) It is in state 0
   - B) It is in state 1
   - C) It is in a combination of state 0 and state 1
   - D) It is not in any state
   - **A:** C
10. **Q: In the quantum state $|\psi\rangle = \alpha|0\rangle + \beta|1\rangle$, what do α and β represent?**
    - A) Probabilities of measuring 0 and 1
    - B) Amplitudes of measuring 0 and 1
    - C) The energy levels
    - D) The spin of the qubit
    - **A:** B
11. **Q: What happens when a qubit in superposition is measured?**
    - A) It remains in superposition
    - B) It collapses to either state 0 or state 1
    - C) It becomes entangled
    - D) It loses its quantum properties
    - **A:** B
12. **Q: The outcome of measuring a qubit in superposition is:**
    - A) Deterministic
    - B) Probabilistic
    - C) Always 0
    - D) Always 1
    - **A:** B
13. **Q: If a qubit is in the state $|\psi\rangle = (1/2)|0\rangle + (\sqrt{3}/2)|1\rangle$, what is the probability of measuring it in the state $|0\rangle$?**
    - A) 1/2
    - B) $\sqrt{3}/2$
    - C) 1/4
    - D) 3/4
    - **A:** C
14. **Q: The act of measuring a qubit causes it to:**
    - A) Entangle
    - B) Superpose
    - C) Collapse
    - D) Rotate
    - **A:** C
15. **Q: Which principle states that a quantum system can exist in multiple states simultaneously?**
    - A) Measurement
    - B) Superposition
    - C) Entanglement
    - D) Collapse
    - **A:** B

Multiple Qubits and Tensor Products

16. **Q: What mathematical operation is used to combine the states of multiple qubits?**
    - A) Addition
    - B) Multiplication
    - C) Tensor product
    - D) Dot product
    - **A:** C
17. **Q: If you have two qubits, how many basis states does the combined system have?**
    - A) 2
    - B) 3
    - C) 4
    - D) 8
    - **A:** C
18. **Q: Two qubits are in the states |0⟩ and |1⟩, respectively. What is their combined state?**
    - A) |0⟩ + |1⟩
    - B) |0⟩ * |1⟩
    - C) |01⟩
    - D) |10⟩
    - **A:** C
19. **Q: How many qubits are needed to represent 8 simultaneous states?**
    - A) 2
    - B) 3
    - C) 4
    - D) 8
    - **A:** B
20. **Q: The tensor product of two qubits results in a state space that is:**
    - A) Smaller
    - B) The same size
    - C) Larger
    - D) Zero
    - **A:** C
21. **Q: Which of the following is a valid representation of two qubits?**
    - A) |0⟩
    - B) |1⟩
    - C) |00⟩
    - D) |+⟩
    - **A:** C

Bloch Sphere Visualization

22. **Q: What does the Bloch sphere represent?**
    - A) The state of a classical bit
    - B) The state of a single qubit
    - C) The state of multiple qubits

- D) The probability of measurement
- **A:** B

23. **Q: On the Bloch sphere, the state |0⟩ is located at the:**
    - A) South Pole
    - B) Equator
    - C) North Pole
    - D) Center
    - **A:** C
24. **Q: The state |1⟩ on the Bloch sphere is located at the:**
    - A) North Pole
    - B) Equator
    - C) South Pole
    - D) Center
    - **A:** C
25. **Q: What angles are used to define a qubit's position on the Bloch sphere?**
    - A) α and β
    - B) x and y
    - C) θ and φ
    - D) 0 and 1
    - **A:** C
26. **Q: The angle θ on the Bloch sphere is measured from the:**
    - A) x-axis
    - B) y-axis
    - C) z-axis
    - D) Equator
    - **A:** C
27. **Q: What does the Bloch sphere help visualize?**
    - A) Quantum entanglement
    - B) Quantum superposition
    - C) Qubit states and quantum gate operations
    - D) Quantum decoherence
    - **A:** C
28. **Q: A qubit in an equal superposition of |0⟩ and |1⟩ lies on the:**
    - A) North Pole
    - B) South Pole
    - C) Equator
    - D) Center
    - **A:** C
29. **Q: Which of the following is NOT represented on the Bloch Sphere?**
    - A) Superposition
    - B) Measurement
    - C) Quantum Gates
    - D) Entanglement
    - **A:** D
30. **Q: The Bloch Sphere is a visualization for:**
    - A) Single classical bits

- B) Multiple classical bits
- C) Single qubits
- D) Multiple qubits
- **A:** C

20 short questions and answers:

Classical Bits vs. Quantum Bits

1. **Q: How many states can a classical bit be in at once?**
   - **A:** One.
2. **Q: How many states can a qubit be in at once?**
   - **A:** A superposition of two states.
3. **Q: What are the two states of a classical bit?**
   - **A:** 0 and 1.
4. **Q: What is the quantum equivalent of a bit?**
   - **A:** A qubit.
5. **Q: Can a classical bit be in a superposition?**
   - **A:** No.

Superposition and Measurement

6. **Q: What is superposition?**
   - **A:** The ability of a qubit to be in multiple states simultaneously.
7. **Q: What happens when a qubit in superposition is measured?**
   - **A:** It collapses to either $|0\rangle$ or $|1\rangle$.
8. **Q: Is the outcome of a quantum measurement deterministic or probabilistic?**
   - **A:** Probabilistic.
9. **Q: What determines the probability of measuring a qubit in a specific state?**
   - **A:** The square of the magnitude of the probability amplitude.
10. **Q: What are the coefficients in the state $|\psi\rangle = \alpha|0\rangle + \beta|1\rangle$ called?**
    - **A:** Probability amplitudes.

Multiple Qubits and Tensor Products

11. **Q: What mathematical operation is used to combine the states of multiple qubits?**
    - **A:** Tensor product.
12. **Q: If you have two qubits, how many states can they represent?**
    - **A:** Four.
13. **Q: What are the basis states of a two-qubit system?**
    - **A:** $|00\rangle$, $|01\rangle$, $|10\rangle$, and $|11\rangle$.
14. **Q: How many states can 'n' qubits represent simultaneously?**
    - **A:** 2^n
15. **Q: What is the combined state of two qubits in states $|0\rangle$ and $|1\rangle$?**

- **A:** $|01\rangle$

Bloch Sphere Visualization

16. **Q: What does the Bloch sphere visualize?**
    - **A:** The state of a single qubit.
17. **Q: Where is the state $|0\rangle$ located on the Bloch sphere?**
    - **A:** The North Pole.
18. **Q: Where is the state $|1\rangle$ located on the Bloch sphere?**
    - **A:** The South Pole.
19. **Q: What angles are used to define a qubit's state on the Bloch sphere?**
    - **A:** θ (theta) and φ (phi).
20. **Q: Do pure states of a single qubit lie on the surface or inside the Bloch sphere?**
    - **A:** On the surface.

10 medium-length questions and answers:

Classical Bits vs. Quantum Bits

1. **Q: Explain the fundamental difference between a classical bit and a qubit, and why this difference is significant for computing.**
    - **A:** A classical bit can only be in one of two states (0 or 1) at any given time. A qubit, however, can exist in a superposition of both states simultaneously. This means a qubit can represent a combination of 0 and 1. This difference is significant because it allows quantum computers to perform certain computations much more efficiently than classical computers by exploring many possibilities in parallel.
2. **Q: Compare and contrast how information is stored and processed in classical computers versus quantum computers.**
    - **A:** Classical computers store and process information using classical bits, which are discrete units representing either 0 or 1. They use logic gates to manipulate these bits. Quantum computers use qubits, which can exist in superpositions. They use quantum gates to perform operations on these superpositions, allowing for parallel processing and potentially exponential speedups for specific types of problems.

Superposition and Measurement

3. **Q: Describe the concept of superposition in quantum mechanics, and provide an example of how it is represented mathematically for a single qubit.**
    - **A:** Superposition is the principle that a quantum system, like a qubit, can exist in a combination of multiple states simultaneously. For a single qubit, this is represented as |\psi\rangle = \alpha|0\rangle + \beta|1\rangle, where α and β are

complex numbers representing the probability amplitudes of the states |0⟩ and |1⟩, respectively.

4. **Q: Explain what happens when a measurement is performed on a qubit in superposition, and how the outcome of the measurement is determined.**
   - **A:** When a measurement is performed on a qubit in superposition, the qubit collapses to one of the basis states, either |0⟩ or |1⟩. The outcome of the measurement is probabilistic. The probability of collapsing to a particular state is given by the square of the magnitude of the corresponding probability amplitude. For example, the probability of measuring |0⟩ is $|\alpha|^2$.

Multiple Qubits and Tensor Products

5. **Q: Describe how the tensor product is used to represent the combined state of multiple qubits, and give an example with two qubits.**
   - **A:** The tensor product is used to combine the state spaces of individual qubits to represent the joint state of a multi-qubit system. For two qubits, if the first is in state |a⟩ and the second in state |b⟩, the combined state is |a⟩ ⊗ |b⟩, often written as |ab⟩. For example, if the first qubit is |0⟩ and the second is |1⟩, the combined state is |01⟩.
6. **Q: Explain how the number of states that can be represented simultaneously scales with the number of qubits, and why this is important for quantum computing.**
   - **A:** 'n' qubits can represent 2n states simultaneously. This exponential scaling is crucial for quantum computing because it allows quantum computers to explore a vast number of possibilities in parallel, offering potential speedups for certain computations compared to classical computers, where the number of states scales linearly.

Bloch Sphere Visualization

7. **Q: Describe how a qubit's state is represented on the Bloch sphere, including the significance of the angles θ and φ.**
   - **A:** A qubit's state is represented as a point on the surface of a unit sphere. The angle θ is the angle from the vertical (z) axis, and φ is the angle around the z-axis. These angles define the direction of the qubit's state vector.
8. **Q: Explain how the Bloch sphere helps visualize quantum gate operations, giving an example of how a quantum gate affects a qubit's state.**
   - **A:** The Bloch sphere helps visualize quantum gate operations as rotations of the qubit's state vector. For example, the Hadamard gate rotates the qubit from the |0⟩ state to a superposition state on the equator of the Bloch sphere. Different quantum gates correspond to rotations around different axes.

More Challenging Questions

9. **Q: Discuss the limitations of the Bloch sphere and why it cannot be used to visualize the states of multiple qubits.**

- **A:** The Bloch sphere is limited to visualizing the state of a *single* qubit. It cannot represent the entangled states of multiple qubits. Entangled states exist in a higher-dimensional space that cannot be accurately depicted on a 3D sphere. The Bloch sphere relies on two angles, which is insufficient to capture the correlations between multiple qubits.

10. **Q: Explain how superposition and measurement are interconnected in quantum computing, and their combined effect on the state of a qubit.**
    - **A:** Superposition allows a qubit to exist in a combination of $|0\rangle$ and $|1\rangle$ simultaneously, enabling parallel processing. Measurement, however, collapses this superposition into a single definite state, either $|0\rangle$ or $|1\rangle$. The probabilities of collapsing to these states are determined by the amplitudes of the superposition. Thus, superposition provides the computational advantage, while measurement extracts the result, albeit probabilistically.

CHAPTER 4: QUANTUM GATES AND CIRCUITS

Single-Qubit Gates

Single-qubit gates are fundamental operations in quantum computing. They operate on individual qubits, manipulating their quantum states. These gates are analogous to logic gates in classical computing but operate on superpositions of quantum states. Here's a breakdown of the common single-qubit gates:

📌 X Gate (Pauli-X) - Quantum NOT Gate

- **Description:** The X gate is the quantum equivalent of the classical NOT gate. It flips the state of a qubit.
- **Matrix Representation:** $$ X = \begin{bmatrix} 0 & 1 \ 1 & 0 \end{bmatrix} $$
- **Operation:**
  - Applies the X gate to the state |0\rangle: $$ X|0\rangle = \begin{bmatrix} 0 & 1 \ 1 & 0 \end{bmatrix} \begin{bmatrix} 1 \ 0 \end{bmatrix} = \begin{bmatrix} 0 \ 1 \end{bmatrix} = |1\rangle $$
  - Applies the X gate to the state |1\rangle: $$ X|1\rangle = \begin{bmatrix} 0 & 1 \ 1 & 0 \end{bmatrix} \begin{bmatrix} 0 \ 1 \end{bmatrix} = \begin{bmatrix} 1 \ 0 \end{bmatrix} = |0\rangle $$
- **Example:** If a qubit is in the state |0\rangle, applying the X gate transforms it to |1\rangle, and vice-versa.

📌 Y Gate (Pauli-Y) - Phase Flip + Bit Flip

- **Description:** The Y gate combines a bit-flip operation (like the X gate) with a phase flip.
- **Matrix Representation:** $$ Y = \begin{bmatrix} 0 & -i \ i & 0 \end{bmatrix} $$
- **Operation:**
  - Applies the Y gate to the state |0\rangle: $$ Y|0\rangle = \begin{bmatrix} 0 & -i \ i & 0 \end{bmatrix} \begin{bmatrix} 1 \ 0 \end{bmatrix} = \begin{bmatrix} 0 \ i \end{bmatrix} = i|1\rangle $$
  - Applies the Y gate to the state |1\rangle: $$ Y|1\rangle = \begin{bmatrix} 0 & -i \ i & 0 \end{bmatrix} \begin{bmatrix} 0 \ 1 \end{bmatrix} = \begin{bmatrix} -i \ 0 \end{bmatrix} = -i|0\rangle $$
- **Example:**
  - If a qubit is in the state |0\rangle, applying the Y gate transforms it to i|1\rangle.
  - If a qubit is in the state |1\rangle, applying the Y gate transforms it to -i|0\rangle.

📌 Z Gate (Pauli-Z) - Phase Flip

- **Description:** The Z gate flips the phase of the state |1\rangle while leaving the state |0\rangle unchanged.
- **Matrix Representation:** $$ Z = \begin{bmatrix} 1 & 0 \ 0 & -1 \end{bmatrix} $$
- **Operation:**

- Applies the Z gate to the state |0\rangle: $$ Z|0\rangle = \begin{bmatrix} 1 & 0 \ 0 & -1 \end{bmatrix} \begin{bmatrix} 1 \ 0 \end{bmatrix} = \begin{bmatrix} 1 \ 0 \end{bmatrix} = |0\rangle $$
    - Applies the Z gate to the state |1\rangle: $$ Z|1\rangle = \begin{bmatrix} 1 & 0 \ 0 & -1 \end{bmatrix} \begin{bmatrix} 0 \ 1 \end{bmatrix} = \begin{bmatrix} 0 \ -1 \end{bmatrix} = -|1\rangle $$
- **Example:**
    - If a qubit is in the state |0\rangle, applying the Z gate leaves it unchanged.
    - If a qubit is in the state |1\rangle, applying the Z gate changes its phase to -|1⟩.

📌 H Gate (Hadamard) - Creates Superposition

- **Description:** The Hadamard gate is a crucial gate in quantum computing. It creates an equal superposition of the basis states |0\rangle and |1\rangle when applied to either |0\rangle or |1\rangle.
- **Matrix Representation:** $$ H = \frac{1}{\sqrt{2}} \begin{bmatrix} 1 & 1 \ 1 & -1 \end{bmatrix} $$
- **Operation:**
    - Applies the H gate to the state |0\rangle: $$ H|0\rangle = \frac{1}{\sqrt{2}} \begin{bmatrix} 1 & 1 \ 1 & -1 \end{bmatrix} \begin{bmatrix} 1 \ 0 \end{bmatrix} = \frac{1}{\sqrt{2}} \begin{bmatrix} 1 \ 1 \end{bmatrix} = \frac{|0\rangle + |1\rangle}{\sqrt{2}} $$
    - Applies the H gate to the state |1\rangle: $$ H|1\rangle = \frac{1}{\sqrt{2}} \begin{bmatrix} 1 & 1 \ 1 & -1 \end{bmatrix} \begin{bmatrix} 0 \ 1 \end{bmatrix} = \frac{1}{\sqrt{2}} \begin{bmatrix} 1 \ -1 \end{bmatrix} = \frac{|0\rangle - |1\rangle}{\sqrt{2}} $$
- **Example:**
    - Applying the Hadamard gate to |0\rangle results in an equal superposition: \frac{|0\rangle + |1\rangle}{\sqrt{2}}.
    - Applying the Hadamard gate to |1\rangle results in another superposition: \frac{|0\rangle - |1\rangle}{\sqrt{2}}.

📌 S Gate (Phase Gate)

- **Description:** The S gate applies a $\pi/2$ (90°) phase shift to the state |1\rangle.
- **Matrix Representation:** $$ S = \begin{bmatrix} 1 & 0 \ 0 & i \end{bmatrix} $$
- **Operation:**
    - Applies the S gate to the state |0\rangle: $$ S|0\rangle = \begin{bmatrix} 1 & 0 \ 0 & i \end{bmatrix} \begin{bmatrix} 1 \ 0 \end{bmatrix} = \begin{bmatrix} 1 \ 0 \end{bmatrix} = |0\rangle $$
    - Applies the S gate to the state |1\rangle: $$ S|1\rangle = \begin{bmatrix} 1 & 0 \ 0 & i \end{bmatrix} \begin{bmatrix} 0 \ 1 \end{bmatrix} = \begin{bmatrix} 0 \ i \end{bmatrix} = i|1\rangle $$
- **Example:**
    - Applying the S gate to |0\rangle leaves it unchanged.
    - Applying the S gate to |1\rangle changes its phase to i|1⟩.

📌 T Gate (π/8 Gate)

- **Description:** The T gate applies a π/4 (45°) phase shift to the state |1\rangle.
- **Matrix Representation:** $$ T = \begin{bmatrix} 1 & 0 \ 0 & e^{i\pi/4} \end{bmatrix} $$
- **Operation:**
  - Applies the T gate to the state |0⟩: $$ T|0\rangle = \begin{bmatrix} 1 & 0 \ 0 & e^{i\pi/4} \end{bmatrix} \begin{bmatrix} 1 \ 0 \end{bmatrix} = \begin{bmatrix} 1 \ 0 \end{bmatrix} = |0\rangle $$
  - Applies the T gate to the state |1⟩:

    $$ T|1\rangle = \begin{bmatrix} 1 & 0 \ 0 & e^{i\pi/4} \end{bmatrix} \begin{bmatrix} 0 \ 1 \end{bmatrix} = \begin{bmatrix} 0 \ e^{i\pi/4} \end{bmatrix} = e^{i\pi/4}|1\rangle $$

- **Example:**
  - Applying the T gate to |0⟩ leaves it unchanged.
  - Applying the T gate to |1⟩ changes its phase to e^{i\pi/4}|1\rangle.
- **Importance of S and T gates:** The S and T gates, along with the Hadamard gate, are crucial for building universal quantum gates, which can perform any quantum computation.

Multi-Qubit Gates

Multi-qubit gates operate on two or more qubits. They are crucial for creating entanglement and performing conditional operations, which are essential for complex quantum computations. Here's a look at the key multi-qubit gates:

📌 CNOT Gate (Controlled-NOT)

- **Description:** The CNOT gate is one of the most fundamental multi-qubit gates. It operates on two qubits: a control qubit and a target qubit. The CNOT gate flips the state of the target qubit *only if* the control qubit is in the state |1\rangle. If the control qubit is in the state |0\rangle, the target qubit is left unchanged.
- **Matrix Representation:** The CNOT gate is represented by a 4x4 matrix:

  $$ \text{CNOT} = \begin{bmatrix} 1 & 0 & 0 & 0 \ 0 & 1 & 0 & 0 \ 0 & 0 & 0 & 1 \ 0 & 0 & 1 & 0 \end{bmatrix} $$

  This matrix operates on the combined state of the two qubits, which can be any of the four basis states: |00\rangle, |01\rangle, |10\rangle, and |11\rangle.

- **Operation:** Let's see how the CNOT gate affects each of the two-qubit basis states:

- **Input: $|00\rangle$ (Control=0, Target=0) → Output: $|00\rangle$** $$ \text{CNOT} |00\rangle = \begin{bmatrix} 1 & 0 & 0 & 0 \ 0 & 1 & 0 & 0 \ 0 & 0 & 0 & 1 \ 0 & 0 & 1 & 0 \end{bmatrix} \begin{bmatrix} 1 \ 0 \ 0 \ 0 \end{bmatrix} = \begin{bmatrix} 1 \ 0 \ 0 \ 0 \end{bmatrix} = |00\rangle $$ Since the control qubit is $|0\rangle$, the target qubit remains unchanged.
- **Input: $|01\rangle$ (Control=0, Target=1) → Output: $|01\rangle$** $$ \text{CNOT} |01\rangle = \begin{bmatrix} 1 & 0 & 0 & 0 \ 0 & 1 & 0 & 0 \ 0 & 0 & 0 & 1 \ 0 & 0 & 1 & 0 \end{bmatrix} \begin{bmatrix} 0 \ 1 \ 0 \ 0 \end{bmatrix} = \begin{bmatrix} 0 \ 1 \ 0 \ 0 \end{bmatrix} = |01\rangle $$ Again, the control qubit is $|0\rangle$, so the target qubit is unchanged.
- **Input: $|10\rangle$ (Control=1, Target=0) → Output: $|11\rangle$** $$ \text{CNOT} |10\rangle = \begin{bmatrix} 1 & 0 & 0 & 0 \ 0 & 1 & 0 & 0 \ 0 & 0 & 0 & 1 \ 0 & 0 & 1 & 0 \end{bmatrix} \begin{bmatrix} 0 \ 0 \ 1 \ 0 \end{bmatrix} = \begin{bmatrix} 0 \ 0 \ 0 \ 1 \end{bmatrix} = |11\rangle $$ Here, the control qubit is $|1\rangle$, so the target qubit is flipped from $|0\rangle$ to $|1\rangle$.
- **Input: $|11\rangle$ (Control=1, Target=1) → Output: $|10\rangle$** $$ \text{CNOT} |11\rangle = \begin{bmatrix} 1 & 0 & 0 & 0 \ 0 & 1 & 0 & 0 \ 0 & 0 & 0 & 1 \ 0 & 0 & 1 & 0 \end{bmatrix} \begin{bmatrix} 0 \ 0 \ 0 \ 1 \end{bmatrix} = \begin{bmatrix} 0 \ 0 \ 1 \ 0 \end{bmatrix} = |10\rangle $$ The control qubit is $|1\rangle$, so the target qubit is flipped from $|1\rangle$ to $|0\rangle$.

- **Entanglement:** The CNOT gate is crucial for creating entanglement between qubits. For example, starting with the state |00\rangle and applying a Hadamard gate to the first qubit followed by a CNOT gate, we can create the Bell state: \frac{|00\rangle + |11\rangle}{\sqrt{2}}, which is a maximally entangled state.

📌 Toffoli Gate (CCNOT)

- **Description:** The Toffoli gate is a three-qubit gate. It has two control qubits and one target qubit. The Toffoli gate flips the state of the target qubit *only if* both control qubits are in the state |1\rangle. Otherwise, the target qubit remains unchanged. It's also known as the controlled-controlled-NOT (CCNOT) gate.
- **Operation:**
  - **Input: $|110\rangle$ → Output: $|111\rangle$** (Both controls are 1, target flips)
  - **Input: $|101\rangle$ → Output: $|101\rangle$** (One control is 0, target remains unchanged)
- **Usefulness:**
  - **Reversible Classical Logic:** The Toffoli gate is important in reversible classical logic, which is a type of logic where no information is lost.
  - **Universal Quantum Gates:** The Toffoli gate, along with single-qubit gates, can be used to construct any quantum circuit. This means it's a key component in building universal quantum computers.
  - **Quantum Arithmetic and Error Correction:** The Toffoli gate is also used in quantum arithmetic operations and quantum error correction codes.

Building Quantum Circuits

A quantum circuit is a sequence of quantum gates applied to qubits to perform a specific quantum computation or execute a quantum algorithm. It's the quantum equivalent of a classical electronic circuit.

Here's a breakdown:

- **Components of a Quantum Circuit:**
  - **Qubits:** The basic units of quantum information.
  - **Quantum Gates:** Operations that manipulate the states of qubits.
  - **Measurements:** Operations that extract classical information from qubits.
- **Process:** A quantum circuit starts with qubits initialized in a known state (usually $|0\rangle$). Then, a series of quantum gates is applied to these qubits, transforming their states and creating superpositions and entanglement. Finally, measurements are performed to obtain the result of the computation.

📌 Example: Bell State Circuit

Let's illustrate this with an example of a quantum circuit that creates a Bell state, a maximally entangled state of two qubits.

- **Goal:** To create the Bell state: $$ |\Phi^+\rangle = \frac{|00\rangle + |11\rangle}{\sqrt{2}} $$
- **Circuit Steps:**
  1. **Initialize Qubits:** Start with two qubits, both initialized to the state $|0\rangle$. The combined state is $|00\rangle$.
  2. **Apply Hadamard Gate to Qubit 0:** Apply the Hadamard gate (H) to the first qubit (Qubit 0).
     - The Hadamard gate transforms the state $|0\rangle$ to an equal superposition of $|0\rangle$ and $|1\rangle$: $$ H|0\rangle = \frac{|0\rangle + |1\rangle}{\sqrt{2}} $$
     - The combined state of the two qubits becomes: $$ \left(\frac{|0\rangle + |1\rangle}{\sqrt{2}} \right) \otimes |0\rangle = \frac{|00\rangle + |10\rangle}{\sqrt{2}} $$
  3. **Apply CNOT Gate:** Apply the CNOT gate to the two qubits, with Qubit 0 as the control qubit and Qubit 1 as the target qubit.
     - The CNOT gate flips the state of the target qubit (Qubit 1) if the control qubit (Qubit 0) is in the state $|1\rangle$.
     - Applying CNOT to the state $\frac{|00\rangle + |10\rangle}{\sqrt{2}}$:
       - When Qubit 0 is $|0\rangle$, Qubit 1 remains $|0\rangle$: $|00\rangle$ remains $|00\rangle$
       - When Qubit 0 is $|1\rangle$, Qubit 1 flips from $|0\rangle$ to $|1\rangle$: $|10\rangle$ becomes $|11\rangle$
     - The final state of the two-qubit system is: $$ \frac{|00\rangle + |11\rangle}{\sqrt{2}} = |\Phi^+\rangle $$

- **Result:** The circuit has successfully created the Bell state |\Phi^+\rangle. In this state, the two qubits are entangled. If you measure Qubit 0 and find it to be in the state |0⟩, you will instantly know that Qubit 1 is also in the state |0⟩. Similarly, if you measure Qubit 0 and find it to be in the state |1⟩, Qubit 1 will also be in the state |1⟩. The measurement outcomes are perfectly correlated.

Quantum Circuit Diagrams and Reversibility

Here's a detailed explanation of quantum circuit diagrams and the reversibility of quantum gates:

📌 Quantum Circuit Diagrams

- **Description:** Quantum circuit diagrams are visual representations of quantum circuits. They provide a way to depict the sequence of quantum gates applied to qubits in a quantum computation.
- **Symbols and Conventions:**
  - **Qubit Wires:** Horizontal lines represent qubits. These lines are often called "wires," analogous to wires in classical circuits, but they represent the flow of quantum information.
  - **Time Flow:** Time flows from left to right in a quantum circuit diagram. The gates on the left act on the qubits first, and the gates on the right act later.
  - **Quantum Gates:** Quantum gates are represented by boxes or symbols. Each box represents a specific quantum gate operation.
    - `–H–`: Hadamard gate
    - `–X–`: Pauli-X gate
    - `–Z–`: Pauli-Z gate
    - `–S–`: S gate
    - `–T–`: T gate
    - –•–⊕–: CNOT gate (The • is the control qubit, and the ⊕ is the target qubit)
- **Example: Bell State Circuit Diagram**

  The Bell state circuit, which creates an entangled pair of qubits, can be represented as:

```
Qubit 0: —H—•—
            |
Qubit 1: ——⊕—
```

  In this diagram:

  - Qubit 0 starts in the state |0⟩, and the Hadamard gate (H) is applied to it first.
  - Then, the CNOT gate is applied, with Qubit 0 as the control qubit (•) and Qubit 1 as the target qubit (⊕).

    - This circuit creates the entangled Bell state: $|\Phi^+\rangle = \frac{|00\rangle + |11\rangle}{\sqrt{2}}$

📌 Reversibility of Quantum Gates

- **Description:** A fundamental property of quantum gates is that they are reversible. This means that for every quantum gate, there exists an inverse gate that can undo the operation of the original gate.
- **Implications of Reversibility:**
    - **Inverse Gates:** Every quantum gate has a corresponding inverse gate. Applying a gate followed by its inverse returns the qubits to their original state.
    - **No Information Loss:** Reversibility implies that no information is lost during quantum operations. This is crucial for maintaining quantum coherence, a property that is essential for quantum computation.
- **Reversibility in Matrix Representation:** Since quantum gates are represented by unitary matrices, and unitary matrices have inverses, quantum gates are reversible.
- **Examples of Gates and Their Inverses:**

    Here's a table showing some common quantum gates and their inverses:

Gate	Inverse
X	X
H	H
Z	Z
S	S† (S-dagger)
T	T† (T-dagger)
CNOT	CNOT

    - **X, H, Z, CNOT:** These gates are their own inverses. Applying them twice returns the qubit(s) to the original state.
    - **S† and T†:** S-dagger (S†) and T-dagger (T†) are the adjoint (conjugate transpose) of the S and T gates, respectively. They "undo" the phase shifts applied by the S and T gates.

✅ Summary and Learning Outcomes

By the end of this chapter, students will:

- Understand the matrix representations and behavior of key **single and multi-qubit gates**.
- Be able to **construct quantum circuits** to perform specific tasks.
- Visualize operations using **circuit diagrams**.
- Appreciate the importance of **reversibility** in quantum computation.

- Start exploring real-world circuits like those used in **quantum teleportation**, **Grover's**, and **Shor's algorithms**.

10 practical questions with detailed solutions:

Single-Qubit Gates

1. **Q: A qubit is initially in the state |0⟩. Apply the following sequence of gates: H, then X. What is the final state of the qubit?**
   - **A:**
     - Step 1: Apply H to |0⟩:
       - H|0⟩ = (|0⟩ + |1⟩)/√2
     - Step 2: Apply X to the result:
       - X((|0⟩ + |1⟩)/√2) = X|0⟩/√2 + X|1⟩/√2 = |1⟩/√2 + |0⟩/√2 = (|1⟩ + |0⟩)/√2
     - Final state: (|0⟩ + |1⟩)/√2
2. **Q: A qubit is in the state |1⟩. Apply the Y gate. What is the resulting state?**
   - **A:**
     - Y|1⟩ = -i|0⟩
     - Resulting state: -i|0⟩

Multi-Qubit Gates

3. **Q: Two qubits are in the state |10⟩. Apply a CNOT gate with the first qubit as the control and the second as the target. What is the final state?**
   - **A:**
     - The CNOT gate flips the target qubit if the control qubit is |1⟩.
     - In |10⟩, the first qubit (control) is |1⟩, and the second qubit (target) is |0⟩.
     - Therefore, the second qubit is flipped from |0⟩ to |1⟩.
     - Final state: |11⟩
4. **Q: Three qubits are in the state |110⟩. Apply a Toffoli gate with the first two qubits as controls and the third as the target. What is the final state?**
   - **A:**
     - The Toffoli gate flips the target qubit if both control qubits are |1⟩.
     - In |110⟩, the first two qubits (controls) are |1⟩, and the third qubit (target) is |0⟩.
     - Therefore, the third qubit is flipped from |0⟩ to |1⟩.
     - Final state: |111⟩

Building Quantum Circuits

5. **Q: Draw a quantum circuit diagram for the following operations: Start with two qubits in the state |00⟩. Apply a Hadamard gate to the first qubit, then a CNOT gate with the first qubit as control and the second as the target.**

- **A:**
- `Qubit 0: —H—•—`
- `             |`
- `Qubit 1: ——⊕—`

6. **Q: Write the sequence of gates to transform the two-qubit state |00⟩ to the state |10⟩ using only single-qubit gates (X) and the CNOT gate.**
   - **A:**
     - Step 1: Apply X to the first qubit. This transforms |00⟩ to |10⟩

Quantum Circuit Diagrams and Reversibility

7. **Q: What is the inverse of the Hadamard gate?**
   - **A:** The Hadamard gate is its own inverse. Applying it twice returns the qubit to its original state.
8. **Q: What is the inverse of the S gate? If the S gate applies a +90° phase shift, what does its inverse do?**
   - **A:** The inverse of the S gate is the S-dagger gate (S†). If the S gate applies a +90° phase shift, S† applies a -90° phase shift.
9. **Q: A quantum circuit consists of a Hadamard gate followed by a CNOT gate. Draw the circuit and then draw the inverse circuit that returns the qubits to their original state.**
   - **A:**
     - Original Circuit:
     - `Qubit 0: —H—•—`
     - `             |`
     - `Qubit 1: ——⊕—`

     - Inverse Circuit: To reverse the circuit, apply the inverse gates in the reverse order. Since H and CNOT are their own inverses:
     - `Qubit 0: —•—H—`
     - `           |`
     - `Qubit 1: —⊕——`

10. **Q: Explain why all quantum gates must be reversible. What is the implication of reversibility in quantum computation?**
    - **A:**
      - Quantum gates must be reversible because they are represented by unitary matrices, which have inverses.
      - Reversibility implies that no information is lost during quantum operations. This is a fundamental requirement to maintain quantum coherence and allows for complex quantum computations to be performed without loss of information.

30 multiple-choice questions with answers:

Single-Qubit Gates

1. **Q: Which gate is known as the Quantum NOT gate?**
   - A) Y gate
   - B) Z gate
   - C) X gate
   - D) H gate
   - **A:** C
2. **Q: What does the X gate do to the state |0⟩?**
   - A) Changes it to |1⟩
   - B) Changes it to -|0⟩
   - C) Leaves it as |0⟩
   - D) Creates a superposition
   - **A:** A
3. **Q: Which gate applies a phase flip and a bit flip?**
   - A) X gate
   - B) Y gate
   - C) Z gate
   - D) H gate
   - **A:** B
4. **Q: What does the Y gate do to the state |1⟩?**
   - A) Changes it to |0⟩
   - B) Changes it to -|1⟩
   - C) Changes it to i|0⟩
   - D) Changes it to -i|0⟩
   - **A:** D
5. **Q: Which gate flips the sign of the state |1⟩?**
   - A) X gate
   - B) Y gate
   - C) Z gate
   - D) H gate
   - **A:** C
6. **Q: What does the Z gate do to the state |0⟩?**
   - A) Changes it to |1⟩
   - B) Changes it to -|0⟩
   - C) Leaves it as |0⟩
   - D) Creates a superposition
   - **A:** C
7. **Q: Which gate creates a superposition of |0⟩ and |1⟩?**
   - A) X gate
   - B) Y gate
   - C) Z gate
   - D) H gate
   - **A:** D

8. **Q: What does the Hadamard gate (H) do to the state |0⟩?**
   - A) Changes it to |1⟩
   - B) Changes it to -|0⟩
   - C) Leaves it as |0⟩
   - D) Changes it to (|0⟩ + |1⟩)/√2
   - **A:** D
9. **Q: Which gate applies a 90° phase shift to the state |1⟩?**
   - A) X gate
   - B) S gate
   - C) Z gate
   - D) T gate
   - **A:** B
10. **Q: What does the S gate do to the state |1⟩?**
   - A) Changes it to |0⟩
   - B) Changes it to -|1⟩
   - C) Changes it to i|1⟩
   - D) Leaves it as |1⟩
   - **A:** C
11. **Q: Which gate applies a 45° phase shift to the state |1⟩?**
   - A) X gate
   - B) S gate
   - C) Z gate
   - D) T gate
   - **A:** D
12. **Q: What does the T gate do to the state |0⟩?**
   - A) Changes it to |1⟩
   - B) Changes it to -|0⟩
   - C) Leaves it as |0⟩
   - D) Changes it to e^(iπ/4)|0⟩
   - **A:** C

Multi-Qubit Gates

13. **Q: Which gate operates on two qubits, a control and a target?**
   - A) X gate
   - B) Y gate
   - C) CNOT gate
   - D) Z gate
   - **A:** C
14. **Q: The CNOT gate flips the target qubit if the control qubit is:**
   - A) |0⟩
   - B) |1⟩
   - C) In superposition
   - D) Measured
   - **A:** B
15. **Q: If the input to a CNOT gate is |10⟩ (control=1, target=0), what is the output?**

- A) |00⟩
- B) |01⟩
- C) |10⟩
- D) |11⟩
- **A:** D

16. **Q: Which gate is a controlled-controlled-NOT gate?**
    - A) CNOT gate
    - B) Hadamard gate
    - C) Toffoli gate
    - D) Z gate
    - **A:** C
17. **Q: The Toffoli gate flips the target qubit if both control qubits are:**
    - A) |0⟩
    - B) |1⟩
    - C) In superposition
    - D) Different
    - **A:** B
18. **Q: If the input to a Toffoli gate is |110⟩, what is the output?**
    - A) |000⟩
    - B) |101⟩
    - C) |110⟩
    - D) |111⟩
    - **A:** D
19. **Q: Which gate is crucial for creating entanglement between qubits?**
    - A) Z gate
    - B) T gate
    - C) CNOT gate
    - D) S gate
    - **A:** C

Building Quantum Circuits

20. **Q: What is a quantum circuit?**
    - A) A sequence of classical logic gates
    - B) A sequence of quantum gates applied to qubits
    - C) A physical arrangement of qubits
    - D) A measurement device
    - **A:** B
21. **Q: In a quantum circuit diagram, what do horizontal lines represent?**
    - A) Quantum gates
    - B) Qubit states
    - C) Qubit wires
    - D) Measurement outcomes
    - **A:** C
22. **Q: In a quantum circuit diagram, time flows from:**
    - A) Left to right

- B) Right to left
- C) Top to bottom
- D) Bottom to top
- **A:** A

23. **Q: A quantum circuit that creates the state (|00⟩ + |11⟩)/√2 uses which gates?**
    - A) X and Z
    - B) H and CNOT
    - C) S and T
    - D) Y and Toffoli
    - **A:** B

Quantum Circuit Diagrams and Reversibility

24. **Q: What does the reversibility of quantum gates mean?**
    - A) Gates can only operate in one direction
    - B) There is always an inverse gate
    - C) Gates can only be applied once
    - D) Gates change the state to zero
    - **A:** B
25. **Q: Which of the following is true about quantum gates?**
    - A) They are irreversible
    - B) They are represented by unitary matrices
    - C) They lose information
    - D) They cannot be inverted
    - **A:** B
26. **Q: Which gate is its own inverse?**
    - A) S gate
    - B) T gate
    - C) X gate
    - D) All of the above
    - **A:** C
27. **Q: If a quantum gate applies a transformation U, its inverse applies the transformation:**
    - A) -U
    - B) U^2
    - C) U†
    - D) 1/U
    - **A:** C
28. **Q: Why are quantum gates required to be reversible?**
    - A) To simplify calculations
    - B) To maintain quantum coherence
    - C) To increase speed
    - D) To allow for classical computation
    - **A:** B
29. **Q: Which of the following gates is NOT its own inverse?** * A) X * B) H * C) Z * D) S * **A:** D

30. **Q: In a quantum circuit, to reverse the operations, you apply the inverse gates in:**
    - A) The same order
    - B) The reverse order
    - C) Any order
    - D) A random order
    - **A:** B

20 short questions and answers:

Single-Qubit Gates

1. **Q: What is the X gate also known as?**
    - **A:** Quantum NOT gate.
2. **Q: What does the Y gate do?**
    - **A:** It combines a bit-flip with a phase-flip.
3. **Q: What does the Z gate do?**
    - **A:** Flips the sign of the $|1\rangle$ state.
4. **Q: Which gate creates a superposition?**
    - **A:** Hadamard gate (H).
5. **Q: What phase shift does the S gate apply?**
    - **A:** 90° phase shift.
6. **Q: What phase shift does the T gate apply?**
    - **A:** 45° phase shift.

Multi-Qubit Gates

7. **Q: Which gate is a controlled-NOT gate?**
    - **A:** CNOT gate.
8. **Q: What does the CNOT gate do?**
    - **A:** Flips the target qubit if the control qubit is $|1\rangle$.
9. **Q: Which gate is a controlled-controlled-NOT gate?**
    - **A:** Toffoli gate.
10. **Q: How many control qubits does the Toffoli gate have?**
    - **A:** Two.

Building Quantum Circuits

11. **Q: What is a quantum circuit?**
    - **A:** A sequence of quantum gates applied to qubits.
12. **Q: What are the components of a quantum circuit?**
    - **A:** Qubits, quantum gates, and measurements.
13. **Q: What is the purpose of a quantum circuit?**
    - **A:** To solve a problem or execute an algorithm.

Quantum Circuit Diagrams and Reversibility

14. **Q: What do horizontal lines in a quantum circuit diagram represent?**
    - **A:** Qubit wires.
15. **Q: In a quantum circuit diagram, which direction does time flow?**
    - **A:** Left to right.
16. **Q: Are quantum gates reversible?**
    - **A:** Yes.
17. **Q: What does the reversibility of quantum gates mean?**
    - **A:** There is always an inverse gate.
18. **Q: What is the inverse of the X gate?**
    - **A:** X gate.
19. **Q: What is the inverse of the Hadamard gate?**
    - **A:** Hadamard gate.
20. **Q: What is the inverse of the S gate?**
    - **A:** S-dagger gate (S†).

10 medium-length questions and answers:

Single-Qubit Gates

1. **Q: Explain the operation of the Pauli-Y gate. How does it affect the basis states |0⟩ and |1⟩, and what is its significance?**
    - **A:** The Pauli-Y gate performs both a bit-flip and a phase flip. It transforms |0⟩ to i|1⟩ and |1⟩ to -i|0⟩. Its significance lies in its role in quantum algorithms and quantum error correction, as it represents a fundamental rotation around the Y-axis of the Bloch sphere.
2. **Q: Describe the Hadamard gate (H) and its importance in quantum computing. What does it do to the states |0⟩ and |1⟩, and why is this useful?**
    - **A:** The Hadamard gate creates superposition. It transforms |0⟩ to (|0⟩ + |1⟩)/√2 and |1⟩ to (|0⟩ - |1⟩)/√2. This is crucial because it allows us to put qubits into a state where they represent a combination of both |0> and |1>, which is essential for quantum algorithms to explore multiple possibilities simultaneously.

Multi-Qubit Gates

3. **Q: Explain how the CNOT gate works. Describe its effect on a two-qubit system, including how it creates entanglement.**
    - **A:** The CNOT gate has a control qubit and a target qubit. If the control qubit is |1⟩, it flips the target qubit; otherwise, it leaves the target qubit unchanged. For example, CNOT applied to (|0⟩ + |1⟩)|0⟩ results in (|00⟩ + |11⟩)/√2, which is an entangled state. This gate is fundamental to creating quantum correlations.
4. **Q: Describe the Toffoli gate and its role in quantum computing. How does it differ from the CNOT gate, and where is it used?**
    - **A:** The Toffoli gate is a three-qubit gate (controlled-controlled-NOT). It flips the target qubit only if both control qubits are |1⟩. Unlike CNOT, it's a three-qubit

gate. It's used in reversible classical logic, quantum arithmetic, and constructing universal quantum gates, allowing it to perform any quantum computation.

Building Quantum Circuits

5. **Q: What is a quantum circuit, and what are its essential components? Explain the process of building a simple quantum circuit with two qubits.**
   - **A:** A quantum circuit is a sequence of quantum gates applied to qubits to perform a quantum computation. Its components are qubits, quantum gates, and measurements. A simple circuit might involve applying a Hadamard gate to one qubit, followed by a CNOT gate to entangle it with a second qubit.
6. **Q: Explain how quantum circuits are used to implement quantum algorithms. Give a simple example of a quantum circuit and its function.**
   - **A:** Quantum circuits implement quantum algorithms by applying a series of quantum gates to manipulate qubits. For instance, a circuit with Hadamard and CNOT gates can create Bell states, which are used in quantum teleportation and superdense coding.

Quantum Circuit Diagrams and Reversibility

7. **Q: Describe how quantum circuit diagrams represent quantum operations. Explain the symbols used for common gates like H and CNOT.**
   - **A:** Quantum circuit diagrams use horizontal lines ("wires") for qubits and boxes for gates, with time flowing left to right. Hadamard is shown as "H", CNOT has a control (•) and target (⊕). This provides a visual representation of the sequence of operations on qubits.
8. **Q: Explain the concept of reversibility in quantum gates. Why is reversibility a fundamental requirement for quantum computation?**
   - **A:** Reversibility means every quantum gate has an inverse. This is because quantum gates are represented by unitary matrices. Reversibility is required to ensure no information is lost during computation, which is essential for maintaining quantum coherence and performing complex quantum operations.

More Challenging Questions

9. **Q: Explain how single-qubit gates can be combined to perform arbitrary rotations on the Bloch sphere. Give an example.**
   - **A:** Any rotation on the Bloch sphere can be achieved by combining rotations around the X, Y, and Z axes, which correspond to the X, Y, and Z gates. For example, a rotation around an arbitrary axis can be decomposed into a sequence of X, Y, and Z gate operations.
10. **Q: Describe how multi-qubit gates, such as CNOT and Toffoli, are essential for creating quantum entanglement, and why entanglement is important in quantum computing.**
    - **A:** Multi-qubit gates create entanglement, a quantum phenomenon where qubits become correlated. CNOT, for instance, can create Bell states. Entanglement is

crucial because it allows quantum computers to perform operations that are impossible for classical computers, enabling exponential speedups in certain algorithms.

CHAPTER 5: QUANTUM MEASUREMENT AND ENTANGLEMENT

Measurement Postulates in Quantum Mechanics

In quantum mechanics, measurement is a fundamental process that governs how we extract information from a quantum system. It's described by a set of postulates that define the rules for what we can observe and how the quantum state changes as a result of the measurement.

Here's a detailed explanation of the measurement postulates:

📌 Postulate 1: Measurement and Collapse

- **Description:** When a measurement is performed on a quantum system, the system's state collapses (or reduces) to one of the eigenstates of the observable being measured.
- **Explanation:**
    - In quantum mechanics, an observable is a physical property that can be measured (e.g., energy, position, spin). Mathematically, observables are represented by Hermitian operators.
    - Each Hermitian operator has a set of eigenstates, which are the special states that, when acted upon by the operator, simply return a multiple of themselves (the eigenvalue).
    - Before measurement, a quantum system can be in a superposition of multiple eigenstates.
    - The act of measurement forces the system to "choose" one of these eigenstates. The system is no longer in a superposition.

📌 Postulate 2: Probability of Outcomes

- **Description:** The probability of obtaining a particular measurement outcome (i.e., a particular eigenvalue) is given by the square of the magnitude (modulus squared) of the probability amplitude associated with the corresponding eigenstate in the system's initial state.
- **Explanation:**
    - If a quantum system is in the state $|\psi\rangle$ and we measure an observable with eigenstates $|e_i\rangle$, the probability of measuring the eigenvalue corresponding to $|e_i\rangle$ is given by $|\langle e_i | \psi \rangle|^2$.
    - $\langle e_i | \psi \rangle$ is the probability amplitude, and $|\langle e_i | \psi \rangle|^2$ is always a real number between 0 and 1, as required for a probability.

📌 Postulate 3: State After Measurement

- **Description:** Immediately after the measurement, the system is left in the eigenstate corresponding to the measured eigenvalue.
- **Explanation:**

   - This postulate formalizes the idea of state collapse. The act of measuring not only gives us a result but also changes the state of the system.
   - If we measure the eigenvalue corresponding to the eigenstate $|e_i\rangle$, the system is now in the state $|e_i\rangle$, and further measurements of the same observable will yield the same eigenvalue with certainty.

✅ Example

Let's consider a qubit in the state:

$$|\psi\rangle = \frac{1}{\sqrt{3}}|0\rangle + \sqrt{\frac{2}{3}}|1\rangle$$

We are measuring in the standard basis, where the eigenstates are $|0\rangle$ and $|1\rangle$.

- **Measurement Outcomes:**
  - **Outcome $|0\rangle$:**
    - Probability $= |\langle 0 | \psi \rangle|^2 = \left| \frac{1}{\sqrt{3}} \right|^2 = \frac{1}{3}$
  - **Outcome $|1\rangle$:**
    - Probability $= |\langle 1 | \psi \rangle|^2 = \left| \sqrt{\frac{2}{3}} \right|^2 = \frac{2}{3}$
- **State After Measurement:**
  - If we measure $|0\rangle$, the qubit collapses to the state $|0\rangle$.
  - If we measure $|1\rangle$, the qubit collapses to the state $|1\rangle$.

Observables and Outcomes in Quantum Mechanics

In quantum mechanics, observables are the physical quantities that can be measured. Unlike classical mechanics, where observables are simply numbers, in quantum mechanics, they are represented by mathematical operators.

Here's a breakdown:

- **Observables:**
  - Measurable quantities in quantum mechanics (e.g., spin, energy, momentum, position).
  - Represented by Hermitian operators.
- **Hermitian Operators:**
  - Operators that are equal to their own conjugate transpose.
  - Have real eigenvalues, which correspond to the possible values that can be measured.

Example: Z Observable

Let's consider the Z observable, which corresponds to measuring the spin of a qubit along the z-axis.

- **Z Operator:** The Z operator is represented by the following 2x2 matrix:

  $$ Z = \begin{bmatrix} 1 & 0 \ 0 & -1 \end{bmatrix} $$

- **Eigenstates and Eigenvalues:**
  - Eigenstates are the special states that, when acted upon by the operator, simply return a multiple of themselves. This multiple is the eigenvalue.
  - For the Z operator:
    - The eigenstate |0\rangle = \begin{bmatrix} 1 \ 0 \end{bmatrix} has an eigenvalue of +1: $$ Z|0\rangle = \begin{bmatrix} 1 & 0 \ 0 & -1 \end{bmatrix} \begin{bmatrix} 1 \ 0 \end{bmatrix} = \begin{bmatrix} 1 \ 0 \end{bmatrix} = +1|0\rangle $$
    - The eigenstate |1\rangle = \begin{bmatrix} 0 \ 1 \end{bmatrix} has an eigenvalue of -1: $$ Z|1\rangle = \begin{bmatrix} 1 & 0 \ 0 & -1 \end{bmatrix} \begin{bmatrix} 0 \ 1 \end{bmatrix} = \begin{bmatrix} 0 \ -1 \end{bmatrix} = -1|1\rangle $$
  - Therefore, the possible outcomes of measuring the Z observable are +1 and -1.
- **Measurement and Collapse:**
  - If a qubit is in a superposition of the eigenstates of Z, such as: $$ |\psi\rangle = \alpha|0\rangle + \beta|1\rangle $$
  - And we measure the Z observable, the result will be either +1 or -1.
  - **Outcome +1:** The qubit collapses to the state |0\rangle.
  - **Outcome -1:** The qubit collapses to the state |1\rangle.
  - The probabilities of these outcomes are given by the square of the magnitudes of the amplitudes:
    - Probability of measuring +1 (and collapsing to $|0\rangle$) = |\alpha|^2
    - Probability of measuring -1 (and collapsing to $|1\rangle$) = |\beta|^2

Quantum Entanglement and EPR Pairs

Entanglement is a peculiar and profound phenomenon in quantum mechanics where two or more qubits become interconnected in such a way that their fates are intertwined. The quantum state of each qubit is dependent on the state of the other(s), regardless of the physical distance separating them.

Here's a detailed explanation:

- **Entanglement Definition:** When qubits are entangled, they form a composite quantum system where the state of one qubit cannot be described independently of the states of the other qubits. Even if the qubits are separated by vast distances, measuring the state of one instantaneously influences the state of the others. This interconnectedness is a key feature that distinguishes quantum systems from classical systems.

✅ Bell State (EPR Pair)

- **Description:** The Bell states are a set of maximally entangled states of two qubits. They are named after John Stewart Bell, who highlighted their significance in demonstrating the non-classical nature of quantum mechanics. One of the most famous Bell states is also known as an EPR pair (named after Einstein, Podolsky, and Rosen, who first described this type of entanglement).
- **Mathematical Representation:** The Bell state (EPR pair) is represented as:

  $$ |\Phi^+\rangle = \frac{|00\rangle + |11\rangle}{\sqrt{2}} $$

- **Properties of the Bell State:**
  - **Indefinite Individual States:** In this state, neither qubit has a definite state on its own. Instead, they exist in a superposition of possibilities, but their states are perfectly correlated.
  - **Correlated Measurements:** If you measure the first qubit and find it to be in the state $|0\rangle$, you will instantly know that the second qubit is also in the state $|0\rangle$. Similarly, if you measure the first qubit and find it to be in the state $|1\rangle$, the second qubit will also be in the state $|1\rangle$. This correlation holds true regardless of the distance between the two qubits.

✅ Circuit to Generate an EPR Pair

- **Steps:** A quantum circuit can be used to create an EPR pair. The circuit consists of the following steps:
  1. **Initialize Qubits:** Start with two qubits, both initialized to the state $|0\rangle$. The combined state is $|00\rangle$.
  2. **Apply Hadamard Gate to Qubit 0:** Apply the Hadamard gate (H) to the first qubit (Qubit 0). This puts Qubit 0 into a superposition:

     $$ H|0\rangle = \frac{|0\rangle + |1\rangle}{\sqrt{2}} $$

     The combined state becomes: $\frac{|00\rangle + |10\rangle}{\sqrt{2}}$

  3. **Apply CNOT Gate:** Apply the CNOT gate to the two qubits, with Qubit 0 as the control qubit and Qubit 1 as the target qubit. This entangles the two qubits.
- **Circuit Diagram:**
- `Qubit 0: ---H---•---`
- `               |`
- `Qubit 1: -------⊕---`

- **Resulting State:** After applying these gates, the resulting state of the two-qubit system is the Bell state:

  $$ \frac{|00\rangle + |11\rangle}{\sqrt{2}} $$

□ Practical Significance

- **Quantum Information Processing:** Entanglement is a crucial resource in various quantum technologies:
  - **Quantum Teleportation:** Entanglement enables the transfer of a quantum state from one location to another, even if the two locations are far apart.
  - **Superdense Coding:** Entanglement allows two bits of classical information to be transmitted using only one qubit.
  - **Quantum Cryptography:** Entanglement can be used to create highly secure communication channels.
- **Quantum Computation:** Entanglement is essential for achieving quantum advantage in many quantum algorithms:
  - **Shor's Algorithm:** Entanglement plays a key role in factoring large numbers, which has implications for cryptography.
  - **Grover's Search Algorithm:** Entanglement helps speed up the search for a specific item in an unsorted database.

Bell's Inequality and Experiments

Bell's inequality is a crucial concept in quantum mechanics that highlights the fundamental difference between quantum predictions and classical local theories. It provides a way to experimentally test whether nature behaves according to classical intuition or the seemingly bizarre rules of quantum mechanics.

Here's a detailed explanation:

- **Classical Local Realism:**
  - **Realism:** Assumes that physical properties have definite values, regardless of whether they are measured.
  - **Locality:** Assumes that measurements on one system cannot instantaneously affect the outcomes of measurements on another system, if they are separated by a large enough distance.
- **Bell's Theorem:**
  - Bell's theorem states that if classical local realism is true, then certain statistical correlations between measurement outcomes on entangled particles must satisfy a specific mathematical inequality (Bell's inequality).
  - In simpler terms, if the world behaves classically, there are limits to how strongly the results of measurements on separated particles can be correlated.

📌 Bell's Inequality

- **Mathematical Formulation:** Bell formulated a mathematical inequality that sets an upper bound on the correlations between measurement outcomes, assuming local realism. There are several forms of Bell's inequality.

📌 CHSH Inequality (A Simplified Bell Inequality)

- **Description:** The Clauser-Horne-Shimony-Holt (CHSH) inequality is a simplified version of Bell's inequality that is often used in experiments.
- **Mathematical Formulation:** Let A and B be measurements on two particles (e.g., measuring the spin of two entangled electrons) with possible outcomes of +1 or -1. A' and B' are alternative measurements on the same particles. The CHSH inequality states:

  $$ |E(A, B) + E(A', B) + E(A, B') - E(A', B')| \leq 2 $$

  Where E(X, Y) represents the expected value (correlation) of the measurement outcomes for measurements X and Y.

- **Classical Limit:** According to classical local realism, the value of the expression on the left-hand side of the inequality cannot exceed 2.
- **Quantum Prediction:** Quantum mechanics predicts that for certain entangled states, the value of this expression can be as high as $2\sqrt{2}$. This value violates the classical limit of 2.

□ Bell Test Experiments

- **EPR Paradox:** The idea behind Bell's inequality and its violation was first discussed in a 1935 paper by Albert Einstein, Boris Podolsky, and Nathan Rosen (EPR). They proposed a thought experiment to argue that quantum mechanics was incomplete because it seemed to allow for "spooky action at a distance."
- **Experimental Verification:** John Bell later formalized this idea into a testable inequality. The first conclusive experimental tests of Bell's inequality were performed by Alain Aspect and his team in the early 1980s. These experiments measured the polarization of entangled photons.
- **Results:** Aspect's experiments, and many subsequent experiments, have consistently shown that Bell's inequality is violated. The measured correlations between the entangled particles were stronger than any correlations allowed by classical local realism.

✅ Summary and Key Takeaways

By the end of this chapter, students should be able to:

- Understand how quantum measurement differs from classical observation.
- Use postulates to predict outcomes and probabilities.
- Explain quantum entanglement and its mathematical representation.
- Generate entangled states using circuits.
- Understand the philosophical and practical implications of Bell's inequality.

10 practical questions with detailed answers:

Measurement Postulates

1. **Q: A qubit is in the state $|\psi\rangle = (1/\sqrt{5})|0\rangle + (2/\sqrt{5})|1\rangle$. If you measure this qubit in the standard basis, what are the possible outcomes and their probabilities? What state is the qubit in after each possible measurement?**
    - **A:**
        - Possible Outcomes: $|0\rangle$ and $|1\rangle$.
        - Probabilities:
            - $P(|0\rangle) = |1/\sqrt{5}|^2 = 1/5$
            - $P(|1\rangle) = |2/\sqrt{5}|^2 = 4/5$
        - State After Measurement:
            - If $|0\rangle$ is measured, the qubit collapses to $|0\rangle$.
            - If $|1\rangle$ is measured, the qubit collapses to $|1\rangle$.
2. **Q: A quantum system is in the state $|\psi\rangle = (1/\sqrt{2})|00\rangle + (1/\sqrt{2})|11\rangle$. If you measure the first qubit, what are the possible outcomes for that measurement, their probabilities, and the resulting state of the system after each outcome?**
    - **A:**
        - Possible Outcomes: $|0\rangle$ and $|1\rangle$ for the first qubit.
        - Probabilities:
            - $P(|0\rangle$ for first qubit$) = |(1/\sqrt{2})|^2 = 1/2$ (The state becomes $|00\rangle$)
            - $P(|1\rangle$ for first qubit$) = |(1/\sqrt{2})|^2 = 1/2$ (The state becomes $|11\rangle$)
        - Resulting State:
            - If $|0\rangle$ is measured, the system collapses to $|00\rangle$.
            - If $|1\rangle$ is measured, the system collapses to $|11\rangle$.

Observables and Outcomes

3. **Q: The observable Sz for a spin-1/2 particle is represented by the matrix Z = [[1, 0], [0, -1]]. What are the possible outcomes of measuring Sz, and what are the corresponding eigenstates?**
    - **A:**
        - Possible Outcomes: The eigenvalues of Z, which are +1 and -1.
        - Eigenstates:
            - For eigenvalue +1: $|0\rangle$ = [[1], [0]]
            - For eigenvalue -1: $|1\rangle$ = [[0], [1]]
4. **Q: A qubit is in the state $|\psi\rangle = (\sqrt{3}/2)|+\rangle + (1/2)|-\rangle$, where $|+\rangle$ and $|-\rangle$ are the eigenstates of the X operator with eigenvalues +1 and -1, respectively. If you**

measure the observable X, what are the probabilities of obtaining the outcomes +1 and -1?

- **A:**
  - P(+1) = |√3/2|² = 3/4
  - P(-1) = |1/2|² = 1/4

Quantum Entanglement and EPR Pairs

5. **Q: Describe the Bell state |Φ+⟩ = (|00⟩ + |11⟩)/√2. Explain why it is an entangled state and what this means for measurements on the individual qubits.**
   - **A:**
     - Description: It's a two-qubit state where both qubits are in a superposition, and their states are correlated.
     - Entanglement: Neither qubit has a definite state on its own; they are interconnected.
     - Measurements: If you measure the first qubit as |0⟩, the second is guaranteed to be |0⟩. If the first is |1⟩, the second is |1⟩. The measurement outcomes are perfectly correlated.
6. **Q: How can you create the Bell state |Φ+⟩ = (|00⟩ + |11⟩)/√2 using a quantum circuit? Start with two qubits in the state |00⟩ and specify the necessary quantum gates.**
   - **A:**
     - Step 1: Apply a Hadamard gate (H) to the first qubit: H|00⟩ = (|0⟩ + |1⟩)|0⟩ / √2
     - Step 2: Apply a CNOT gate with the first qubit as control and the second as target.
     - Result: The circuit creates the state (|00⟩ + |11⟩)/√2

Bell's Inequality and Experiments

7. **Q: State the CHSH inequality. Explain what it implies about the limits of correlations between measurement outcomes if local realism is assumed.**
   - **A:**
     - CHSH Inequality: |E(A, B) + E(A', B) + E(A, B') - E(A', B')| ≤ 2
     - Implication: If local realism is true, the correlations between the measurement outcomes on the two sides cannot exceed a certain limit.
8. **Q: How does quantum mechanics violate the CHSH inequality? What is the maximum value that the CHSH expression can reach in quantum mechanics, and what does this violation imply about the nature of the quantum world?**
   - **A:**
     - Violation: Quantum mechanics predicts correlations that exceed the classical bound of 2.
     - Maximum Value: 2√2
     - Implication: The quantum world is non-local; entangled particles are interconnected in a way that classical physics cannot explain.

9. **Q: Describe the key elements of a Bell test experiment. What did the experiments conducted by Alain Aspect and others demonstrate, and what are the implications of these results?**
    - **A:**
        - Key Elements: A source of entangled particles, measurements on each particle at separate locations, and a way to measure correlations.
        - Aspect's Results: Violation of Bell's inequality.
        - Implications: Confirmed the non-local nature of quantum mechanics and ruled out local realism.
10. **Q: Explain the concept of "local realism" and how Bell's inequality challenges this concept. Why is the violation of Bell's inequality considered a fundamental result in quantum physics?**
    - **A:**
        - Local Realism: The assumption that physical properties have definite values independent of measurement (realism) and that measurements at one location cannot instantaneously affect measurements at another (locality).
        - Challenge: Bell's inequality shows that local realism places limits on correlations that quantum mechanics violates.
        - Fundamental Result: It demonstrates the non-local nature of the quantum world, a concept that has profound implications for our understanding of reality.

30 multiple-choice questions with answers:

Measurement Postulates

1. **Q: According to the measurement postulates, what happens when a measurement is performed on a quantum system?**
    - A) The system remains in superposition.
    - B) The system collapses to one of the eigenstates of the observable.
    - C) The system becomes entangled with the measurement apparatus.
    - D) The system's state is unchanged.
    - **A:** B
2. **Q: The probability of obtaining a particular outcome in a quantum measurement is given by:**
    - A) The amplitude of the corresponding eigenstate.
    - B) The square of the amplitude of the corresponding eigenstate.
    - C) The eigenvalue of the corresponding eigenstate.
    - D) The sum of the amplitudes.
    - **A:** B
3. **Q: After a measurement, the quantum system is left in:**
    - A) A superposition of all possible states.
    - B) The initial state.
    - C) The eigenstate corresponding to the measured value.
    - D) A random state.

- **A: C**

4. **Q: If a qubit is in the state $|\psi\rangle = (1/\sqrt{7})|0\rangle + (\sqrt{6}/\sqrt{7})|1\rangle$, what is the probability of measuring it in the state $|1\rangle$?**
    - A) 1/7
    - B) $\sqrt{6}/\sqrt{7}$
    - C) 6/7
    - D) 1
    - **A: C**
5. **Q: Measurement in quantum mechanics is inherently:**
    - A) Deterministic
    - B) Probabilistic
    - C) Reversible
    - D) Classical
    - **A: B**

Observables and Outcomes

6. **Q: In quantum mechanics, observables are represented by:**
    - A) Complex numbers
    - B) Hermitian operators
    - C) Unitary matrices
    - D) Probability amplitudes
    - **A: B**
7. **Q: The possible outcomes of a quantum measurement correspond to the ________ of the operator representing the observable.**
    - A) Eigenstates
    - B) Eigenvalues
    - C) Amplitudes
    - D) Probabilities
    - **A: B**
8. **Q: The Z operator for a qubit has eigenvalues:**
    - A) 0 and 1
    - B) +1 and -1
    - C) +i and -i
    - D) 0 and -1
    - **A: B**
9. **Q: If a qubit is in a superposition and we measure the observable X, the result will be one of the eigenvalues of X, and the qubit will collapse to the corresponding:**
    - A) Superposition
    - B) Eigenstate
    - C) Amplitude
    - D) Probability
    - **A: B**
10. **Q: Which of the following is a measurable quantity in quantum mechanics?**
    - A) Probability amplitude
    - B) Eigenstate

- C) Observable
- D) Unitary matrix
- **A:** C

Quantum Entanglement and EPR Pairs

11. **Q: What is quantum entanglement?**
    - A) The superposition of a single qubit
    - B) A correlation between two or more qubits where their states are interconnected
    - C) The collapse of a quantum state upon measurement
    - D) The process of applying quantum gates
    - **A:** B
12. **Q: In an entangled state:**
    - A) Each qubit has a definite state.
    - B) The qubits are independent of each other.
    - C) The state of one qubit cannot be described independently of the others.
    - D) The qubits are always in the same state.
    - **A:** C
13. **Q: Which of the following is a Bell state?**
    - A) $|0\rangle$
    - B) $|1\rangle$
    - C) $(|00\rangle + |11\rangle)/\sqrt{2}$
    - D) $(|0\rangle + |1\rangle)/\sqrt{2}$
    - **A:** C
14. **Q: If two qubits are in the Bell state $(|00\rangle + |11\rangle)/\sqrt{2}$ and you measure the first qubit to be $|1\rangle$, what will the state of the second qubit be?**
    - A) $|0\rangle$
    - B) $|1\rangle$
    - C) A superposition of $|0\rangle$ and $|1\rangle$
    - D) Undefined
    - **A:** B
15. **Q: The Bell state is also known as:**
    - A) A superposition state
    - B) An EPR pair
    - C) A classical state
    - D) A measurement outcome
    - **A:** B

Bell's Inequality and Experiments

16. **Q: Bell's inequality provides a limit on correlations between measurement outcomes based on:**
    - A) Quantum mechanics
    - B) Classical local theories
    - C) Quantum entanglement
    - D) The uncertainty principle

- **A:** B

17. **Q: If reality is local and realistic, certain statistical correlations are bounded by:**
    - A) The Schrödinger equation
    - B) Bell's inequality
    - C) Heisenberg's principle
    - D) The Pauli exclusion principle
    - **A:** B
18. **Q: Quantum entanglement ________ Bell's inequality.**
    - A) Satisfies
    - B) Violates
    - C) Ignores
    - D) Is independent of
    - **A:** B
19. **Q: The CHSH inequality is a simplified version of:**
    - A) Schrödinger's equation
    - B) Bell's inequality
    - C) Heisenberg's uncertainty principle
    - D) Pauli's exclusion principle
    - **A:** B
20. **Q: According to classical local realism, the CHSH inequality is bounded by:**
    - A) $2\sqrt{2}$
    - B) 2
    - C) 1
    - D) $\sqrt{2}$
    - **A:** B
21. **Q: Quantum mechanics predicts that the CHSH inequality can reach a maximum value of:**
    - A) 2
    - B) $\sqrt{2}$
    - C) $2\sqrt{2}$
    - D) 4
    - **A:** C
22. **Q: The violation of Bell's inequality implies that nature is not governed by:**
    - A) Quantum mechanics
    - B) Classical local hidden variables
    - C) Quantum entanglement
    - D) The uncertainty principle
    - **A:** B
23. **Q: The first experimental tests of Bell's inequality were conducted by:**
    - A) Albert Einstein
    - B) John Bell
    - C) Alain Aspect
    - D) Erwin Schrödinger
    - **A:** C
24. **Q: Bell test experiments confirm:** * A) Local realism * B) Quantum nonlocality * C) Classical physics * D) The absence of entanglement * **A:** B

25. **Q: The EPR paradox was proposed by:**
    - A) Bohr, Heisenberg, and Pauli
    - B) Einstein, Podolsky, and Rosen
    - C) Schrödinger, Dirac, and Feynman
    - D) Bell, Aspect, and Clauser
    - **A:** B
26. **Q: Bell's inequality helps distinguish between:**
    - A) Quantum and classical states of a single particle
    - B) Entangled and unentangled states
    - C) Quantum mechanics and classical local theories
    - D) Different types of quantum gates
    - **A:** C
27. **Q: The concept of "spooky action at a distance" is related to:**
    - A) Superposition
    - B) Entanglement
    - C) Measurement
    - D) Quantum tunneling
    - **A:** B
28. **Q: In Bell test experiments, what is typically measured?**
    - A) Energy levels of atoms
    - B) Polarization of photons or spin of particles
    - C) Wavelength of light
    - D) Magnetic fields
    - **A:** B
29. **Q: The violation of Bell's inequality suggests that:**
    - A) Quantum mechanics is incorrect
    - B) Information can travel faster than light
    - C) Quantum systems can be correlated in ways that classical physics cannot explain
    - D) Classical physics is complete
    - **A:** C
30. **Q: Which of the following is NOT a consequence of the violation of Bell's inequality?**
    - A) Quantum nonlocality
    - B) Rejection of local realism
    - C) The existence of entanglement
    - D) The validity of classical physics at all scales
    - **A:** D

20 short questions and answers:

Measurement Postulates

1. **Q: What happens to a quantum state when measured?**
    - **A:** It collapses to an eigenstate.
2. **Q: How is the probability of a measurement outcome determined?**

- **A:** By the square of the amplitude's modulus.

3. **Q: What does a measurement leave the system in?**
   - **A:** The corresponding eigenstate.
4. **Q: Is quantum measurement deterministic or probabilistic?**
   - **A:** Probabilistic.
5. **Q: What mathematical objects represent possible measurement results?**
   - **A:** Eigenvalues.

Observables and Outcomes

6. **Q: What mathematical objects represent observables in quantum mechanics?**
   - **A:** Hermitian operators.
7. **Q: What type of values do eigenvalues of Hermitian operators have?**
   - **A:** Real values.
8. **Q: What do the eigenvalues of an observable correspond to?**
   - **A:** Possible measurement outcomes.
9. **Q: What are the eigenstates of the Z operator?**
   - **A:** $|0\rangle$ and $|1\rangle$.
10. **Q: What are the possible outcomes of measuring the Z observable?**
    - **A:** +1 and -1.

Quantum Entanglement and EPR Pairs

11. **Q: What is quantum entanglement?**
    - **A:** Interconnectedness of qubits.
12. **Q: Can the state of one entangled qubit be described independently of the other?**
    - **A:** No.
13. **Q: What is a famous example of an entangled state?**
    - **A:** A Bell state (EPR pair).
14. **Q: What is the Bell state ($|\Phi+\rangle$)?**
    - **A:** $(|00\rangle + |11\rangle)/\sqrt{2}$
15. **Q: What happens when you measure one qubit in an EPR pair?**
    - **A:** It instantly determines the state of the other.

Bell's Inequality and Experiments

16. **Q: What does Bell's inequality provide a limit on?**
    - **A:** Correlations in local realistic theories.
17. **Q: What type of theories does Bell's inequality challenge?**
    - **A:** Classical local realistic theories.
18. **Q: Does quantum mechanics violate Bell's inequality?**
    - **A:** Yes.
19. **Q: What does the violation of Bell's inequality imply?**
    - **A:** Non-locality.
20. **Q: Who conducted key experiments testing Bell's inequality?**
    - **A:** Alain Aspect.

10 medium-length questions and answers:

Measurement Postulates

1. **Q: Explain the concept of state collapse in quantum measurement. How does it differ from measurement in classical physics?**
   - **A:** In quantum measurement, a system in a superposition collapses to a single eigenstate of the measured observable. This is unlike classical physics, where measurement simply reveals a pre-existing value without altering the system's state.
2. **Q: Describe how the Born rule is used to determine the probabilities of measurement outcomes. Provide an example.**
   - **A:** The Born rule states that the probability of measuring a particular eigenvalue is the square of the magnitude of the corresponding probability amplitude. For example, in the state $\alpha|0\rangle + \beta|1\rangle$, the probability of measuring $|1\rangle$ is $|\beta|^2$.

Observables and Outcomes

3. **Q: What is a Hermitian operator, and why is it used to represent an observable in quantum mechanics?**
   - **A:** A Hermitian operator equals its conjugate transpose. It's used because its eigenvalues are real (corresponding to measurable values), and its eigenstates form a complete basis.
4. **Q: Explain the relationship between the eigenvalues and eigenstates of an observable and the possible outcomes of a measurement.**
   - **A:** The eigenvalues of an observable's operator represent the possible measurement outcomes, and the system collapses into the corresponding eigenstate after the measurement.

Quantum Entanglement and EPR Pairs

5. **Q: Describe the characteristics of an EPR pair. Why is it considered a maximally entangled state?**
   - **A:** An EPR pair (like the Bell state $(|00\rangle + |11\rangle)/\sqrt{2}$) exhibits perfect correlations: measuring one qubit instantly determines the other's state. It's maximally entangled because the qubits have no independent definite states.
6. **Q: Explain how entanglement is used in quantum teleportation. What role does the EPR pair play in this process?**
   - **A:** In quantum teleportation, an EPR pair is shared between sender and receiver. The sender performs a joint measurement on the qubit to be teleported and her half of the EPR pair, sending the classical result to the receiver, who then performs operations on his half of the EPR pair to get the teleported qubit.

Bell's Inequality and Experiments

7. **Q: State Bell's inequality and explain the assumptions about the physical world that it tests.**
   - **A:** Bell's inequality sets a limit on correlations assuming local realism: that measurement outcomes are predetermined (realism) and that distant measurements can't affect each other instantaneously (locality).
8. **Q: Describe the CHSH inequality and how it simplifies the test of Bell's theorem. What values can the CHSH expression take in a classical vs. a quantum system?**
   - **A:** The CHSH inequality is a simplified form of Bell's inequality. Classically, it's bounded by 2; quantum mechanically, it can reach up to $2\sqrt{2}$.
9. **Q: Explain the significance of Aspect's experiments in the context of Bell's inequality. What did these experiments demonstrate about the nature of quantum mechanics?**
   - **A:** Aspect's experiments showed a clear violation of Bell's inequality, confirming quantum nonlocality and ruling out local realistic theories.
10. **Q: Discuss the implications of the violation of Bell's inequality for our understanding of space, time, and causality.**
    - **A:** The violation implies that entangled particles are connected in a way that transcends classical notions of space and time, suggesting that quantum correlations are non-local and challenging our understanding of causality.

CHAPTER 6: QUANTUM ALGORITHMS – INTRODUCTION

Oracle Model and Black-box Functions

In quantum computing, many algorithms are designed to solve problems by querying a special kind of function known as a "black-box function" or an "oracle." This approach is particularly useful for understanding the power of quantum computation, even when the specific implementation of the function is unknown.

Here's a detailed explanation:

📌 What is an Oracle?

- **Classical Oracle:** In the classical setting, an oracle is a function *f(x)* that takes an input *x* and returns a value *f(x)*. You can think of it as a black box: you provide an input, and it gives you an output, but you don't know how it computes that output.
- **Quantum Oracle:** In quantum computing, the oracle is implemented as a unitary operator, denoted as *Uf*. This operator acts on quantum states. It's still a "black box" in the sense that the internal workings of *f(x)* are hidden, but it can be queried in superposition.
- **Oracle Operation:** The quantum oracle *Uf* acts on a two-part quantum state: $|x\rangle|y\rangle$, where:
  - $|x\rangle$ is the input register, representing the input to the function.
  - $|y\rangle$ is the output register, which will store the result of the function.

  The oracle transforms this state as follows:

  $$ U_f|x\rangle|y\rangle = |x\rangle|y \oplus f(x)\rangle $$

  Where ⊕ represents the bitwise XOR (exclusive OR) operation.

- **Explanation of the Oracle Operation:**
  - The oracle leaves the input register $|x\rangle$ unchanged.
  - It modifies the output register $|y\rangle$ by XORing it with the value of the function *f(x)*. This means that if *f(x)* is 0, $|y\rangle$ remains unchanged. If *f(x)* is 1, $|y\rangle$ is flipped.

✅ Example

Suppose we have a function *f(x)* that calculates the parity of the first two bits of the input *x*. Let's say *x* has two bits, $x1$ and $x2$, and $f(x) = x1 \oplus x2$.

- **Classical Setting:** To learn anything about *f(x)*, you would have to evaluate it for different inputs:
  - $f(00) = 0 \oplus 0 = 0$

- $f(01) = 0 \oplus 1 = 1$
- $f(10) = 1 \oplus 0 = 1$
- $f(11) = 1 \oplus 1 = 0$

You would need to make multiple queries to the function to understand its behavior.

- **Quantum Setting:** In a quantum setting, we can use superposition to evaluate *f(x)* for all possible inputs "at once."

0. **Prepare Superposition:** Start with the input register in a superposition of all possible inputs:

$$ \frac{|00\rangle + |01\rangle + |10\rangle + |11\rangle}{2} $$

And the output register in the state $|0\rangle$.

1. **Apply the Oracle:** Apply the oracle *Uf* to this state:

$$ U_f \left(\frac{|00\rangle + |01\rangle + |10\rangle + |11\rangle}{2} \otimes |0\rangle \right) $$

The oracle will compute *f(x)* for each term in the superposition and XOR it with the output register:

$$ = \frac{|00\rangle|0 \oplus f(00)\rangle + |01\rangle|0 \oplus f(01)\rangle + |10\rangle|0 \oplus f(10)\rangle + |11\rangle|0 \oplus f(11)\rangle}{2} $$

$$ = \frac{|00\rangle|0\rangle + |01\rangle|1\rangle + |10\rangle|1\rangle + |11\rangle|0\rangle}{2} $$

2. The result is a superposition where the output register contains the function's value for all possible inputs.

Deutsch-Jozsa Algorithm

The Deutsch-Jozsa algorithm is a quantum algorithm that solves a specific problem with an exponential speedup compared to the best possible classical algorithm. It was one of the first algorithms to showcase the potential power of quantum computation.

✅ Problem Statement:

The problem involves a "black-box" function *f(x)*, where the input *x* is an *n*-bit string (x ∈ {0, 1}n), and the output *f(x)* is either 0 or 1. We are guaranteed that the function *f(x)* is either:

- **Constant:** The function returns the same value (either 0 or 1) for all possible inputs *x*.
- **Balanced:** The function returns 0 for exactly half of the possible inputs *x*, and 1 for the other half.

The goal is to determine whether the function *f(x)* is constant or balanced.

□ Classical Solution:

Classically, in the worst-case scenario, you would need to query the function *f(x)* more than half the time to determine if it is constant or balanced.

- If the first half of the inputs all return the same value, you still need to check one more input to be sure if the function is constant.
- In the worst case, you need to check 2n-1 + 1 inputs.

⚡ Quantum Solution:

The Deutsch-Jozsa algorithm can determine whether *f(x)* is constant or balanced with just **one** query to the function, regardless of the number of input bits *n*. This exponential speedup is a significant advantage of quantum computation.

✓ Algorithm Steps (n = 1 case)

Here are the steps of the Deutsch-Jozsa algorithm, simplified for the case where n = 1 (i.e., the input x is a single bit):

1. **Initialize Qubits:** Start with two qubits. The first qubit is initialized to the state |0⟩, and the second qubit is initialized to the state |1⟩. $$ |0\rangle^{\otimes n} \otimes |1\rangle $$
2. **Apply Hadamard Gates:** Apply the Hadamard gate (H) to both qubits.
   - Applying H to |0⟩ results in (|0⟩ + |1⟩)/√2
   - Applying H to |1⟩ results in (|0⟩ - |1⟩)/√2
3. **Apply Oracle Gate Uf:** Apply the quantum oracle *Uf* to the qubits. Recall that the oracle acts as: $$ U_f|x\rangle|y\rangle = |x\rangle|y \oplus f(x)\rangle $$
4. **Apply Hadamard Gate to the First Qubit:** Apply the Hadamard gate (H) again, but only to the *first* qubit.
5. **Measure:** Measure the first qubit.
   - If the measurement result is |0⟩, the function *f(x)* is constant.
   - If the measurement result is |1⟩, the function *f(x)* is balanced.

✓ Example

Let's consider two possible functions for the n=1 case:

- **f(x) = 0 (Constant):** The function always returns 0.

- **f(x) = x (Balanced):** The function returns the input bit itself.

For **f(x) = 0 (Constant)**

- The final state after applying the oracle and Hadamard gates will result in the state |0>.

For **f(x) = x (Balanced)**

- The final state after applying the oracle and Hadamard gates will result in the state |1>.

Bernstein-Vazirani Algorithm

The Bernstein-Vazirani algorithm is a quantum algorithm that efficiently solves a problem related to finding a hidden bit string. It's a simplified version of Simon's algorithm and provides a clear demonstration of quantum speedup.

✅ Problem Statement:

We are given a black-box function *fs(x)* defined as:

$$ f_s(x) = s \cdot x \mod 2 $$

Where:

- *s* is a hidden *n*-bit string (s ∈ {0, 1}n).
- *x* is an *n*-bit input string (x ∈ {0, 1}n).
- '·' represents the bitwise dot product (modulo 2). The bitwise dot product is calculated by taking the sum (modulo 2) of the bitwise AND of *s* and *x*.

The goal is to find the hidden bit string *s*.

□ Classical Solution:

Classically, to determine the *n*-bit string *s*, you would need to query the function *fs(x) n* times. You could query the function with inputs *x* = 00...01, 00...10, ..., 10...0. Each query would reveal one bit of *s*.

⚡ Quantum Solution:

The Bernstein-Vazirani algorithm can find the hidden string *s* with just **one** query to the function *fs(x)*.

✅ Algorithm Steps:

Here are the steps of the Bernstein-Vazirani algorithm:

1. **Initialize Qubits:** Start with n qubits initialized to the state $|0\rangle$ and one auxiliary qubit initialized to the state $|1\rangle$. The initial state is: $$ |0\rangle^{\otimes n} \otimes |1\rangle $$
2. **Apply Hadamard Gates:** Apply the Hadamard gate (H) to all $n + 1$ qubits. This creates a superposition of all possible input strings for the first n qubits and transforms the last qubit.
3. **Apply Oracle Uf:** Apply the quantum oracle Uf to the qubits. The oracle acts as: $$ U_f|x\rangle|y\rangle = |x\rangle|y \oplus f_s(x)\rangle $$
4. **Apply Hadamard Gates to Input Register:** Apply the Hadamard gate (H) again to the first n qubits (the input register).
5. **Measure:** Measure the first n qubits. The measurement result will be the hidden bit string s.

✅ Example

Let's say the hidden string $s = 101$ (n = 3). Then the function is $fs(x) = s \cdot x \bmod 2$.

- $fs(000) = 101 \cdot 000 \bmod 2 = 0$
- $fs(101) = 101 \cdot 101 \bmod 2 = (1 + 0 + 1) \bmod 2 = 0$
- $fs(110) = 101 \cdot 110 \bmod 2 = (1 + 0 + 0) \bmod 2 = 1$

Classically, you would need to evaluate $fs(x)$ three times with $x = 100, 010,$ and 001 to find each bit of s.

Quantumly, the Bernstein-Vazirani algorithm outputs the string $s = 101$ with a single query to the quantum oracle.

Basic Complexity Concepts

To understand the speed advantage of quantum algorithms, it's essential to grasp some fundamental concepts from complexity theory. Complexity theory classifies computational problems based on how their required resources (time, memory) scale with the size of the input.

✅ Classical vs. Quantum Complexity

Here's a comparison of some important complexity classes in classical and quantum computing:

Class	Meaning	Example
P	Solvable in polynomial time	Sorting
NP	Verifiable in polynomial time	SAT (Boolean Satisfiability)

BQP	Problems solvable on a quantum computer in polynomial time with high probability	Shor's algorithm, Grover's algorithm

- **P (Polynomial Time):** This class contains problems that classical computers can solve in a time that grows polynomially with the size of the input. For example, sorting a list of *n* items can be done in O(n2) time (or even better, O(n log n)), which is polynomial. These problems are considered efficiently solvable.
- **NP (Nondeterministic Polynomial Time):** This class contains problems for which a *solution* can be *verified* in polynomial time by a classical computer. However, finding the solution itself might take much longer. The Boolean Satisfiability Problem (SAT) is a classic example. Given a Boolean formula, it's easy to check if a proposed assignment of truth values to the variables satisfies the formula, but finding such an assignment can be very hard.
- **BQP (Bounded-Error Quantum Polynomial Time):** This is the quantum counterpart of P. It contains problems that a quantum computer can solve in polynomial time with a probability of error that is bounded away from 1/2. In other words, BQP problems are efficiently solvable by quantum computers.

✅ Speed Comparison

Here's a table comparing the time complexity of some problems when solved classically versus quantumly:

Problem	Classical Time	Quantum Time
Deutsch-Jozsa	O(2n)	O(1)
Bernstein-Vazirani	O(n)	O(1)
Grover's Search	O(N)	O(√N)
Shor's Factoring	Exponential	Polynomial

- **Deutsch-Jozsa:** Classically, this problem requires an exponential number of queries. Quantumly, it can be solved with a single query.
- **Bernstein-Vazirani:** Classically, finding the hidden bit string requires a linear number of queries. Quantumly, it takes only one query.
- **Grover's Search:** Classically, searching an unsorted database of *N* items requires O(N) time. Grover's algorithm achieves a quadratic speedup, solving it in O(√N) time.
- **Shor's Factoring:** Factoring large numbers is believed to be exponentially hard for classical computers. Shor's algorithm can factor numbers in polynomial time, which has significant implications for cryptography.

✅ Summary and Learning Outcomes

By the end of this chapter, students will:

- Understand the **oracle model** and how it's used in quantum algorithms.
- Explain and implement the **Deutsch-Jozsa** and **Bernstein-Vazirani** algorithms.
- Compare **quantum and classical complexities** for specific problems.
- Appreciate the **power of quantum parallelism** and **interference**.

10 practical questions with detailed answers:

Oracle Model and Black-box Functions

1. **Q: Explain the concept of a quantum oracle. How does it differ from a classical black-box function, and what is its role in quantum algorithms?**
   - **A:** A quantum oracle is a unitary operator that implements a function *f(x)*. Unlike a classical black-box function, it can be queried on a superposition of inputs. Its role is to provide access to the function's output within a quantum circuit, allowing quantum algorithms to exploit superposition and interference.
2. ***Q: Describe the action of a quantum oracle Uf on a two-part quantum state $|x\rangle|y\rangle$. Provide the equation and explain the meaning of each term.***
   - **A:** The oracle acts as: $U_f|x\rangle|y\rangle = |x\rangle|y \oplus f(x)\rangle$.
     - $|x\rangle$ is the input register, unchanged by the oracle.
     - $|y\rangle$ is the output register, which is XORed with the function's output *f(x)*.
     - $\oplus$ is the bitwise XOR operation.
     - The oracle encodes the function's information into the phase of the quantum state.

Deutsch-Jozsa Algorithm

3. **Q: State the Deutsch-Jozsa problem. What are the possible types of functions, and what is the goal of the algorithm?**
   - **A:** The Deutsch-Jozsa problem asks whether a given black-box function *f(x)* is constant (same output for all inputs) or balanced (half 0s, half 1s). The goal is to determine this property with the minimum number of queries.
4. **Q: Explain the steps of the Deutsch-Jozsa algorithm. How does it achieve an exponential speedup compared to classical solutions?**
   - **A:**
     1. Initialize qubits.
     2. Apply Hadamard gates.
     3. Apply the oracle *Uf.*
     4. Apply Hadamard gates to the input qubits.
     5. Measure. The algorithm achieves exponential speedup by querying the oracle in superposition, effectively evaluating the function for all inputs simultaneously.

Bernstein-Vazirani Algorithm

5. ***Q: Describe the Bernstein-Vazirani problem. What is the goal, and how is the function fs(x) defined?***

- **A:** The Bernstein-Vazirani problem asks to find a hidden bit string s, given a function $fs(x) = s \cdot x$ mod 2, where '·' is the bitwise dot product.

6. **Q: Outline the steps of the Bernstein-Vazirani algorithm. Why does it require only one query to the oracle?**
   - **A:**
     1. Initialize qubits.
     2. Apply Hadamard gates.
     3. Apply the oracle Uf.
     4. Apply Hadamard gates to the input qubits.
     5. Measure. It requires only one query because the quantum algorithm leverages superposition and interference to extract all the bits of s in a single measurement.

Basic Complexity Concepts

7. **Q: Explain the classical complexity classes P and NP. How do they differ in terms of solvability and verifiability?**
   - **A:**
     - P: Problems solvable in polynomial time (efficiently solvable).
     - NP: Problems whose solutions can be verified in polynomial time. P problems are also in NP (if you can solve a problem efficiently, you can certainly check the answer efficiently), but it is unknown if all problems in NP are also in P.
8. **Q: What is the quantum complexity class BQP? How does it relate to the classical complexity class P, and what are some examples of problems in BQP?**
   - **A:** BQP (Bounded-Error Quantum Polynomial Time) is the class of problems solvable by a quantum computer in polynomial time with a bounded probability of error. It's the quantum counterpart of P. Examples include Shor's algorithm (factoring) and Grover's algorithm (database search).
9. **Q: Compare the classical and quantum time complexity of Grover's search algorithm. What type of speedup does it achieve?**
   - **A:**
     - Classical: O(N) for searching an unsorted database of size N.
     - Quantum (Grover's): $O(\sqrt{N})$. Grover's algorithm achieves a quadratic speedup.
10. **Q: Compare the classical and quantum time complexity of Shor's algorithm for factoring large numbers. Why is this significant?**
    - **A:**
      - Classical: Exponential time.
      - Quantum (Shor's): Polynomial time. This is significant because it implies that quantum computers could break many of the public-key cryptosystems (like RSA) that are currently used to secure the internet.

30 multiple-choice questions with answers:

Oracle Model and Black-box Functions

1. **Q: In quantum computing, an oracle is implemented as a:**
    - A) Classical function
    - B) Unitary operator
    - C) Measurement device
    - D) Register
    - **A:** B
2. ***Q: What does a quantum oracle Uf do to the state |x⟩|y⟩?***
    - A) |f(x)⟩|y⟩
    - B) |x⟩|f(y)⟩
    - C) |x⟩|y ⊕ f(x)⟩
    - D) |y⟩|x ⊕ f(x)⟩
    - **A:** C
3. **Q: A quantum oracle can be queried in:**
    - A) Classical bits
    - B) Superposition
    - C) A single state only
    - D) A measurement basis
    - **A:** B
4. **Q: The output register |y⟩ in a quantum oracle operation is modified by:**
    - A) Adding f(x)
    - B) Multiplying by f(x)
    - C) XORing with f(x)
    - D) Inverting f(x)
    - **A:** C
5. **Q: What is the primary role of an oracle in quantum algorithms?**
    - A) To perform measurements
    - B) To provide access to a function's output
    - C) To initialize qubits
    - D) To apply Hadamard gates
    - **A:** B

Deutsch-Jozsa Algorithm

6. **Q: The Deutsch-Jozsa algorithm determines whether a function is:**
    - A) Injective or surjective
    - B) Constant or balanced
    - C) Linear or non-linear
    - D) Reversible or irreversible
    - **A:** B
7. **Q: How many queries does the Deutsch-Jozsa algorithm require?**
    - A) n
    - B) 2n
    - C) 1
    - D) n2
    - **A:** C

8. **Q: What is the classical worst-case query complexity for the Deutsch-Jozsa problem?**
   - A) O(1)
   - B) O(n)
   - C) O(2n)
   - D) O(2n-1 + 1)
   - **A:** D
9. **Q: In the Deutsch-Jozsa algorithm, Hadamard gates are applied:**
   - A) Only before the oracle
   - B) Only after the oracle
   - C) Before and after the oracle
   - D) Only to the output qubit
   - **A:** C
10. **Q: If the measurement result in the Deutsch-Jozsa algorithm is |0⟩, the function is:**
    - A) Balanced
    - B) Constant
    - C) Both
    - D) Neither
    - **A:** B

Bernstein-Vazirani Algorithm

11. **Q: The Bernstein-Vazirani algorithm finds a hidden:**
    - A) Function
    - B) Bit string
    - C) State
    - D) Gate
    - **A:** B
12. **Q: The function in the Bernstein-Vazirani algorithm is defined as:**
    - A) f(x) = x2
    - B) f(x) = s · x mod 2
    - C) f(x) = s + x
    - D) f(x) = s XOR x
    - **A:** B
13. **Q: How many queries does the Bernstein-Vazirani algorithm require?**
    - A) n
    - B) 2n
    - C) 1
    - D) n2
    - **A:** C
14. **Q: Classically, how many queries are needed to find the hidden bit string in the Bernstein-Vazirani problem?**
    - A) 1
    - B) n
    - C) 2n
    - D) n2

- **A:** B

15. **Q: The output of the Bernstein-Vazirani algorithm is obtained by:**
    - A) Measuring the output qubit
    - B) Measuring the input qubits
    - C) Applying a CNOT gate
    - D) Applying a Z gate
    - **A:** B

Basic Complexity Concepts

16. **Q: The complexity class P represents problems solvable in:**
    - A) Exponential time
    - B) Polynomial time
    - C) Constant time
    - D) Logarithmic time
    - **A:** B
17. **Q: Which of the following is an example of a problem in class P?**
    - A) Factoring
    - B) Searching an unsorted list
    - C) Sorting
    - D) Boolean Satisfiability (SAT)
    - **A:** C
18. **Q: The complexity class NP represents problems:**
    - A) Solvable in polynomial time
    - B) Verifiable in polynomial time
    - C) Solvable in exponential time
    - D) Solvable on a quantum computer
    - **A:** B
19. **Q: Which of the following is an example of a problem in class NP?**
    - A) Sorting
    - B) Searching a sorted list
    - C) Boolean Satisfiability (SAT)
    - D) Matrix multiplication
    - **A:** C
20. **Q: The quantum complexity class BQP represents problems solvable in polynomial time on a:**
    - A) Classical computer
    - B) Quantum computer
    - C) Turing machine
    - D) Finite state machine
    - **A:** B
21. **Q: Which of the following algorithms is in BQP?**
    - A) Classical sorting
    - B) Grover's algorithm
    - C) Traveling salesman problem
    - D) Classical matrix multiplication

- **A:** B

22. **Q: Grover's search algorithm achieves a speedup of:**
    - A) Exponential
    - B) Quadratic
    - C) Linear
    - D) No speedup
    - **A:** B
23. **Q: If N is the size of the search space, Grover's algorithm runs in time:**
    - A) O(N)
    - B) O(log N)
    - C) O(√N)
    - D) O(N2)
    - **A:** C
24. **Q: Shor's algorithm provides a polynomial-time solution for:**
    - A) Searching
    - B) Sorting
    - C) Factoring
    - D) Boolean Satisfiability
    - **A:** C
25. **Q: The classical time complexity of Shor's algorithm is:**
    - A) Polynomial
    - B) Exponential
    - C) Linear
    - D) Logarithmic
    - **A:** B
26. **Q: Quantum computers offer a potential _________ speedup for certain problems.**
    - A) Sub-linear
    - B) Linear
    - C) Polynomial
    - D) Exponential
    - **A:** D
27. **Q: Which problem has an exponential speedup in the Deutsch-Jozsa algorithm?**
    - A) Searching
    - B) Sorting
    - C) Determining function type
    - D) Finding hidden bit string
    - **A:** C
28. **Q: Which problem has a quadratic speedup in Grover's algorithm?**
    - A) Searching
    - B) Sorting
    - C) Determining function type
    - D) Finding hidden bit string
    - **A:** A
29. **Q: Which problem has a polynomial time solution in Shor's algorithm?**
    - A) Searching
    - B) Sorting

- C) Factoring
- D) Boolean Satisfiability
- **A:** C

30. **Q: Bernstein-Vazirani algorithm provides a speedup of:**
    - A) Exponential
    - B) Quadratic
    - C) Linear
    - D) No speedup
    - **A:** A

20 short questions and answers:

Oracle Model and Black-box Functions

1. **Q: What is a quantum oracle?**
    - **A:** A unitary operator representing a function.
2. **Q: How does a quantum oracle act on input states?**
    - **A:** It encodes the function's output into the phase.
3. **Q: Can a quantum oracle be queried in superposition?**
    - **A:** Yes.
4. **Q: What is the output of a quantum oracle operation?**
    - **A:** $|x\rangle|y \oplus f(x)\rangle$
5. **Q: What does the symbol $\oplus$ represent?**
    - **A:** Bitwise XOR.

Deutsch-Jozsa Algorithm

6. **Q: What problem does the Deutsch-Jozsa algorithm solve?**
    - **A:** Determining if a function is constant or balanced.
7. **Q: How many queries does the Deutsch-Jozsa algorithm need?**
    - **A:** One.
8. **Q: What is the classical complexity of the Deutsch-Jozsa problem?**
    - **A:** Exponential.
9. **Q: What gates are used in the Deutsch-Jozsa algorithm?**
    - **A:** Hadamard gates.
10. **Q: What are the two types of functions in the Deutsch-Jozsa problem?**
    - **A:** Constant and balanced.

Bernstein-Vazirani Algorithm

11. **Q: What does the Bernstein-Vazirani algorithm find?**
    - **A:** A hidden bit string.
12. **Q: How many queries does the Bernstein-Vazirani algorithm require?**
    - **A:** One.
13. **Q: What is the classical complexity of the Bernstein-Vazirani problem?**
    - **A:** Linear.

14. **Q: What is the function used in the Bernstein-Vazirani algorithm?**
    - **A:** $f(x) = s \cdot x \mod 2$
15. **Q: What is 's' in the Bernstein-Vazirani algorithm?**
    - **A:** The hidden bit string.

Basic Complexity Concepts

16. **Q: What does the complexity class P represent?**
    - **A:** Polynomial time.
17. **Q: What does the complexity class NP represent?**
    - **A:** Verifiable in polynomial time.
18. **Q: What does the complexity class BQP represent?**
    - **A:** Quantum polynomial time.
19. **Q: What type of speedup does Grover's algorithm achieve?**
    - **A:** Quadratic.
20. **Q: What problem does Shor's algorithm solve efficiently?**
    - **A:** Factoring.

10 medium-length questions and answers:

Oracle Model and Black-box Functions

1. **Q: Explain the concept of a black-box function in the context of quantum computing. Why is it useful to model problems using oracles?**
    - **A:** A black-box function hides the internal workings of a function; we only have access to its input-output behavior. This is useful for analyzing the inherent difficulty of a problem and understanding the power of quantum computation independent of specific implementations.
2. ***Q: Describe how a quantum oracle Uf operates on a quantum state. What is the role of the XOR operation, and why is the oracle required to be unitary?***
    - **A:** *Uf* transforms $|x\rangle|y\rangle$ to $|x\rangle|y \oplus f(x)\rangle$. XOR encodes the function's output into the phase. Unitarity is required to ensure the reversibility of quantum operations and the conservation of probability.

Deutsch-Jozsa Algorithm

3. **Q: State the Deutsch-Jozsa problem and explain why it demonstrates a quantum speedup. What are the limitations of the algorithm?**
    - **A:** It determines if a function is constant or balanced. It demonstrates a speedup because it solves the problem with one query, while a classical solution requires exponential time. A limitation is that it only works for functions that are *guaranteed* to be either constant or balanced.
4. **Q: Explain the quantum circuit for the Deutsch-Jozsa algorithm in detail. How do the Hadamard gates and the oracle contribute to the solution?**
    - **A:** The circuit involves applying Hadamard gates to create a superposition, querying the oracle to encode the function's global property, and applying

Hadamard gates again to extract the answer. The Hadamards create and manipulate the superposition, enabling the single-query solution.

Bernstein-Vazirani Algorithm

5. ***Q: Describe the Bernstein-Vazirani problem and its goal. How does the function fs(x) encode the hidden bit string s?***
   - **A:** The problem is to find a hidden bit string s, given $fs(x) = s \cdot x \bmod 2$. The function encodes s through the bitwise dot product; each bit of s influences the output based on the corresponding bits of x.
6. ***Q: Explain how the Bernstein-Vazirani algorithm efficiently finds the hidden bit string s. Why is it more efficient than a classical approach?***
   - **A:** The algorithm leverages superposition to query $fs(x)$ for all inputs simultaneously. The final Hadamard transform and measurement extract all bits of s in one step, whereas a classical approach requires n queries.

Basic Complexity Concepts

7. **Q: Differentiate between the classical complexity classes P and NP. Why is the question of whether P = NP a major unsolved problem in computer science?**
   - **A:** P is for problems solvable in polynomial time; NP is for problems whose solutions can be *verified* in polynomial time. P=NP is unsolved because it's unknown if every problem whose solution can be *checked* efficiently can also be *solved* efficiently.
8. **Q: What is the quantum complexity class BQP, and how does it relate to the classical complexity class P? Give an example of a problem believed to be in BQP but not in P.**
   - **A:** BQP is for problems solvable by a quantum computer in polynomial time. It's the quantum counterpart to P. Factoring (Shor's algorithm) is believed to be in BQP but not in P.
9. **Q: Compare the time complexity of classical search with Grover's search algorithm. Explain the implications of this speedup.**
   - **A:** Classical search is O(N); Grover's is O(√N). This quadratic speedup means quantum computers can search unsorted databases significantly faster than classical computers, though not exponentially faster.
10. **Q: Explain the significance of Shor's algorithm for factoring large numbers. What are the potential consequences for modern cryptography?**
    - **A:** Shor's algorithm factors in polynomial time, which is exponentially faster than the best-known classical algorithm. This is significant because it threatens the security of widely used public-key cryptosystems like RSA, which rely on the difficulty of factoring.

CHAPTER 7: GROVER'S SEARCH ALGORITHM

Grover's Algorithm: Problem Statement and Quadratic Speedup

Grover's algorithm is a quantum algorithm designed for searching an unstructured database or, more generally, for finding a specific item within a large collection where the only way to identify the item is by checking each entry. It offers a significant speedup over classical search methods.

✅ Problem Statement:

- **Unstructured Search:** Imagine you have a list of *N* items, and you're looking for one particular item that satisfies a certain condition. This is called an "unstructured" search because there's no organization or pattern in the list that you can exploit to narrow down your search. You have to check each item individually.
- **Black-Box Function (Oracle):** In the context of Grover's algorithm, this search problem is formalized using a black-box function (or an oracle) *f(x)*.
    - The function *f(x)* takes an input *x* (representing an item in the list) and returns:
        - 0, if *x* is not the item you're looking for.
        - 1, if *x* is the item you're looking for (the "target" item, often denoted as *x0*).
- **Goal:** The goal is to find the specific input *x0* for which *f(x0)* = 1.

□ Classical Approach:

- **Linear Time Complexity:** Classically, since the database is unstructured, you have to check each item one by one. In the worst case, you might have to check all *N* items before finding the target. Therefore, the classical time complexity is O(N).
    - If *N* = 2n (where *n* is the number of bits needed to represent each item), the classical time complexity is O(2n).

⚡ Grover's Quantum Approach:

- **Quadratic Time Complexity:** Grover's algorithm leverages quantum principles like superposition and amplitude amplification to find the target item with a time complexity of O(√N). This is a significant improvement over the classical O(N) complexity.
- **Example:**
    - Suppose you have a list of 1 million (106) items.
        - **Classical:** On average, you'd need to check around 500,000 items, and in the worst case, you'd need to check all 1,000,000 items.
        - **Quantum (Grover's):** Grover's algorithm would find the target item in approximately √(106) = 1,000 steps.

📌 Intuition:

Grover's algorithm works by iteratively manipulating the probabilities (amplitudes) of the quantum states representing the items in the search space.

1. **Start with Uniform Superposition:** The algorithm begins by putting the quantum system into a superposition where all N items have equal probability.
2. **Grover Iteration:** The core of the algorithm is the "Grover iteration," which is applied repeatedly. Each iteration consists of two main steps:
   - **Oracle Application:** The oracle marks the target state ($x0$) by inverting its amplitude.
   - **Amplitude Amplification:** This step selectively increases the amplitude of the target state while decreasing the amplitudes of the other states.
3. **Amplification:** By repeating the Grover iteration approximately $\sqrt{N}$ times, the amplitude (and thus the probability) of measuring the target state becomes significantly higher than the amplitudes of the other states.
4. **Measurement:** Finally, when you measure the quantum system, you are very likely to obtain the target state $x0$.

Grover's Algorithm: Grover Iteration and Circuit Design

Grover's algorithm efficiently searches an unstructured database by repeatedly applying a sequence of quantum operations called the "Grover iteration." This iteration manipulates the probabilities (amplitudes) of different states to amplify the probability of measuring the desired state.

✅ Step-by-Step Grover's Algorithm

Here's a detailed walkthrough of the algorithm:

Step 1: Initialize Qubits

- **Initialization:** Start with n qubits, all initialized to the state $|0\rangle$: $$ |0\rangle^{\otimes n} = |0\rangle \otimes |0\rangle \otimes ... \otimes |0\rangle $$
- **Uniform Superposition:** Apply the Hadamard gate (H) to each of the n qubits. This creates a uniform superposition of all possible states: $$ |\psi\rangle = \frac{1}{\sqrt{N}} \sum_{x=0}^{N-1} |x\rangle $$ Where $N = 2n$ is the total number of possible states (items in the database). This means each state $|x\rangle$ has an equal amplitude of $1/\sqrt{N}$.

Step 2: Oracle Of

- **Oracle Function:** The oracle *Of* is a unitary operator that marks the target state |x0⟩. It does this by inverting the phase of the target state: $$ O_f|x\rangle = \begin{cases} -|x\rangle & \text{if } x = x_0 \\ |x\rangle & \text{otherwise} \end{cases} $$
- **Phase Inversion:** The oracle doesn't change the amplitudes directly; instead, it flips the sign of the amplitude of the state |x0⟩. This is a crucial step in marking the target state.

Step 3: Diffusion Operator (D)

- **Diffusion Operator:** The diffusion operator *D*, also known as "inversion about the mean," is another unitary operator that amplifies the amplitude of the marked state. It's defined as: $$ D = 2|\psi\rangle\langle\psi| - I $$ Where:
    - |ψ⟩ is the initial uniform superposition.
    - I is the identity operator.
- **Action of the Diffusion Operator:** The diffusion operator performs the following transformation:
    - It calculates the average amplitude of all the states.
    - It reflects the amplitude of each state about this average amplitude.
    - The amplitude of the marked state |x0⟩ increases, while the amplitudes of the other states decrease slightly.

Step 4: Repeat the Iteration

- **Grover Iteration:** The Grover iteration consists of applying the oracle *Of* followed by the diffusion operator *D*. This iteration is repeated approximately: $$ r \approx \frac{\pi}{4} \sqrt{N} $$ times.
- **Measurement:** After repeating the Grover iteration *r* times, the probability of measuring the target state |x0⟩ is very high. Measuring the qubits at this point will, with high probability, give the correct answer.

✅ Example: 2-Qubit Grover (Search among 4 elements)

Let's say we have a 2-qubit system (N = 4), and we want to find the state |10⟩. The function *f(x)* returns 1 if *x* = 10 and 0 otherwise.

x	State Amplitude (Initial)
00	00⟩
01	01⟩
10	10⟩
11	11⟩

- **After one iteration:** The amplitude of |10⟩ increases, and the amplitudes of |00⟩, |01⟩, and |11⟩ decrease.
- **After the second iteration:** The amplitude of |10⟩ is very close to 1, and the probability of measuring |10⟩ is very high.

✅ Quantum Circuit

The quantum circuit for Grover's algorithm consists of the following elements:

```
Qubit 0: ---H---●---------------------------H---■---H---Measure
                |                               |
Qubit 1: ---H---|--- Oracle --- Diffusion ---|---Measure
```

- **H:** Hadamard gates to create the initial superposition.
- **Oracle:** Implements the *Of* operation.
- **Diffusion:** Implements the *D* operation.
- **Measure:** Measures the qubits to obtain the result.

The oracle and diffusion operators are constructed using standard quantum gates like Z, X, H, and CNOT.

Grover's Algorithm: Use Cases and Limitations

Grover's algorithm is a powerful quantum algorithm that provides a quadratic speedup for unstructured search problems. While it offers a significant advantage over classical search, it's important to understand its specific use cases and inherent limitations.

✅ Use Cases

Grover's algorithm is applicable to a variety of problems where you need to find a specific item within a large, unsorted collection.

- **Unstructured Search:** This is the most direct application. Any problem where you're looking for a "needle in a haystack" can potentially benefit from Grover's algorithm.
  - **Example:** Imagine searching for a specific name in a very large phone book where the names are not sorted. Grover's algorithm could find the name faster than a classical linear search.
- **Cryptanalysis:** Grover's algorithm can be used to speed up the process of cracking symmetric key cryptography.
  - **Example:**
    - **Symmetric Key Cracking:** Algorithms like AES (Advanced Encryption Standard) use a secret key to encrypt data. Grover's algorithm can be used to perform a brute-force search for the correct key. While it doesn't provide an exponential speedup like Shor's algorithm does for factoring (which affects asymmetric cryptography like RSA), it still offers a quadratic speedup, making brute-force attacks more feasible (though still challenging) for attackers with quantum computers.

- **NP Problems:** Grover's algorithm can be applied to certain problems in the complexity class NP (Nondeterministic Polynomial time).
  - **Example:**
    - **NP Search:** Many NP problems involve searching for a solution from a set of possibilities. For instance, in the Boolean Satisfiability Problem (SAT), you need to find a set of variable assignments that satisfy a given logical formula. Grover's algorithm can speed up the search for such a satisfying assignment, but it doesn't solve NP-complete problems efficiently in the general case. It can speed up the search, but it doesn't guarantee a polynomial-time solution for all NP problems.

⚠️ Limitations

While Grover's algorithm offers a valuable speedup, it has some limitations:

- **Oracle Requirement:** Grover's algorithm relies on the existence of a "black-box" function (the oracle) $f(x)$ that can efficiently check whether a given item x is the solution.
  - **Limitation:** It only works for problems where it's easy to *verify* a solution. If checking a solution is computationally hard, Grover's algorithm doesn't help.
- **Number of Solutions:** The algorithm's efficiency is affected by the number of solutions.
  - **Limitation:**
    - Grover's algorithm performs optimally when you know (or can approximate) the number of solutions. If you don't know how many solutions exist, the algorithm might "overshoot" the optimal number of iterations, reducing its effectiveness.
    - If there are multiple solutions, the algorithm can be adapted, but it adds complexity.
- **Quadratic Speedup:** Grover's algorithm provides a quadratic speedup ($O(\sqrt{N})$) compared to classical linear search ($O(N)$).
  - **Limitation:** While a quadratic speedup is significant, it's not as dramatic as the exponential speedup offered by some other quantum algorithms, such as Shor's algorithm for factoring. Grover's speedup is substantial, but it doesn't revolutionize all computational problems.
- .

✅ Summary

Feature	Grover's Algorithm
Problem Type	Unstructured Search
Speedup	Quadratic ($\sqrt{N}$ vs N)
Uses Oracle?	Yes

Feature	Grover's Algorithm
Key Component	Amplitude Amplification
Applications	Cryptography, Search

10 practical questions with detailed explanation answers on Grover's Algorithm:

Problem Statement and Quadratic Speedup

1. **Q: Explain the unstructured search problem that Grover's algorithm addresses. Provide a real-world example and contrast the classical and quantum approaches to solving it.**
    - **A:** Grover's algorithm solves the problem of finding a specific item in an unsorted database.
        - **Example:** Imagine searching for a particular contact in a phonebook where the entries are not ordered.
        - **Classical:** You'd have to check each entry one by one (linear search), taking O(N) time in the worst case.
        - **Quantum:** Grover's algorithm allows you to find the contact in $O(\sqrt{N})$ time, offering a quadratic speedup.
2. **Q: How does Grover's algorithm achieve a speedup over classical search? Explain the concept of amplitude amplification and its role in the algorithm's efficiency.**
    - **A:** Grover's algorithm achieves speedup through amplitude amplification.
        - It starts with a uniform superposition, giving each item an equal probability.
        - The Grover iteration selectively increases the probability amplitude of the target item while decreasing the others.
        - By repeating this process, the target item's amplitude is amplified, making it much more likely to be measured.

Grover Iteration and Circuit Design

3. **Q: Describe the steps involved in a single Grover iteration. What is the purpose of the oracle and the diffusion operator in this iteration?**
    - **A:** A Grover iteration consists of two main steps:
        - **Oracle:** Marks the target state by inverting its phase.
        - **Diffusion operator:** Inverts the amplitudes about their mean, further amplifying the target state's amplitude.
        - The oracle identifies the target, and the diffusion operator boosts its probability.
4. **Q: Explain how the diffusion operator works in Grover's algorithm. How does it amplify the amplitude of the marked state?**
    - **A:** The diffusion operator:
        - Calculates the average amplitude of all states.
        - Reflects each state's amplitude around this average.
        - This reflection increases the target state's amplitude while reducing the others, effectively amplifying it.

5. **Q: Draw a basic quantum circuit for Grover's algorithm. Label the key components (Hadamard gates, oracle, diffusion operator) and explain their functions.**
   - **A:**
   - `Qubits: ---H---Oracle---Diffusion---Measure`
   - `        ---H---Oracle---Diffusion---Measure`
   - `        ...`
     - **Hadamard gates:** Create the initial superposition.
     - **Oracle:** Marks the target state.
     - **Diffusion operator:** Amplifies the target state's amplitude.
     - **Measure:** Outputs the result.

Use Cases and Limitations

6. **Q: What are some practical applications of Grover's algorithm beyond searching a database? Provide examples of how it can be used in other domains.**
   - **A:**
     - **Cryptanalysis:** Speeding up brute-force attacks on symmetric key ciphers.
     - **Optimization:** Searching the solution space of certain optimization problems.
     - **Pattern Matching:** Finding specific patterns in large datasets.
7. **Q: Explain how Grover's algorithm can be applied to solve NP problems. Does it provide a general solution for all NP-complete problems?**
   - **A:** Grover's can speed up the search for a solution within the solution space of some NP problems. However, it doesn't solve NP-complete problems in polynomial time. It offers a speedup, but not a complete solution.
8. **Q: What are the key limitations of Grover's algorithm? Describe the conditions under which it can be effectively applied and when it might not be suitable.**
   - **A:**
     - **Oracle requirement:** Requires an efficient oracle to identify solutions.
     - **Number of solutions:** Performance depends on knowing (or estimating) the number of solutions.
     - **Quadratic speedup:** Offers a speedup, but not exponential.
9. **Q: Discuss the impact of knowing (or not knowing) the number of solutions on the performance of Grover's algorithm. How does this affect the number of iterations required?**
   - **A:**
     - **Knowing the number of solutions:** Allows for precise calculation of the optimal number of iterations.
     - **Not knowing the number of solutions:** Can lead to overshooting or undershooting, reducing the algorithm's effectiveness.
10. **Q: Compare and contrast the speedup offered by Grover's algorithm with that of Shor's algorithm. In what types of problems is each algorithm most effective?**
    - **A:**
      - **Grover's:** Quadratic speedup ($O(\sqrt{N})$), effective for unstructured search.

- **Shor's:** Exponential speedup, effective for factoring large numbers.
- Shor's provides a more significant speedup but applies to a narrower range of problems.

30 multiple-choice questions with answers on Grover's Algorithm:

Problem Statement and Quadratic Speedup

1. **Q: Grover's algorithm is designed for what type of search problem?**
   - A) Sorted search
   - B) Unstructured search
   - C) Graph search
   - D) Dynamic programming
   - **A:** B
2. **Q: In Grover's algorithm, the input is accessed through a:**
   - A) Classical function
   - B) Quantum oracle
   - C) Measurement device
   - D) Register
   - **A:** B
3. **Q: If there are N items, the classical search time is:**
   - A) O(log N)
   - B) O(√N)
   - C) O(N)
   - D) O(N2)
   - **A:** C
4. **Q: Grover's algorithm provides a speedup of:**
   - A) Exponential
   - B) Quadratic
   - C) Linear
   - D) No speedup
   - **A:** B
5. **Q: Grover's algorithm's time complexity is:**
   - A) O(log N)
   - B) O(√N)
   - C) O(N)
   - D) O(N2)
   - **A:** B
6. **Q: Amplitude amplification in Grover's algorithm increases the probability of measuring the:**
   - A) Initial state
   - B) Target state
   - C) Superposition state
   - D) All states equally
   - **A:** B
7. **Q: Grover's algorithm starts with the qubits in a:**

- A) Specific state
- B) Uniform superposition
- C) Entangled state
- D) Mixed state
- **A:** B

8. **Q: For a search space of 16 items, Grover's algorithm takes approximately how many iterations?**
   - A) 2
   - B) 4
   - C) 8
   - D) 16
   - **A:** B
9. **Q: The problem Grover's algorithm solves is analogous to finding a:**
   - A) Specific word in a dictionary
   - B) Maximum value in a sorted list
   - C) Needle in a haystack
   - D) Shortest path in a graph
   - **A:** C
10. **Q: Compared to classical search, Grover's algorithm offers a:**
    - A) Exponential speedup
    - B) Quadratic speedup
    - C) Linear speedup
    - D) No speedup
    - **A:** B

Grover Iteration and Circuit Design

11. **Q: A Grover iteration consists of applying the oracle and the:**
    - A) Hadamard gate
    - B) Diffusion operator
    - C) Measurement
    - D) CNOT gate
    - **A:** B
12. **Q: The oracle in Grover's algorithm does what to the target state?**
    - A) Inverts its amplitude
    - B) Sets its amplitude to zero
    - C) Leaves its amplitude unchanged
    - D) Entangles it with another qubit
    - **A:** A
13. **Q: The diffusion operator is also known as:**
    - A) Phase inversion
    - B) Amplitude amplification
    - C) Inversion about the mean
    - D) Hadamard transform
    - **A:** C
14. **Q: The diffusion operator amplifies the amplitude of the:**

- A) Initial state
- B) Target state
- C) Superposition state
- D) All states equally
- **A:** B

15. **Q: The number of Grover iterations is approximately proportional to:**
    - A) log N
    - B) √N
    - C) N
    - D) N2
    - **A:** B
16. **Q: In the quantum circuit for Grover's algorithm, Hadamard gates are used to create the:**
    - A) Oracle
    - B) Diffusion operator
    - C) Initial superposition
    - D) Measurement basis
    - **A:** C
17. **Q: The oracle in Grover's algorithm is implemented using standard quantum:**
    - A) Measurements
    - B) Gates
    - C) Registers
    - D) Qubits
    - **A:** B
18. **Q: The diffusion operator involves reflecting amplitudes around the:**
    - A) Maximum amplitude
    - B) Minimum amplitude
    - C) Average amplitude
    - D) Initial amplitude
    - **A:** C
19. **Q: After applying the Grover iteration multiple times, measuring the qubits gives the:**
    - A) Initial state
    - B) Target state
    - C) Superposition state
    - D) A random state
    - **A:** B
20. **Q: The Grover iteration is repeated approximately:**
    - A) log N times
    - B) √N times
    - C) N times
    - D) N2 times
    - **A:** B

Use Cases and Limitations

21. **Q: Grover's algorithm is useful for:**
    - A) Sorting
    - B) Factoring
    - C) Unstructured search
    - D) Finding the shortest path
    - **A:** C
22. **Q: Grover's algorithm can be applied to speed up:**
    - A) Classical sorting
    - B) Symmetric key cryptanalysis
    - C) Shor's algorithm
    - D) Solving linear equations
    - **A:** B
23. **Q: Grover's algorithm can assist in searching the solution space of some problems in the complexity class:**
    - A) P
    - B) NP
    - C) BQP
    - D) BPP
    - **A:** B
24. **Q: A limitation of Grover's algorithm is that it requires an efficient:**
    - A) Measurement device
    - B) Quantum oracle
    - C) Classical computer
    - D) Qubit initialization
    - **A:** B
25. **Q: Grover's algorithm performs optimally when the number of solutions is:**
    - A) Unknown
    - B) Known or approximated
    - C) Always one
    - D) Always more than half
    - **A:** B
26. **Q: Grover's algorithm provides a speedup that is:**
    - A) Exponential
    - B) Quadratic
    - C) Linear
    - D) No speedup
    - **A:** B
27. **Q: Grover's algorithm does NOT provide exponential speedup like:**
    - A) Classical search
    - B) Grover's algorithm
    - C) Shor's algorithm
    - D) Quantum simulation
    - **A:** C
28. **Q: If the number of solutions is not known, Grover's algorithm may:**
    - A) Fail to find a solution
    - B) Find all solutions

- C) Overshoot the optimal number of iterations
- D) Provide an exponential speedup
- **A:** C

29. **Q: Grover's algorithm is most effective when it is easy to:**
    - A) Find a solution
    - B) Verify a solution
    - C) Calculate a solution
    - D) Store a solution
    - **A:** B
30. **Q: Grover's algorithm can be used for:**
    - A) Factoring large numbers
    - B) Searching unsorted databases
    - C) Solving linear equations
    - D) Sorting lists
    - **A:** B

20 short questions and answers on Grover's Algorithm:

Problem Statement and Quadratic Speedup

1. **Q: What type of search problem does Grover's algorithm solve?**
    - **A:** Unstructured search.
2. **Q: How is the input accessed in Grover's algorithm?**
    - **A:** Quantum oracle.
3. **Q: What is the classical search time for N items?**
    - **A:** O(N).
4. **Q: What type of speedup does Grover's algorithm provide?**
    - **A:** Quadratic.
5. **Q: What is the time complexity of Grover's algorithm?**
    - **A:** $O(\sqrt{N})$.

Grover Iteration and Circuit Design

6. **Q: What are the two main steps in a Grover iteration?**
    - **A:** Oracle and diffusion operator.
7. **Q: What does the oracle do to the target state's amplitude?**
    - **A:** Inverts it.
8. **Q: What is another name for the diffusion operator?**
    - **A:** Inversion about the mean.
9. **Q: What does the diffusion operator amplify?**
    - **A:** Target state amplitude.
10. **Q: How many times is the Grover iteration repeated?**
    - **A:** Approximately $\sqrt{N}$ times.
11. **Q: What gates are used to create the initial superposition?**
    - **A:** Hadamard gates.
12. **Q: What type of gates are used to construct the oracle and diffusion operator?**

- **A:** Standard quantum gates.

13. **Q: What is measured at the end of Grover's algorithm?**
    - **A:** The qubits.
14. **Q: What is the approximate number of iterations for a search space of 9?**
    - **A:** 3

Use Cases and Limitations

15. **Q: What is a primary use case for Grover's algorithm?**
    - **A:** Unstructured search.
16. **Q: Can Grover's algorithm be used in cryptanalysis?**
    - **A:** Yes.
17. **Q: Does Grover's algorithm solve NP-complete problems efficiently?**
    - **A:** No.
18. **Q: What is a key requirement for the problem structure for Grover's?**
    - **A:** Easy to check if a solution is correct.
19. **Q: What happens if the number of solutions is unknown in Grover's algorithm?**
    - **A:** Performance may be affected.
20. **Q: Does Grover's algorithm provide an exponential speedup?**
    - **A:** No.

10 medium-size questions with answers on Grover's Algorithm:

Problem Statement and Quadratic Speedup

1. **Q: Explain the problem statement for Grover's algorithm in detail. What are the inputs and outputs, and what is the key characteristic of the search space?**
    - **A:** Grover's algorithm searches for a specific item in an unstructured database. The input is a black-box function (oracle) that identifies the target item. The output is the index of the target item. The search space is unstructured, meaning there's no known order or pattern to exploit.
2. **Q: Describe how Grover's algorithm achieves a quadratic speedup compared to classical search. Explain the concept of amplitude amplification and how it reduces the search time.**
    - **A:** Grover's achieves speedup by manipulating quantum probabilities. Amplitude amplification starts with a uniform superposition, then iteratively increases the probability amplitude of the target state. This amplification concentrates the probability, allowing the target to be found in $O(\sqrt{N})$ time, a quadratic improvement over the classical $O(N)$.

Grover Iteration and Circuit Design

3. **Q: Explain the role of the oracle in Grover's algorithm. How does it mark the target state, and what is the effect of this marking on the quantum state?**
    - **A:** The oracle identifies the target state. It marks it by inverting its phase. This phase inversion doesn't change the probability of measuring the state, but it allows

the diffusion operator to amplify the target state's amplitude in subsequent iterations.

4. **Q: Describe the diffusion operator in Grover's algorithm. How does it work, and why is it essential for the algorithm's success?**
   - **A:** The diffusion operator reflects the amplitudes of all states around the average amplitude. This reflection boosts the amplitude of the marked state while reducing the amplitudes of others. It's essential because it amplifies the target state's probability, making it measurable.
5. **Q: Draw a quantum circuit for Grover's algorithm and explain the function of each component. How do the Hadamard gates, oracle, and diffusion operator work together?**
   - **A:**
   - `Qubits: ---H---Oracle---Diffusion---Measure`
   - `        ---H---Oracle---Diffusion---Measure`
   - `        ...`

       - Hadamard gates create the initial superposition.
       - The oracle marks the target state.
       - The diffusion operator amplifies the target state's amplitude.
       - Measurement yields the target state.

Use Cases and Limitations

6. **Q: Discuss the practical applications of Grover's algorithm beyond simple database searching. Provide examples of how it can be used in other fields.**
   - **A:**
       - Cryptanalysis: Speeding up brute-force attacks on symmetric ciphers.
       - Optimization: Searching solution spaces for optimization problems.
       - Pattern Matching: Finding specific patterns in data.
7. **Q: Explain how Grover's algorithm can be used to solve NP problems. What type of speedup does it offer, and what are the limitations in this context?**
   - **A:** Grover's can speed up the search for a solution within an NP problem's solution space. It offers a quadratic speedup. However, it doesn't guarantee a polynomial-time solution for all NP-complete problems, so it doesn't "solve" NP-complete.
8. **Q: What are the key limitations of Grover's algorithm? Discuss the requirements for the oracle and the impact of knowing (or not knowing) the number of solutions.**
   - **A:**
       - Oracle: Requires an efficient oracle to identify solutions.
       - Solutions: Knowing the number of solutions is crucial for optimal performance. If unknown, the algorithm may overshoot.
9. **Q: Compare and contrast Grover's algorithm with classical search algorithms. What are the advantages and disadvantages of using Grover's algorithm in a real-world search scenario?**
   - **A:** Grover's offers a quadratic speedup over classical search.
       - Advantage: Faster for large, unstructured searches.

- Disadvantage: Requires a quantum computer and an efficient oracle, which may not always be available.

10. **Q: Discuss the potential impact of Grover's algorithm on cryptography. How does it affect the security of symmetric key ciphers, and what are the implications for key lengths and security practices?**
    - **A:** Grover's reduces the effective key length of symmetric ciphers by half. For example, a 128-bit key would have the security of a 64-bit key against a quantum attack. This necessitates the use of longer key lengths to maintain security in a quantum era.

CHAPTER 8: SHOR'S ALGORITHM AND QUANTUM FOURIER TRANSFORM

Shor's Algorithm: Introduction

Shor's algorithm is a quantum algorithm that provides an exponential speedup over the best-known classical algorithms for the problem of integer factorization. This has significant implications for cryptography, as the security of many widely used public-key cryptosystems relies on the difficulty of factoring large numbers.

✅ Problem Statement:

The problem that Shor's algorithm solves is:

- **Input:** Given a composite integer N.
- **Output:** Find its prime factors.

For example:

- Input: $N = 15$
- Output: 3×5

□ Why Is It Important?

- **RSA Cryptography:** The security of the RSA (Rivest–Shamir–Adleman) cryptosystem, a widely used public-key encryption method, is based on the assumption that factoring large integers is computationally difficult for classical computers.
- **Classical Difficulty:** Classical algorithms for factoring large numbers take sub-exponential time. This means that as the size of the number to be factored increases, the time required to factor it grows faster than any polynomial function, but slower than an exponential function. Examples of classical factoring algorithms include the General Number Field Sieve (GNFS).
- **Shor's Algorithm's Speedup:** Shor's algorithm, running on a quantum computer, can factor integers in polynomial time, specifically O((log N)3). Here, log N represents the number of bits needed to represent N, so this is considered a polynomial time complexity. This is an exponential speedup compared to the best-known classical algorithms.

□ High-Level Idea:

Shor's algorithm cleverly reduces the factoring problem to a period-finding problem. Here's a simplified overview:

1. **Reduction to Period Finding:** Shor's algorithm transforms the problem of finding the factors of N into the problem of finding the period of a certain function. This function is based on modular exponentiation.

2. **Quantum Fourier Transform (QFT):** The period of this function can be efficiently found using the Quantum Fourier Transform (QFT). The QFT is the quantum analogue of the classical Discrete Fourier Transform (DFT) and can be implemented efficiently on a quantum computer.
3. **Factor Extraction:** Once the period is found, the factors of N can be determined through some classical post-processing.

Quantum Fourier Transform (QFT) Basics

The Quantum Fourier Transform (QFT) is the quantum analogue of the classical Discrete Fourier Transform (DFT). It's a fundamental quantum algorithm used in various quantum computations, most notably in Shor's algorithm for factoring.

✓ QFT Definition:

- **Transformation:** The QFT transforms the amplitudes of a quantum state into their frequency components. For an n-qubit state $|x\rangle$, the QFT is defined as:

  $$ |x\rangle \rightarrow \frac{1}{\sqrt{2^n}} \sum_{y=0}^{2^n-1} e^{2\pi i xy / 2^n} |y\rangle $$

  Where:

  - x is an integer representing the input state.
  - n is the number of qubits.
  - y is an integer representing the output state.
  - i is the imaginary unit.
  - The summation is over all possible output states y.
- **Purpose:** In Shor's algorithm, the QFT is used to efficiently extract the period of a function. The period is a crucial value needed to determine the factors of the number being factored.

✓ QFT Circuit (3-Qubit Example):

Here's a simplified quantum circuit for a 3-qubit QFT:

```
|x2⟩ ---H---●--------●-----Swap---|y0⟩
            |        |
|x1⟩ ---H---R2---●---Swap---|y1⟩
                 |
|x0⟩ ---H--------R3--------Swap---|y2⟩
```

- **Hadamard Gates (H):** Apply a Hadamard gate to each qubit.

- **Controlled Phase Gates (Rk):** These gates apply a phase rotation to a target qubit, controlled by another qubit. The rotation angle depends on the control qubit and the value of *k*.
- **Swap Gates:** Swap the order of the output qubits to obtain the correct output order.
    - Rk gate: The general form of the controlled phase gate is: Rk = $$ \begin{bmatrix} 1 & 0 \ 0 & e^{2\pi i / 2^k} \bmatrix} $$

✓ QFT vs. Classical DFT:

- **Computational Cost:** The QFT offers a significant speedup over the classical Discrete Fourier Transform (DFT):
    - QFT: Requires O(n2) quantum operations, where n is the number of qubits.
    - Classical DFT: Requires O(n · 2n) operations.
- **Speedup:** The QFT's quadratic scaling in the number of qubits, compared to the DFT's scaling that is linear in the number of inputs (2n), demonstrates the exponential advantage of the quantum algorithm. This efficiency is crucial in Shor's algorithm for factoring large numbers.

Shor's Algorithm: Period Finding and Integer Factoring

Shor's algorithm's genius lies in its ability to transform the hard problem of factoring into a much easier problem for a quantum computer: finding the period of a function. Let's explore this in detail.

✓ Core Insight:

1. **Random Number Selection:** To factor a composite number N, we first pick a random number a that is less than N.
2. **Coprime Condition:** It's crucial that a and N are coprime, meaning their greatest common divisor (GCD) is 1: gcd(a, N) = 1. If they are not coprime, then gcd(a, N) will directly give you a factor of N.
3. **Periodic Function:** We then define a function: $$ f(x) = a^x \mod N $$ This function exhibits a periodic behavior. The "period" (r) is the smallest positive integer such that $f(x + r) = f(x)$ for all x. In other words, $ax+r$ mod $N = ax$ mod N.
4. **Period and Factoring:** The key insight is that finding this period r allows us to determine the factors of N.

□ Why Does the Period Help?

If the period r satisfies two conditions:

- r is even, and
- $ar/2$ is not congruent to -1 modulo N (ar/2 ≢ -1 mod N),

Then we can use the following to find non-trivial factors of N:

- gcd($ar/2$ - 1, N)
- gcd($ar/2$ + 1, N)

These GCD calculations will yield factors of N that are neither 1 nor N itself (non-trivial factors).

✓ Step-by-Step Shor's Algorithm:

Here's a breakdown of the factoring process:

1. **Choose a Random Number:** Pick a random number $a < N$ such that gcd(a, N) = 1.
2. **Quantum Period Finding:** Use a quantum computer (specifically, the Quantum Fourier Transform) to find the period r of the function $f(x) = ax$ mod N.
3. **Check Conditions and Compute Factors:**
    - If r is even and $ar/2 \not\equiv -1$ mod N, compute:
        - gcd($ar/2$ - 1, N)
        - gcd($ar/2$ + 1, N)
    - These will give you the factors of N.
    - If the conditions on r are not met, go back to step 1 and choose a different random a.

✓ Example: Factor N = 15

Let's factor $N = 15$ using Shor's algorithm.

1. **Choose a:** We choose $a = 2$. gcd(2, 15) = 1.
2. **Define Function:** $f(x) = 2x$ mod 15.
3. **Compute Function Values:**
    - $x = 0$, $f(0) = 20$ mod 15 = 1
    - $x = 1$, $f(1) = 21$ mod 15 = 2
    - $x = 2$, $f(2) = 22$ mod 15 = 4
    - $x = 3$, $f(3) = 23$ mod 15 = 8
    - $x = 4$, $f(4) = 24$ mod 15 = 1
    - ...
4. **Find Period:** We see that the function repeats after $r = 4$. The period is 4.
5. **Check Conditions and Compute GCDs:**
    - $r = 4$ is even.
    - 24/2 mod 15 = 22 mod 15 = 4. 4 is not congruent to -1 mod 15 (which is 14).
    - Calculate the GCDs:
        - gcd(24/2 - 1, 15) = gcd(22 - 1, 15) = gcd(3, 15) = 3
        - gcd(24/2 + 1, 15) = gcd(22 + 1, 15) = gcd(5, 15) = 5
6. **Factors:** The factors of 15 are 3 and 5.

✓ Quantum Role:

The quantum part of Shor's algorithm is crucial for efficiently finding the period r. It does this using:

- **Superposition:** Creating a superposition of all possible input values for x.
- **Function Evaluation:** Computing $f(x) = ax \bmod N$ for all these values in superposition.
- **Quantum Fourier Transform (QFT):** Applying the QFT to the resulting state to reveal the period r as an interference pattern.
- **Measurement:** Measuring the quantum state to obtain information related to the period.

Shor's Algorithm: Impact on Cryptography

Shor's algorithm, a quantum algorithm capable of efficiently factoring large integers, poses a significant threat to many of the public-key cryptosystems that currently secure our digital world.

✅ RSA Security:

- **Factoring Difficulty:** The RSA (Rivest–Shamir–Adleman) encryption scheme is a cornerstone of modern cryptography. Its security relies on the computational difficulty of factoring large numbers.
- **Key Generation:** In RSA:
  - A public key (N) is generated by multiplying two large prime numbers, p and q: $N = p \cdot q$.
  - The private key is derived from knowing p and q.
- **Encryption and Decryption:** Encryption uses the public key (N), while decryption requires the private key (which depends on knowing the prime factors p and q).
- **Classical Security:** Classically, factoring N to obtain p and q is extremely difficult for sufficiently large numbers, making RSA secure against classical attacks.

⚠︎ Quantum Risk:

- **Shor's Algorithm Threat:** A sufficiently powerful quantum computer running Shor's algorithm could efficiently factor the large integer N, thereby compromising the security of RSA.
- **Vulnerable Systems:** This vulnerability extends beyond RSA. Other widely used public-key cryptosystems, including:
  - DSA (Digital Signature Algorithm)
  - ECC (Elliptic Curve Cryptography) are also susceptible to quantum attacks, as Shor's algorithm (or related quantum algorithms) can break the mathematical problems upon which their security relies.
- **Post-Quantum Cryptography (PQC):** The realization of this quantum threat has spurred research and development in Post-Quantum Cryptography (PQC). PQC aims to develop cryptographic algorithms that are believed to be secure against attacks from both classical and quantum computers.

✅ Quantum-Safe Cryptography Approaches:

Researchers are exploring several promising approaches to create quantum-safe cryptographic systems:

- **Lattice-based Cryptography:** These schemes rely on the difficulty of solving problems related to lattices in high-dimensional spaces.
  - Examples: NTRU, Kyber
- **Code-based Cryptography:** These schemes are based on the difficulty of decoding general linear codes.
  - Example: McEliece
- **Multivariate Polynomial Cryptography:** These schemes use the difficulty of solving systems of multivariate polynomial equations.

NIST Standardization:

The National Institute of Standards and Technology (NIST) is actively working to standardize a new generation of cryptographic algorithms that will be resistant to quantum attacks. They have evaluated and selected several PQC algorithms, and the process of standardizing these algorithms is underway to prepare for the post-quantum era.

✅ Summary

Concept	Description
Shor's Algorithm	Factors large integers using period finding
QFT	Used to extract period from quantum state
Complexity	Polynomial O((log⁡N)3)O((\log N)^3)O((logN)3)
Real-world Impact	Breaks RSA, ECC, and other cryptosystems
Quantum Prerequisite	A scalable quantum computer

10 practical questions with detailed explanation answers on Shor's Algorithm:

Introduction to Shor's Algorithm

1. **Q: Explain the integer factorization problem and why it is important in cryptography. How does Shor's algorithm change the complexity of this problem?**
   - **A:** The integer factorization problem is finding the prime factors of a composite number. It's crucial in cryptography because RSA's security relies on the classical difficulty of this problem. Shor's algorithm reduces the complexity from sub-exponential to polynomial time, posing a threat to RSA.

Quantum Fourier Transform (QFT) Basics

2. **Q: Describe the Quantum Fourier Transform (QFT). What is its purpose, and how does it differ from the classical Discrete Fourier Transform (DFT)?**
    - **A:** The QFT is the quantum analogue of the DFT. Its purpose is to transform a quantum state's amplitudes into their frequency components. Unlike the DFT, which has a complexity of O(n * 2n), the QFT has a complexity of O(n2), offering an exponential speedup.
3. **Q: Explain how the QFT is used within Shor's algorithm. What specific information does it help to extract, and why is this information crucial for factoring?**
    - **A:** The QFT is used to find the period of the function f(x) = ax mod N. The period 'r' is crucial because, if 'r' is even and ar/2 is not congruent to -1 mod N, it allows us to compute factors of N using gcd(ar/2 ± 1, N).

Period Finding and Integer Factoring

4. **Q: Explain the concept of period finding in Shor's algorithm. How is the function f(x) = ax mod N used, and what does its period tell us about the factors of N?**
    - **A:** Period finding involves determining the smallest 'r' for which ax+r mod N = ax mod N. If 'r' is even and ar/2 ≠ -1 mod N, then gcd(ar/2 ± 1, N) yields non-trivial factors of N.
5. **Q: Walk through the steps of Shor's algorithm with an example. Show how a random number 'a' is chosen, the period is found (conceptually), and how the factors are extracted.**
    - **A:** Example: Factor N = 15.
        1. Choose a = 2 (gcd(2, 15) = 1).
        2. Find the period of f(x) = 2x mod 15 (which is 4).
        3. Since 4 is even and 22 ≠ -1 mod 15, compute gcd(22 - 1, 15) = 3 and gcd(22 + 1, 15) = 5.
        4. Factors are 3 and 5.
6. **Q: Describe the conditions under which the period 'r' can be used to find the factors of N. What happens if 'r' is odd, or if ar/2 is congruent to -1 mod N?**
    - **A:** Factors are found if 'r' is even and ar/2 ≠ -1 mod N. If 'r' is odd or ar/2 ≡ -1 mod N, the algorithm fails to produce useful factors, and a different 'a' must be chosen.

Impact on Cryptography

7. **Q: Explain how Shor's algorithm threatens the security of the RSA cryptosystem. What is the underlying mathematical problem that RSA relies on, and how does Shor's algorithm compromise it?**
    - **A:** RSA relies on the difficulty of factoring large numbers. Shor's algorithm efficiently factors these numbers, allowing an attacker to determine the private key from the public key, thus breaking the encryption.
8. **Q: Discuss the implications of Shor's algorithm for other public-key cryptosystems beyond RSA. Which other cryptographic schemes are vulnerable, and why?**

- **A:** DSA and ECC are also vulnerable. DSA's security relies on the difficulty of the discrete logarithm problem, and ECC's on the difficulty of the elliptic curve discrete logarithm problem, both of which quantum computers can solve efficiently.

9. **Q: What is Post-Quantum Cryptography (PQC)? Describe the main approaches being explored to develop quantum-resistant cryptographic algorithms.**
   - **A:** PQC develops crypto systems secure against both classical and quantum computers. Approaches include:
     - Lattice-based cryptography
     - Code-based cryptography
     - Multivariate polynomial cryptography
10. **Q: Explain the efforts being made to standardize Post-Quantum Cryptography. Which organizations are involved, and what is the goal of this standardization process?**
    - **A:** NIST is leading the standardization effort. The goal is to select and standardize new cryptographic algorithms that will remain secure in the presence of quantum computers, ensuring long-term data security.

30 multiple-choice questions with answers on Shor’s Algorithm:

Introduction to Shor’s Algorithm

1. **Q: Shor's algorithm solves which problem?**
   - A) Searching
   - B) Sorting
   - C) Integer factorization
   - D) Graph coloring
   - **A:** C
2. **Q: The input to Shor's algorithm is a:**
   - A) Prime number
   - B) Composite integer
   - C) Quantum state
   - D) Graph
   - **A:** B
3. **Q: Shor's algorithm provides what type of speedup over classical factoring algorithms?**
   - A) Linear
   - B) Quadratic
   - C) Sub-exponential
   - D) Exponential
   - **A:** D
4. **Q: Shor's algorithm reduces factoring to a:**
   - A) Searching problem
   - B) Sorting problem

- C) Period-finding problem
- D) Graph coloring problem
- **A:** C

5. **Q: The efficiency of Shor's algorithm is:**
   - A) Exponential time
   - B) Sub-exponential time
   - C) Polynomial time
   - D) Linear time
   - **A:** C

Quantum Fourier Transform (QFT) Basics

6. **Q: QFT stands for:**
   - A) Quantum Filtering Transform
   - B) Quantum Fourier Transform
   - C) Quantum Factoring Transform
   - D) Quantum Frequency Transform
   - **A:** B
7. **Q: The QFT is the quantum analogue of the classical:**
   - A) Fast Fourier Transform (FFT)
   - B) Discrete Fourier Transform (DFT)
   - C) Laplace Transform
   - D) Z-Transform
   - **A:** B
8. **Q: What does the QFT transform?**
   - A) Classical bits
   - B) Quantum state amplitudes
   - C) Qubit positions
   - D) Quantum gates
   - **A:** B
9. **Q: The QFT is used in Shor's algorithm to extract the _________ of a function.**
   - A) Maximum value
   - B) Minimum value
   - C) Period
   - D) Derivative
   - **A:** C
10. **Q: The time complexity of QFT is:**
    - A) O(n)
    - B) O(n log n)
    - C) O(n2)
    - D) O(2n)
    - **A:** C

Period Finding and Integer Factoring

11. **Q: In Shor's algorithm, we pick a random number 'a' such that gcd(a, N) = ?**

- A) 0
- B) 1
- C) N
- D) a
- **A:** B

12. **Q: The function used in Shor's algorithm for period finding is f(x) = ?**
    - A) ax + N
    - B) ax - N
    - C) ax * N
    - D) ax mod N
    - **A:** D
13. **Q: The period 'r' of the function f(x) is the smallest positive integer such that f(x + r) = ?**
    - A) f(x) + r
    - B) f(x) - r
    - C) f(x) * r
    - D) f(x)
    - **A:** D
14. **Q: If 'r' is even and ar/2 ≠ -1 mod N, then the factors of N can be found using gcd(ar/2 ± 1, ?)**
    - A) a
    - B) r
    - C) N
    - D) x
    - **A:** C
15. **Q: The quantum part of Shor's algorithm finds the __________ of the function.**
    - A) Maximum value
    - B) Minimum value
    - C) Period
    - D) Derivative
    - **A:** C

Impact on Cryptography

16. **Q: Shor's algorithm poses a threat to which encryption scheme?**
    - A) AES
    - B) DES
    - C) RSA
    - D) SHA-256
    - **A:** C
17. **Q: RSA security is based on the difficulty of factoring large:**
    - A) Prime numbers
    - B) Composite numbers
    - C) Quantum states
    - D) Graphs
    - **A:** B

18. **Q: A powerful quantum computer running Shor's algorithm could break:**
    - A) Symmetric key cryptography
    - B) Public-key cryptography
    - C) Hash functions
    - D) Classical algorithms
    - **A:** B
19. **Q: The acronym PQC stands for:**
    - A) Post-Quantum Computing
    - B) Post-Quantum Cryptography
    - C) Pre-Quantum Computing
    - D) Pre-Quantum Cryptography
    - **A:** B
20. **Q: PQC aims to develop algorithms secure against attacks from both _________ and quantum computers.**
    - A) Analog
    - B) Classical
    - C) Hybrid
    - D) Optical
    - **A:** B
21. **Q: Which of the following is a Post-Quantum Cryptography approach?**
    - A) RSA
    - B) AES
    - C) Lattice-based cryptography
    - D) DES
    - **A:** C
22. **Q: Which organization is standardizing Post-Quantum Cryptography?**
    - A) ISO
    - B) IEEE
    - C) NIST
    - D) IETF
    - **A:** C
23. **Q: Shor's algorithm has significant implications for:**
    - A) Data compression
    - B) Quantum simulation
    - C) Cryptography
    - D) Database searching
    - **A:** C
24. **Q: The public key in RSA is N, which is the product of two large _________ numbers.**
    - A) Even
    - B) Odd
    - C) Prime
    - D) Composite
    - **A:** C
25. **Q: The private key in RSA depends on knowing the _________ of N.**
    - A) Sum

- B) Product
- C) Factors
- D) Square root
- **A:** C

26. **Q: Which cryptographic schemes are vulnerable to Shor's algorithm?**
    - A) AES
    - B) DES
    - C) RSA, DSA, ECC
    - D) SHA-256
    - **A:** C
27. **Q: Lattice-based cryptography relies on the difficulty of solving problems related to _________ in high-dimensional spaces.**
    - A) Graphs
    - B) Matrices
    - C) Lattices
    - D) Polynomials
    - **A:** C
28. **Q: Code-based cryptography is based on the difficulty of _________ general linear codes.**
    - A) Encoding
    - B) Decoding
    - C) Compressing
    - D) Encrypting
    - **A:** B
29. **Q: NIST is working to standardize cryptographic algorithms that are resistant to _________ attacks.**
    - A) Classical
    - B) Quantum
    - C) Analog
    - D) Optical
    - **A:** B
30. **Q: Multivariate polynomial schemes use the difficulty of solving systems of _________ equations.** * A) Linear * B) Quadratic * C) Differential * D) Polynomial * **A:** D

20 short questions and answers on Shor's Algorithm:

Introduction to Shor's Algorithm

1. **Q: What problem does Shor's algorithm solve?**
    - **A:** Integer factorization.
2. **Q: What type of speedup does Shor's algorithm provide?**
    - **A:** Exponential.
3. **Q: What is the input to Shor's algorithm?**

- **A:** A composite integer.

4. **Q: Shor's algorithm reduces factoring to what problem?**
    - **A:** Period finding.
5. **Q: Is Shor's algorithm polynomial or exponential time?**
    - **A:** Polynomial time.

Quantum Fourier Transform (QFT) Basics

6. **Q: What does QFT stand for?**
    - **A:** Quantum Fourier Transform.
7. **Q: What is the quantum analogue of the DFT?**
    - **A:** QFT.
8. **Q: What does the QFT transform?**
    - **A:** Quantum state amplitudes.
9. **Q: What is QFT used for in Shor's algorithm?**
    - **A:** To find the period of a function.
10. **Q: Is QFT faster or slower than DFT?**
    - **A:** Faster.

Period Finding and Integer Factoring

11. **Q: What must the gcd of 'a' and 'N' be in Shor's algorithm?**
    - **A:** 1.
12. **Q: What is the function used in Shor's algorithm for period finding?**
    - **A:** ax mod N.
13. **Q: What is 'r' in Shor's algorithm?**
    - **A:** The period.
14. **Q: What must 'r' be to find factors?**
    - **A:** Even.
15. **Q: What operation is used to extract factors?**
    - **A:** GCD.

Impact on Cryptography

16. **Q: Which cryptosystem does Shor's algorithm threaten?**
    - **A:** RSA.
17. **Q: What is RSA security based on?**
    - **A:** Difficulty of factoring.
18. **Q: What does PQC stand for?**
    - **A:** Post-Quantum Cryptography.
19. **Q: Name a PQC approach.**
    - **A:** Lattice-based cryptography (or Code-based, or Multivariate Polynomial).
20. **Q: Which organization is standardizing PQC?**

A: NIST. 10 medium-size questions with answers on Shor's Algorithm:

Introduction to Shor's Algorithm

1. **Q: Explain the integer factorization problem and its significance in cryptography. How does Shor's algorithm address this problem, and what is its impact on computational complexity?**
   - **A:** Integer factorization is finding the prime factors of a composite number. It's crucial for RSA security. Shor's algorithm uses a quantum computer to solve this in polynomial time, an exponential speedup over classical algorithms.

Quantum Fourier Transform (QFT) Basics

2. **Q: Describe the Quantum Fourier Transform (QFT). What is its purpose in Shor's algorithm, and how does its efficiency compare to the classical Discrete Fourier Transform (DFT)?**
   - **A:** The QFT transforms quantum state amplitudes into frequency components. In Shor's, it finds the period of a function. QFT is much more efficient, O(n^2) vs. DFT's O(n * 2^n), where n is the number of qubits.
3. **Q: Explain, in general terms, how the Quantum Fourier Transform (QFT) is implemented in a quantum circuit. What are the key quantum gates involved?**
   - **A:** QFT uses Hadamard gates and controlled phase rotation gates. Hadamard creates superpositions, and the controlled phase gates manipulate the phases based on qubit values.

Period Finding and Integer Factoring

4. **Q: Explain the process of period finding in Shor's algorithm. How is the function f(x) = a^x mod N used, and what is the relationship between its period and the factors of N?**
   - **A:** We find the smallest 'r' where a^(x+r) mod N = a^x mod N. If 'r' is even and a^(r/2) is not congruent to -1 mod N, then the GCD of (a^(r/2) ± 1, N) gives the factors of N.
5. **Q: Walk through the steps of Shor's algorithm to factor a small composite number (e.g., 21). Clearly show how the period is used to obtain the factors.**
   - **A:** To factor 21:
     1. Choose a = 2 (gcd(2, 21) = 1).
     2. Find the period of f(x) = 2^x mod 21 (which is 6).
     3. Since 6 is even and 2^3 is not congruent to -1 mod 21, compute gcd(2^3 - 1, 21) = 7 and gcd(2^3 + 1, 21) = 3.
     4. Factors are 3 and 7.
6. **Q: What are the conditions that the period 'r' must satisfy to be useful in factoring N? What happens if these conditions are not met, and what is the solution?**
   - **A:** 'r' must be even, and a^(r/2) must not be congruent to -1 mod N. If these aren't met, the algorithm might not produce useful factors, and a different random 'a' is chosen.

Impact on Cryptography

7. **Q: Explain how Shor's algorithm poses a threat to the security of the RSA cryptosystem. What are the implications for secure communication over the internet?**
   - **A:** RSA relies on the difficulty of factoring large numbers. Shor's can efficiently factor these, allowing a quantum computer to derive the private key from the public key, compromising secure communication.
8. **Q: Discuss the vulnerability of other public-key cryptosystems, such as DSA and ECC, to quantum attacks. What common mathematical problem underlies their security?**
   - **A:** DSA and ECC are vulnerable because their security relies on the difficulty of the discrete logarithm problem, which quantum computers can solve efficiently.
9. **Q: What is Post-Quantum Cryptography (PQC), and what are its goals? Describe two different approaches being pursued in PQC research.**
   - **A:** PQC aims to develop crypto systems secure against both classical and quantum computers. Two approaches are lattice-based cryptography and code-based cryptography.
10. **Q: Describe the efforts to standardize Post-Quantum Cryptography. Which organizations are involved, and what is the timeline for the transition to quantum-resistant cryptography?**
    - **A:** NIST is standardizing PQC algorithms. The goal is to have new standards ready before powerful quantum computers become a threat. The timeline involves ongoing evaluation and standardization.

CHAPTER 9: QUANTUM ERROR CORRECTION AND DECOHERENCE

Sources of Error in Quantum Systems

Quantum systems are notoriously susceptible to errors. Unlike classical bits, which are relatively stable, qubits are delicate and can easily lose their quantum properties. Here are some of the primary sources of errors in quantum systems:

✓ A. Decoherence

- **Description:** Decoherence is the loss of quantum coherence. Quantum coherence refers to the ability of a quantum system to exist in a superposition of states or to be entangled with other systems. When a qubit interacts with its surrounding environment, it starts to lose these quantum properties. The environment can be anything: stray electromagnetic fields, thermal vibrations, or even the measurement apparatus itself. This interaction causes the qubit to "leak" its quantum information into the environment, effectively collapsing its superposition into a classical state (either $|0\rangle$ or $|1\rangle$).
- **Coherence Time:** The time it takes for a qubit to lose its quantum coherence is called the coherence time. This is a crucial metric for quantum systems. The longer the coherence time, the more complex quantum computations can be performed before errors become dominant. Different types of qubits have different coherence times. For example, superconducting qubits might have coherence times on the order of tens or hundreds of microseconds, while some trapped ion qubits can maintain coherence for seconds or even minutes.
- **Example:** Imagine a qubit in a superposition of $|0\rangle$ and $|1\rangle$. If a stray electromagnetic field interacts with this qubit, it might "observe" the qubit's state. This observation, even without a formal measurement, causes the superposition to collapse. The qubit will then be in either the $|0\rangle$ state or the $|1\rangle$ state, and the quantum information encoded in the superposition is lost.

✓ B. Gate Errors

- **Description:** Quantum gates are the fundamental operations that manipulate qubits. Ideally, these gates should perform their intended operations perfectly. However, in reality, quantum gates are imperfect. This means that when a gate is applied to a qubit, it doesn't always perform the exact rotation or transformation that it's supposed to. These small inaccuracies accumulate over the course of a quantum computation, leading to errors in the final result.
- **Types of Gate Errors:** Gate errors can arise from various sources, including:
    - **Calibration errors:** Imperfect control over the physical parameters (e.g., pulse duration, amplitude) used to implement the gates.
    - **Noise:** Fluctuations in the control signals or the environment can affect the gate's performance.
    - **Crosstalk:** Unintended interactions with neighboring qubits can distort the gate operation.

- **Example:** Consider a quantum NOT gate (X gate), which should flip a qubit from |0⟩ to |1⟩ and vice versa. A gate error might cause the X gate to only partially flip the qubit, resulting in a state that is neither |0⟩ nor |1⟩, but a superposition with incorrect amplitudes.

✅ C. Measurement Errors

- **Description:** Measurement is the process of extracting classical information from a quantum state. In a perfect measurement, a qubit in the state |0⟩ would always be measured as 0, and a qubit in the state |1⟩ would always be measured as 1. However, in practice, measurements are not always accurate. Measurement errors occur when a qubit in the state |0⟩ is incorrectly measured as 1, or vice versa.
- **Sources of Measurement Errors:** These errors can be caused by:
  - **Imperfect detectors:** The detectors used to measure the qubits might have limited sensitivity or accuracy.
  - **Noise:** External noise can interfere with the measurement process.
  - **State preparation errors:** If the qubit was not in a pure |0⟩ or |1⟩ state before the measurement (due to previous gate errors or decoherence), the measurement result will be probabilistic and potentially incorrect.
- **Example:** Suppose a qubit is actually in the state |0⟩. Due to a measurement error, the measurement apparatus might incorrectly register it as a 1. This incorrect reading can lead to wrong conclusions about the outcome of the quantum computation.

✅ D. Crosstalk

- **Description:** Crosstalk is a particularly problematic error in multi-qubit systems. It refers to unintended interactions between qubits that are not supposed to be interacting. When performing an operation on one qubit, the operation can unintentionally affect the state of nearby qubits. This is similar to how nearby wires can sometimes interfere with each other, causing unwanted signals.
- **Causes of Crosstalk:** Crosstalk can be caused by:
  - **Electromagnetic interference:** Control signals applied to one qubit can induce electromagnetic fields that affect neighboring qubits.
  - **Physical proximity:** Qubits that are physically close to each other are more susceptible to crosstalk.
  - **Imperfect isolation:** Insufficient shielding or isolation between qubits can exacerbate crosstalk.
- **Example:** Imagine you want to apply a NOT gate (X gate) to qubit 1 in a system with three qubits. Due to crosstalk, the operation might also slightly rotate the states of qubits 2 and 3, even though they were not intended to be involved in the operation. This unintended interaction introduces errors into the overall quantum computation.

Accumulation of Errors

These errors, whether from decoherence, imperfect gates, faulty measurements, or crosstalk, accumulate during a quantum computation. If left uncorrected, they can quickly overwhelm the quantum system, rendering the final result meaningless. This is why quantum error correction is a critical area of research in quantum computing.

Quantum Error Correction: Bit Flip and Phase Flip Codes

Quantum error correction is essential for building fault-tolerant quantum computers. Because qubits are so sensitive, errors are much more common than in classical computers. Quantum error correction uses techniques to detect and correct these errors without directly measuring the qubit (which would destroy its quantum state).

✅ A. Bit Flip Code

- **Bit Flip Error:** A bit flip error changes a qubit from |0⟩ to |1⟩ or vice versa. This is analogous to a bit flip in classical computing.
- **Strategy:** The bit flip code protects against this type of error by encoding one logical qubit into three physical qubits.
  - |0⟩ is encoded as |000⟩
  - |1⟩ is encoded as |111⟩
- **Encoding:** We take the state we want to protect, and repeat it three times.
- **Error Detection and Correction:** If a bit flip occurs in one of the physical qubits, we can detect and correct it using majority voting. We measure the parity of the first and second qubits, and the parity of the second and third qubits.
- **Example:**
  - Suppose we encode the logical state |1⟩ as the physical state |111⟩.
  - If a bit flip error occurs on the second qubit, the state becomes |101⟩.
  - To correct this, we perform a majority vote:
    - Compare the first and second qubits: they disagree.
    - Compare the second and third qubits: they disagree.
    - Since the first and third qubits agree, we assume the second qubit is the one that flipped.
  - We flip the second qubit back, recovering the original state |111⟩.

✅ B. Phase Flip Code

- **Phase Flip Error:** A phase flip error changes the phase of a qubit. Recall that a qubit can be in a superposition of |0⟩ and |1⟩, such as |+⟩ = (|0⟩ + |1⟩)/√2. A phase flip error changes the sign between these states: |+⟩ becomes (|0⟩ - |1⟩)/√2 = |−⟩.
- **Detection Challenge:** Unlike bit flip errors, phase flip errors cannot be detected by directly measuring the qubits in the computational basis (|0⟩, |1⟩). Measuring in this basis would collapse the superposition, destroying the quantum information.

- **Strategy:** To protect against phase flip errors, we use a clever trick: we transform phase flips into bit flips using Hadamard gates.
- **Hadamard Transformation:** The Hadamard gate (H) has the property that:
    - H · Z · H = X Where:
        - Z is the Pauli-Z gate, which induces a phase flip.
        - X is the Pauli-X gate, which induces a bit flip.
- **Encoding and Correction:**

0. **Hadamard Transform:** Apply Hadamard gates to the qubit. This transforms a phase flip error (Z) into a bit flip error (X).
1. **Bit Flip Code:** Apply the bit flip code to the Hadamard-transformed state. This protects against the now-transformed phase flip errors.
2. **Inverse Hadamard Transform:** Apply Hadamard gates again to return to the original basis.

- **In essence:** By sandwiching the phase flip error (Z) with Hadamard gates, we've converted it into a bit flip error (X), which we can then correct using the bit flip code.

Shor Code and Fault-Tolerant Quantum Computing

✅ A. Shor Code (9-Qubit Code)

- **Pioneering Code:** Invented by Peter Shor, the Shor code was the first quantum error-correcting code. It was a major breakthrough in the field, demonstrating that quantum errors could, in principle, be corrected.
- **Error Correction Capability:** The Shor code can protect against:
    - One arbitrary error (a bit-flip, a phase-flip, or a combination of both) on any single qubit within the encoded block of qubits.

✅ Encoding in Shor Code:

The Shor code encodes a single logical qubit (the qubit we want to protect) into nine physical qubits. The encoding process involves two steps:

- **Step 1: Bit-Flip Protection:** First, we encode the logical qubit using the bit-flip code:
    - $|\psi\rangle = \alpha|0\rangle + \beta|1\rangle \rightarrow \alpha|000\rangle + \beta|111\rangle$ This step protects against bit-flip errors.
- **Step 2: Phase-Flip Protection:** Next, we protect against phase-flip errors. We encode each of the three qubits from the previous step into a three-qubit group using a specific encoding:
    - $|000\rangle \rightarrow 1/\sqrt{2}\,(|000\rangle + |111\rangle) \otimes 1/\sqrt{2}\,(|000\rangle + |111\rangle) \otimes 1/\sqrt{2}\,(|000\rangle + |111\rangle)$
    - $|000\rangle \rightarrow 1/2\sqrt{2}\,[|000000000\rangle + |000000111\rangle + |000111000\rangle + |000111111\rangle + |111000000\rangle + |111000111\rangle + |111111000\rangle + |111111111\rangle]$
- **Final Encoding:** After these two steps, the logical qubit $|\psi\rangle$ is encoded into a 9-qubit state. This 9-qubit state can tolerate one arbitrary error on any of its qubits.

✅ Error Detection and Correction

The Shor code can:

- **Detect Error Location:** Determine which of the nine physical qubits has experienced an error.
- **Correct the Error:** Apply the appropriate inverse gate (either X for a bit-flip or Z for a phase-flip) to correct the error.
- **Preserve Logical Qubit:** Perform error correction without collapsing the state of the logical qubit, which is crucial for maintaining quantum information.

This error detection and correction are achieved using ancilla qubits (auxiliary qubits) and syndrome measurements. Syndrome measurements extract information about the error (which qubit was affected, and what type of error occurred) without directly measuring the data qubits in a way that would destroy their superposition.

✅ Example:

- Suppose we want to encode the logical qubit $|\psi\rangle = \alpha|0\rangle + \beta|1\rangle$ using the Shor code. This logical qubit is transformed into a specific 9-qubit state. If, for example, the fifth qubit in this 9-qubit state experiences a phase-flip error, the Shor code's structure allows us to:
  - Detect that the error occurred on the fifth qubit.
  - Apply a Z gate to the fifth qubit to correct the phase flip.
  - Recover the original 9-qubit state (and thus the original logical qubit $|\psi\rangle$) with high fidelity.

✅ Visual Summary of Shor Code:

```
Logical qubit → Encoded in 9 qubits
|ψ⟩ = α|0⟩ + β|1⟩
|0⟩ → (|000⟩ + |111⟩) ⊗ (|000⟩ + |111⟩) ⊗ (|000⟩ + |111⟩)
```

✅ B. Fault-Tolerant Quantum Computing

- **Beyond Error Correction:** Even error correction circuits themselves can be susceptible to errors. Fault-tolerant quantum computing is a set of techniques that allow us to perform quantum computations in a way that not only corrects errors but also prevents errors from spreading or amplifying.
- **Key Ideas:**
  - **Fault-Tolerant Gates:** Design quantum gates and circuits such that a single error in one gate does not lead to multiple errors in subsequent gates. This often involves encoding qubits and performing operations on the encoded qubits in a way that limits error propagation.

- **Encoded Operations:** Perform quantum operations on encoded logical qubits rather than directly on physical qubits. This helps to preserve the encoded quantum information even in the presence of errors.
- **Error Correction Cycles:** Apply error correction procedures periodically throughout the computation. This prevents errors from accumulating to the point where they can no longer be corrected.

✅ Threshold Theorem

- **Error Threshold:** The threshold theorem of quantum computation states that if the error rate per qubit per gate is below a certain threshold (estimated to be around 10-4), it becomes possible to build a scalable quantum computer that can perform arbitrarily long computations with high reliability.
- **Practical Implications:** This theorem is a cornerstone of quantum computing. It means that if we can build quantum hardware with sufficiently low error rates, we can use quantum error correction to overcome the inherent fragility of quantum systems and build powerful, fault-tolerant quantum computers.

✅ Summary

Concept	Description
Bit Flip Code	Protects against bit-flip errors using 3 qubits
Phase Flip Code	Uses Hadamard basis to detect phase errors
Shor Code	9-qubit code that corrects arbitrary single-qubit error
Fault-Tolerant Computing	Prevents errors from spreading in circuits
Decoherence	Loss of quantum information due to environment

10 practical questions with detailed explanation answers on Quantum Error Correction:

Sources of Error in Quantum Systems

1. **Q: Describe the phenomenon of decoherence in quantum systems. How does it affect the coherence time of a qubit, and why is coherence time important for quantum computation?**
   - **A:** Decoherence is the loss of quantum coherence (superposition and entanglement) due to interactions with the environment. It reduces a qubit's

coherence time, which is the duration a qubit can maintain quantum properties. Longer coherence times allow for more complex and longer quantum computations before errors dominate.

2. **Q: Explain how gate imperfections can introduce errors in quantum computations. What are some sources of these gate errors, and how do they accumulate over a series of quantum operations?**
   - **A:** Gate imperfections cause slight deviations from intended operations. Sources include calibration errors, noise, and crosstalk. These errors accumulate with each gate application, degrading the final result.

Bit Flip and Phase Flip Codes

3. **Q: Describe the bit flip code. How does it encode a logical qubit, and how does it detect and correct a bit flip error? Provide a simple example.**
   - **A:** The bit flip code encodes $|0\rangle$ as $|000\rangle$ and $|1\rangle$ as $|111\rangle$. If a bit flips (e.g., $|111\rangle \rightarrow |101\rangle$), majority voting on the three physical qubits identifies and corrects the error.
4. **Q: Explain the phase flip error and why it cannot be directly detected using the bit flip code. How does the phase flip code address this issue, and what role do Hadamard gates play in this process?**
   - **A:** A phase flip error changes the relative phase between $|0\rangle$ and $|1\rangle$. It can't be detected like a bit flip. The phase flip code uses Hadamard gates to convert phase flips into bit flips (HZH = X), allowing the bit flip code to correct them.

Shor Code and Fault-Tolerant Computing

5. **Q: Describe the Shor code. How many physical qubits are used to encode one logical qubit, and what types of errors can it correct?**
   - **A:** The Shor code uses 9 physical qubits to encode 1 logical qubit. It can correct any single-qubit error: bit flip, phase flip, or a combination of both.
6. **Q: Explain the encoding process in the Shor code. What are the two main steps involved, and how do they provide protection against both bit flip and phase flip errors?**
   - **A:**
     - Step 1 (Bit-flip protection): Encode |0> to |000>, |1> to |111>.
     - Step 2 (Phase-flip protection): Encode each of those to a superposition. This two-step process allows the code to correct against both types of errors.
7. **Q: How does the Shor code detect and correct errors? What are ancilla qubits and syndrome measurements, and how do they help in this process?**
   - **A:** The Shor code uses ancilla qubits and syndrome measurements. Syndrome measurements, performed with ancilla qubits, extract error information (which qubit and error type) without collapsing the logical qubit's state, enabling correction.
8. **Q: What is fault-tolerant quantum computing? Why is it important, and what are the key ideas involved in achieving fault tolerance?**

- **A:** Fault-tolerant quantum computing performs computations that prevent errors from spreading. Key ideas include:
    - Fault-tolerant gates
    - Encoded operations
    - Periodic error correction

9. **Q: Explain the threshold theorem in quantum computing. What does it state, and why is it a crucial concept for the future of quantum computers?**
    - **A:** The threshold theorem states that if the error rate is below a certain threshold (around 10-4), arbitrarily long quantum computations are possible. This is crucial because it means we can build scalable quantum computers.
10. **Q: Compare and contrast quantum error correction with classical error correction. What are the key differences, and why is quantum error correction more challenging?**

```
* **A:**
    * Classical error correction copies bits.
    * Quantum error correction must deal with superposition, entanglement,
and the no-cloning theorem, making it more complex.
```

30 multiple-choice questions with answers on Quantum Error Correction:

Sources of Error in Quantum Systems

1. **Q: What is the primary cause of decoherence?**
    - A) Imperfect gates
    - B) Measurement errors
    - C) Interaction with the environment
    - D) Crosstalk
    - **A:** C
2. **Q: The time it takes for a qubit to lose its quantum coherence is called:**
    - A) Gate time
    - B) Measurement time
    - C) Coherence time
    - D) Error time
    - **A:** C
3. **Q: Imperfect operations on qubits lead to:**
    - A) Decoherence
    - B) Gate errors
    - C) Measurement errors
    - D) Crosstalk
    - **A:** B
4. **Q: Which type of error occurs during the process of extracting classical information from a qubit?**
    - A) Decoherence
    - B) Gate errors
    - C) Measurement errors

- D) Crosstalk
- **A:** C

5. **Q: Unintended interactions between qubits are known as:**
    - A) Decoherence
    - B) Gate errors
    - C) Measurement errors
    - D) Crosstalk
    - **A:** D
6. **Q: Which error is most like a classical bit flip?**
    - A) Phase flip
    - B) Bit flip
    - C) Decoherence
    - D) Crosstalk
    - **A:** B
7. **Q: Which error involves loss of superposition?**
    - A) Bit flip
    - B) Phase flip
    - C) Decoherence
    - D) Crosstalk
    - **A:** C
8. **Q: Which error is specific to multi-qubit systems?**
    - A) Bit flip
    - B) Phase flip
    - C) Decoherence
    - D) Crosstalk
    - **A:** D
9. **Q: What is the impact of gate errors on a quantum computation?**
    - A) They cause the computer to crash
    - B) They introduce inaccuracies
    - C) They are easily corrected
    - D) They have no impact.
    - **A:** B
10. **Q: What is a major challenge in quantum measurement?**
    - A) Speed
    - B) Accuracy
    - C) Cost
    - D) Size
    - **A:** B

Bit Flip and Phase Flip Codes

11. **Q: A bit flip error changes a qubit from $|0\rangle$ to $|1\rangle$ or vice versa. How does the bit flip code protect against this?**
    - A) By using Hadamard gates
    - B) By encoding $|0\rangle$ to $|000\rangle$ and $|1\rangle$ to $|111\rangle$
    - C) By measuring the qubit multiple times

- D) By entangling the qubit with an ancilla
- **A:** B

12. **Q: In the bit flip code, if we encode |1⟩ as |111⟩ and one qubit flips to |0⟩, the state becomes:**
    - A) |000⟩
    - B) |101⟩
    - C) |011⟩
    - D) |110⟩
    - **A:** B
13. **Q: How does the bit flip code correct the error in the previous question?**
    - A) By applying a Hadamard gate
    - B) By measuring the qubit directly
    - C) By using majority voting
    - D) By entangling with an ancilla
    - **A:** C
14. **Q: A phase flip error changes the:**
    - A) Amplitude of the qubit
    - B) Phase of the qubit
    - C) State of the qubit
    - D) Energy of the qubit
    - **A:** B
15. **Q: How does a phase flip error affect the state |+⟩ = (|0⟩ + |1⟩)/√2?**
    - A) It becomes |0⟩
    - B) It becomes |1⟩
    - C) It becomes |−⟩ = (|0⟩ - |1⟩)/√2
    - D) It remains unchanged
    - **A:** C
16. **Q: What gate is used to transform a phase flip error into a bit flip error?**
    - A) X gate
    - B) Y gate
    - C) Z gate
    - D) Hadamard gate
    - **A:** D
17. **Q: The Hadamard gate transforms the Pauli-Z gate (Z) into which gate?**
    - A) X gate
    - B) Y gate
    - C) Z gate
    - D) I gate
    - **A:** A
18. **Q: After transforming a phase flip into a bit flip, which code is applied?**
    - A) Phase flip code
    - B) Bit flip code
    - C) Shor code
    - D) Surface code
    - **A:** B
19. **Q: In the phase flip code, Hadamard gates are applied:**

- A) Only at the beginning
- B) Only at the end
- C) Both at the beginning and the end
- D) Never
- **A:** C

20. **Q: The bit flip code protects against errors in qubit..., while phase flip code protects against errors in qubit...**
    - A) Phase, state
    - B) State, phase
    - C) Amplitude, phase
    - D) Phase, amplitude
    - **A:** B

Shor Code and Fault-Tolerant Computing

21. **Q: Who invented the Shor code?**
    - A) Peter Shor
    - B) Richard Feynman
    - C) David Deutsch
    - D) Charles Bennett
    - **A:** A
22. **Q: The Shor code uses how many physical qubits to encode one logical qubit?**
    - A) 3
    - B) 5
    - C) 7
    - D) 9
    - **A:** D
23. **Q: The Shor code protects against:**
    - A) Only bit-flip errors
    - B) Only phase-flip errors
    - C) Only measurement errors
    - D) Any single-qubit error
    - **A:** D
24. **Q: In the Shor code, the first step of encoding uses:**
    - A) Phase flip code
    - B) Bit flip code
    - C) Surface code
    - D) Repetition code
    - **A:** B
25. **Q: In the Shor code, the second step of encoding protects against:**
    - A) Bit-flip errors
    - B) Phase-flip errors
    - C) Measurement errors
    - D) Crosstalk
    - **A:** B
26. **Q: The Shor code uses... qubits and... qubits for encoding.**

- A) 3, 6
- B) 6, 3
- C) 9, 3
- D) 3, 9
- **A:** C

27. **Q: What are used in Shor code for error detection and correction?**
    - A) Only Hadamard gates
    - B) Ancilla qubits and syndrome measurements
    - C) Only CNOT gates
    - D) Direct measurement of data qubits
    - **A:** B
28. **Q: Fault-tolerant quantum computing aims to prevent errors from:**
    - A) Occurring
    - B) Being corrected
    - C) Spreading
    - D) Being detected
    - **A:** C
29. **Q: According to the threshold theorem, reliable quantum computation is possible if the error rate is below approximately:**
    - A) 10-1
    - B) 10-2
    - C) 10-4
    - D) 10-6
    - **A:** C
30. **Q: Fault-tolerant quantum computing involves:**
    - A) Using only classical error correction
    - B) Designing gates that do not amplify errors
    - C) Avoiding error correction entirely
    - D) Measuring qubits very frequently
    - **A:** B

20 short questions and answers on Quantum Error Correction:

Sources of Error in Quantum Systems

1. **Q: What is the main cause of decoherence?**
    - **A:** Environmental interaction.
2. **Q: What is coherence time?**
    - **A:** Time a qubit maintains quantum properties.
3. **Q: What do imperfect operations cause?**
    - **A:** Gate errors.
4. **Q: What errors occur during qubit measurement?**
    - **A:** Measurement errors.
5. **Q: What is unintended qubit interaction called?**
    - **A:** Crosstalk.

Bit Flip and Phase Flip Codes

6. **Q: What error does bit flip code correct?**
   - **A:** Bit flip.
7. **Q: How does bit flip code encode |0⟩?**
   - **A:** |000⟩.
8. **Q: What is used for correction in bit flip code?**
   - **A:** Majority voting.
9. **Q: What error does phase flip code correct?**
   - **A:** Phase flip.
10. **Q: What gate transforms phase flips to bit flips?**
    - **A:** Hadamard gate.
11. **Q: What code is applied after the Hadamard transform in phase flip correction?**
    - **A:** Bit flip code.

Shor Code and Fault-Tolerant Computing

12. **Q: Who invented the Shor code?**
    - **A:** Peter Shor.
13. **Q: How many qubits does the Shor code use?**
    - **A:** 9.
14. **Q: What type of error does Shor code correct?**
    - **A:** Any single-qubit error.
15. **Q: What are used for error detection in Shor code?**
    - **A:** Ancilla qubits.
16. **Q: What measurements are used in Shor code?**
    - **A:** Syndrome measurements.
17. **Q: What does fault-tolerant computing prevent?**
    - **A:** Error spreading.
18. **Q: What kind of gates are used in fault-tolerant computing?**
    - **A:** Gates that do not amplify errors.
19. **Q: What does the threshold theorem define?**
    - **A:** Maximum error rate.
20. **Q: What is the approximate error threshold?**
    -

10 medium-size questions with answers on Quantum Error Correction:

Sources of Error in Quantum Systems

1. **Q: Explain the concept of decoherence and its impact on quantum systems. How does it differ from classical noise, and why is it a significant challenge for quantum computing?**
   - **A:** Decoherence is the loss of quantum superposition and entanglement due to environmental interaction. Unlike classical noise, it directly affects the quantum

state, making it a major challenge because it destroys the very properties quantum computers rely on.

2. **Q: Describe gate errors in quantum systems. What are some of the primary sources of these errors, and how do they affect the accuracy of quantum computations?**
    - **A:** Gate errors are imperfections in quantum gate operations. Sources include calibration errors, noise, and crosstalk. They reduce computational accuracy by causing qubits to deviate from their intended states, accumulating errors over time.

Bit Flip and Phase Flip Codes

3. **Q: Explain the bit flip code in detail. How does it encode a logical qubit, and how does it detect and correct bit flip errors? Provide an example of how this code corrects an error.**
    - **A:** The bit flip code encodes $|0\rangle$ as $|000\rangle$ and $|1\rangle$ as $|111\rangle$. If a bit flips (e.g., $|111\rangle$ to $|101\rangle$), majority voting identifies the flipped bit, which is then flipped back to correct the error.
4. **Q: Describe the phase flip error and explain why it cannot be corrected using the bit flip code directly. How does the phase flip code address this issue, and what is the role of the Hadamard gate in this process?**
    - **A:** A phase flip changes the relative phase between $|0\rangle$ and $|1\rangle$. The bit flip code can't detect this. The phase flip code uses Hadamard gates to transform phase flips into bit flips ($HZH = X$), allowing the bit flip code to be used for correction.

Shor Code and Fault-Tolerant Computing

5. **Q: Explain the Shor code in detail. How does it encode a logical qubit into nine physical qubits, and how does this encoding protect against both bit flip and phase flip errors?**
    - **A:** The Shor code encodes a logical qubit into nine physical qubits in two steps: first encoding with a bit flip code and then encoding each of those qubits to protect against phase flips. This combined encoding protects against any single-qubit error.
6. **Q: Describe the error detection and correction process in the Shor code. What are ancilla qubits and syndrome measurements, and how do they enable error correction without collapsing the state of the logical qubit?**
    - **A:** The Shor code uses ancilla qubits and syndrome measurements. Syndrome measurements use the ancilla qubits to extract information about errors (type and location) without directly measuring the data qubits, thus preventing collapse.
7. **Q: What is fault-tolerant quantum computing? Why is it necessary for building large-scale quantum computers, and what are the key principles involved in achieving fault tolerance?**
    - **A:** Fault-tolerant quantum computing enables reliable computation by preventing errors from spreading. It's necessary for scalable quantum computers and involves fault-tolerant gates, encoded operations, and periodic error correction.

8. **Q: Explain the quantum threshold theorem. What does it state about the relationship between error rates and the feasibility of building large-scale quantum computers, and why is this significant?**
   - **A:** The threshold theorem states that if the error rate per gate is below a certain threshold (around 10^-4), arbitrarily long quantum computations are possible. This is significant because it provides a target for hardware development.
9. **Q: Compare and contrast classical error correction and quantum error correction. What are the fundamental differences that make quantum error correction more challenging?**
   - **A:** Classical error correction copies bits, while quantum error correction must deal with superposition, entanglement, and the no-cloning theorem. This makes quantum error correction more complex, requiring more sophisticated techniques.
10. **Q: Discuss the challenges and future directions in quantum error correction. What are some of the current research efforts, and what are the potential long-term impacts of achieving effective quantum error correction?**
    - **A:** Challenges include reducing error rates below the threshold and developing more efficient codes. Current research focuses on topological codes and improved hardware. Effective quantum error correction is crucial for realizing practical, large-scale quantum computers.

CHAPTER 10: QUANTUM COMPUTING HARDWARE

Types of Quantum Computers

Several companies and research labs are actively developing various hardware architectures for building quantum computers. Here are some of the most prominent ones:

✅ A. Superconducting Qubits

- **Used by:** IBM, Google, Rigetti
- 💡 **How It Works:**
  - Superconducting qubits are created using superconducting circuits, which are cooled to extremely low temperatures, very close to absolute zero.
  - At these temperatures, the circuits exhibit quantum mechanical properties and behave like artificial atoms with quantized energy levels.
  - **Josephson junctions:** These special electrical circuit elements are crucial for controlling the quantum states of these qubits. They act like switches that allow us to manipulate the flow of quantum information.
- ✅ **Example:**
  - IBM's Quantum Experience makes use of transmon qubits, which are a specific type of superconducting qubit. These transmon qubits are designed to be less sensitive to charge noise, a common source of errors.
  - Google's Sycamore processor, which contained 53 qubits, was used to demonstrate "quantum supremacy" in 2019. This experiment showcased the potential of superconducting qubits to perform certain calculations much faster than the most powerful classical computers.
- ✅ **Pros:**
  - **Fast gate times:** Superconducting qubits can perform quantum operations very quickly, typically on the order of nanoseconds. This speed is crucial for executing complex quantum algorithms.
  - **Scalable fabrication:** These qubits can be manufactured using standard microfabrication techniques similar to those used to make classical computer chips. This makes it potentially easier to scale up the number of qubits in a system.
- ⚠️ **Cons:**
  - **Sensitive to noise and decoherence:** Superconducting qubits are susceptible to various forms of noise from their environment, which can cause them to lose their quantum information (decoherence).
  - **Requires cryogenic cooling:** These systems need to be cooled to extremely low temperatures (around 15 millikelvin, which is colder than interstellar space) using specialized equipment called dilution refrigerators. This cooling requirement adds complexity and cost.

✅ B. Ion Trap Qubits

- **Used by:** IonQ, Honeywell
- 💡 **How It Works:**
  - Ion trap quantum computers use individual charged atoms, or ions, as qubits.
  - These ions are held in place, or "trapped," using electromagnetic fields within a vacuum chamber.
  - Quantum information is stored in the internal energy states of the ions, such as the electron's energy levels.
  - **Lasers:** Precisely controlled lasers are used to manipulate the quantum states of the ions and to read out (measure) the results of quantum computations.
- ✅ **Example:**
  - IonQ's quantum systems employ Ytterbium ions, which have desirable properties for quantum computing, including relatively long coherence times.
  - In an ion trap system, each ion represents a qubit, and quantum gates are implemented by applying carefully timed laser pulses to entangle and manipulate these ions.
- ✅ **Pros:**
  - **Very low error rates:** Ion trap systems are known for their high fidelity, meaning they can perform quantum operations with very low error rates.
  - **Long coherence times:** Ions can maintain their quantum states for relatively long periods, often on the order of seconds. This long coherence time is a significant advantage for performing complex quantum computations.
- ⚠️ **Cons:**
  - **Slower gate speeds:** Compared to superconducting qubits, ion trap systems typically have slower gate speeds, on the order of microseconds.
  - **Scaling challenges:** Scaling up ion trap systems to include a large number of qubits is more challenging due to the complexity of controlling and addressing individual ions.

✅ C. Photonic Quantum Computers

- **Used by:** Xanadu, PsiQuantum
- 💡 **How It Works:**
  - Photonic quantum computers use photons, or light particles, as qubits.
  - Quantum information is encoded in various properties of photons, such as their polarization (the direction of the light wave's oscillation), time-bin (whether the photon arrives in an early or late time window), or path (which optical path the photon travels through).
  - **Optical circuits:** These systems use optical components like mirrors, beam splitters, and phase shifters to manipulate the photons and perform quantum operations.
- ✅ **Example:**
  - Xanadu's Borealis system uses continuous-variable photonic qubits. Unlike discrete qubits (which are either $|0\rangle$ or $|1\rangle$), continuous-variable qubits can take on a range of values.

- PsiQuantum is pursuing a different approach, aiming to build a large-scale photonic quantum computer using silicon photonics, leveraging existing semiconductor manufacturing techniques.

- ✅ **Pros:**
  - **Room-temperature operation:** Photonic quantum computers can operate at room temperature, eliminating the need for expensive and complex cryogenic cooling.
  - **Natural compatibility with quantum networks:** Photons are the natural carriers of information in optical communications, making photonic qubits well-suited for building future quantum networks.
- ⚠️ **Cons:**
  - **Photon loss and detection inefficiency:** One of the main challenges is minimizing the loss of photons as they travel through the optical circuits and efficiently detecting the photons at the end of the computation.
  - **Harder to implement deterministic entangling gates:** Creating reliable and deterministic entangling gates (gates that create entanglement between photons) is more challenging compared to other qubit technologies.

Noise, Decoherence, and Scalability in Quantum Computing

Quantum systems are inherently delicate and face several fundamental physical limitations that pose significant challenges to building practical quantum computers.

✅ A. Noise

- **Fragile Quantum States:** Quantum states, such as superpositions and entanglement, are extremely fragile and can be easily disrupted by even the smallest disturbances from the environment.
- **Sources of Noise:**
  - **Thermal noise:** Random fluctuations in temperature can cause qubits to change their states.
  - **Electromagnetic interference:** Stray electromagnetic fields can interact with qubits, leading to errors.
  - **Imperfect gates or measurements:** As discussed earlier, quantum gates and measurement devices are not perfect and can introduce errors into the system.

✅ B. Decoherence

- **Loss of Quantum Properties:** Decoherence is the process by which qubits lose their quantum properties, such as superposition and entanglement, due to their interaction with the surrounding environment. In essence, the quantum information stored in the qubits "leaks" into the environment, causing the qubits to behave more like classical bits.
- **Coherence Times:** Two key metrics characterize decoherence:

    - **T1 (Relaxation Time):** This is the time it takes for a qubit in an excited state to decay to its ground state. It represents how long a qubit can maintain its energy state.
    - **T2 (Dephasing Time):** This is the time it takes for a qubit to lose its phase coherence. Phase coherence is essential for maintaining superpositions. T2 represents how long a qubit can maintain its superposition.
- 📉 **Short Coherence Times:** Short coherence times are a major obstacle in quantum computing. They limit the number of quantum operations (gates) that can be performed on the qubits before errors due to decoherence become dominant and render the computation unreliable.

✅ C. Scalability

- **Scaling to Millions of Qubits:** To solve complex, real-world problems that are beyond the reach of classical computers, quantum computers will need to scale to contain millions of qubits. This presents enormous engineering and scientific challenges.
- **Challenges of Scaling:**
    - **Managing error rates:** As the number of qubits increases, the overall error rate of the system also tends to increase. Maintaining low error rates in large-scale quantum systems is a significant hurdle.
    - **Efficiently entangling large numbers of qubits:** Creating and maintaining entanglement between a large number of qubits is a complex task. Entanglement is crucial for many quantum algorithms, and scaling it up is difficult.
    - **Cooling or isolating large-scale systems:** For technologies like superconducting and trapped ion qubits, which require extremely low temperatures or high vacuum, scaling up the cooling or isolation infrastructure becomes increasingly challenging and expensive.
- □□ **Solutions for Scalability:** Researchers are exploring several approaches to address the scalability challenge:
    - **Modular quantum architectures:** Breaking down a large quantum computer into smaller, interconnected modules. This allows for easier control and scaling.
    - **3D integration:** Stacking qubits and control circuitry in three dimensions to increase density and reduce wiring complexity.
    - **Quantum interconnects:** Developing technologies to efficiently transfer quantum information between different modules or quantum computers.

Quantum Hardware vs. Simulation

Because building and operating quantum computers is still in its early stages and presents many challenges, researchers and students often rely on quantum simulators to study and develop quantum algorithms.

✅ A. Quantum Hardware

- **Real Quantum Processors:** These are physical devices that harness quantum mechanical phenomena to perform computations. Examples include:
  - IBM Q quantum computers, which use superconducting qubits.
  - IonQ's systems, which use trapped ion qubits.
- **Real-World Imperfections:** Quantum hardware is subject to the limitations of the physical world, including:
  - **Noise:** Environmental disturbances that affect qubit states.
  - **Decoherence:** The loss of quantum coherence over time.
  - **Hardware-specific constraints:** Each type of quantum hardware has its own unique set of limitations and imperfections.
- **Best Use:** Quantum hardware is essential for:
  - Testing and validating quantum error correction techniques in a real-world setting.
  - Calibrating and optimizing quantum gates and operations.
  - Benchmarking the performance of actual quantum devices.
  - Exploring the behavior of quantum systems in the presence of real-world noise.

✅ B. Quantum Simulation

- **Classical Simulation of Quantum Circuits:** Quantum simulators are classical computer programs that mimic the behavior of quantum circuits. They use classical algorithms to calculate how quantum states evolve under the action of quantum gates. Examples of quantum simulation software include:
  - Qiskit (developed by IBM)
  - Cirq (developed by Google)
  - QuTiP (Quantum Toolbox in Python)
- ✅ **Pros:**
  - **Noise-free environment:** Simulations are typically free of noise and decoherence, allowing for ideal, error-free computations.
  - **Debug-friendly:** Simulators provide tools and features that make it easier to debug and analyze quantum circuits.
  - **Accessibility:** Quantum simulators are readily accessible and can be run on standard classical computers, making them a valuable tool for learning and experimentation.
- ⚠□ **Cons:**
  - **Exponential scaling:** The computational resources required to simulate a quantum system grow exponentially with the number of qubits. Simulating systems with more than about 30 qubits becomes extremely challenging and often infeasible for even the most powerful supercomputers.
  - **Doesn't capture real-world limitations:** Simulations do not accurately capture the complex and often unpredictable behavior of real quantum hardware, including noise, decoherence, and hardware-specific errors.

✅ Example: Running Grover's Algorithm

Imagine you want to run Grover's algorithm, a quantum algorithm for searching an unstructured database:

- **Simulator:** If you run Grover's algorithm on a quantum simulator, you will get perfect results very quickly (assuming a small number of qubits). You can easily verify the correctness of the algorithm and analyze its behavior without worrying about errors.
- **Hardware:** If you run the same algorithm on real quantum hardware, you will likely get noisy results. The output will be affected by errors due to decoherence, gate imperfections, and other hardware limitations. However, running on hardware provides valuable insights into how the algorithm performs in a real-world setting and helps to identify the challenges that need to be addressed to build practical quantum computers.

```
# Qiskit Example (Simulation vs. Real Hardware)
from qiskit import Aer, IBMQ, execute

# Get a simulator from the Aer provider
simulator = Aer.get_backend('qasm_simulator')

# Load your IBM Quantum account (if you have one)
# and get access to a real quantum device
# provider = IBMQ.load_account()  # This line requires an IBM Quantum account
# real_device = provider.get_backend('ibmq_quito') # Example device


# Example usage (you would define your quantum circuit 'qc' here)
# job_sim = execute(qc, simulator, shots=1024)  # Run on simulator
# result_sim = job_sim.result()
# counts_sim = result_sim.get_counts(qc)
# print("Simulation Results:", counts_sim)


# job_real = execute(qc, real_device, shots=1024)  # Run on real hardware
# result_real = job_real.result()
# counts_real = result_real.get_counts(qc)
# print("Real Hardware Results:", counts_real)
```

✅ Summary Table

Hardware Type	Examples	Pros	Cons
Superconducting	IBM, Google	Fast, scalable	Requires ultra-cold temperatures
Ion Trap	IonQ, Honeywell	Long coherence, precise	Harder to scale, slower gates
Photonic	Xanadu, PsiQ	Room temperature, high connectivity	Photon loss, gate limitations

Hardware Type	Examples	Pros	Cons
Simulation	Qiskit, Cirq	Accessible, noise-free	Not scalable beyond ~30 qubits

10 practical questions with detailed explanation answers on Quantum Computing:

Types of Quantum Computers

1. **Q: Compare and contrast superconducting qubits and ion trap qubits in terms of their physical implementation, gate speeds, coherence times, and scalability. Which technology is currently more mature, and what are the potential long-term advantages of each?**
   - **A:**
     - **Superconducting:** Uses superconducting circuits cooled to near absolute zero. Fast gate speeds (nanoseconds) and scalable fabrication. Shorter coherence times, more sensitive to noise. More mature in terms of qubit count. Potential for large-scale integration.
     - **Ion Trap:** Uses trapped ions in vacuum chambers. Slower gate speeds (microseconds) but very low error rates and long coherence times (seconds). Scaling is challenging. Potential for very high-fidelity operations.
     - **Maturity:** Superconducting is currently more mature in terms of the number of qubits in a single device.
     - **Long-term Advantages:** Superconducting for speed and scalability. Ion trap for accuracy and long coherence.
2. **Q: Explain how photonic quantum computers encode and manipulate quantum information. What are the advantages of using photons as qubits, and what are the main challenges in developing this technology?**
   - **A:** Photonic quantum computers use photons, encoding information in properties like polarization or path. Advantages: room-temperature operation, compatibility with quantum networks. Challenges: photon loss, inefficient entangling gates.

Noise, Decoherence, and Scalability

3. **Q: Describe the primary sources of noise that affect quantum systems. How does noise impact the stability of quantum states, and what are the implications for performing accurate quantum computations?**
   - **A:** Sources of noise: thermal noise, electromagnetic interference, imperfect gates. Noise disrupts fragile quantum states (superpositions, entanglement), leading to errors and limiting the accuracy of computations.
4. **Q: Explain the phenomenon of decoherence. What are T1 and T2 times, and how do they characterize the decoherence process? Why are long coherence times essential for practical quantum computing?**

- **A:** Decoherence is the loss of quantum properties due to environmental interaction. T1 (relaxation time) measures how long a qubit stays excited. T2 (dephasing time) measures how long a qubit retains phase coherence. Long coherence times are essential to perform enough quantum operations before errors overwhelm the computation.

5. **Q: What are the main challenges in scaling quantum computers to millions of qubits? Discuss the issues related to error management, entanglement, and physical implementation.**
    - **A:** Challenges: managing increasing error rates, efficiently entangling many qubits, and the physical difficulties of cooling and controlling large systems. Solutions involve modular architectures, 3D integration, and quantum interconnects.

Quantum Hardware vs. Simulation

6. **Q: Compare and contrast quantum hardware and quantum simulators. What are the key advantages and disadvantages of each, and in what situations is it more appropriate to use one over the other?**
    - **A:**
        - **Hardware:** Real quantum processors. Subject to noise and decoherence. Best for real-world testing.
        - **Simulators:** Classical computers mimicking quantum circuits. Noise-free, debug-friendly, accessible. Limited by exponential scaling.
    - Use simulators for algorithm development and testing; use hardware for real-world validation and benchmarking.
7. **Q: Explain the limitations of quantum simulators in accurately representing the behavior of real quantum hardware. How do factors like noise and decoherence affect the performance of quantum algorithms on actual quantum computers compared to simulations?**
    - **A:** Simulators don't capture real-world noise, decoherence, and hardware imperfections. Algorithms that work perfectly in simulation may fail on real hardware due to these factors, highlighting the need for quantum error correction and fault-tolerant techniques.
8. **Q: Describe how quantum computers are cooled and why they need to be kept so cold. What are dilution refrigerators, and what role do they play in superconducting quantum computing?**
    - **A:** Superconducting quantum computers need to be kept extremely cold (millikelvins) to suppress thermal noise and maintain superconductivity. Dilution refrigerators are specialized cryogenic devices that achieve these ultra-low temperatures.
9. **Q: Explain the concept of quantum supremacy (or quantum advantage). What was the significance of Google's Sycamore experiment, and what are the challenges in demonstrating a practical quantum advantage for real-world applications?**
    - **A:** Quantum supremacy (or advantage) is the point where a quantum computer can solve a problem that is practically impossible for any classical computer.

Google's Sycamore experiment demonstrated this for a specific, contrived problem. The challenge is to show this advantage for useful, real-world problems.

10. **Q: Discuss the potential applications of quantum computers in various fields, such as materials science, drug discovery, and finance. How do the different quantum computing architectures (superconducting, ion trap, photonic) lend themselves to specific types of applications?**
    - **A:**
        - Materials Science: Simulating molecular structures (all architectures).
        - Drug Discovery: Molecular simulation, optimization (all architectures).
        - Finance: Optimization, risk analysis (superconducting, photonic for speed).
        - Superconducting: Fast computation, good for optimization.
        - Ion Trap: High-fidelity, good for complex simulations.
        - Photonic: Quantum networking, room-temperature operation.

30 medium-length multiple-choice questions with answers on Quantum Computing:

Types of Quantum Computers

1. **Q: Which type of qubit is created using superconducting circuits cooled to near absolute zero?**
    - A) Ion Trap Qubits
    - B) Photonic Qubits
    - C) Superconducting Qubits
    - D) Trapped Neutral Atoms
    - **A:** C
2. **Q: What are Josephson junctions, and what role do they play in superconducting quantum computers?**
    - A) Light detectors; measuring photon states
    - B) Charged atoms; storing quantum information
    - C) Special electrical circuits; controlling quantum states
    - D) Magnetic fields; trapping ions
    - **A:** C
3. **Q: Which quantum computing technology is known for its fast gate times (nanoseconds) and scalable fabrication using standard chip technologies?**
    - A) Ion Trap Qubits
    - B) Photonic Qubits
    - C) Superconducting Qubits
    - D) Trapped Neutral Atoms
    - **A:** C
4. **Q: What is a major disadvantage of superconducting qubits in terms of their operational requirements?**
    - A) Slow gate speeds
    - B) High error rates
    - C) Requirement for dilution refrigerators
    - D) Difficulty in scaling

- **A:** C

5. **Q: Which type of qubit uses charged atoms trapped using electric/magnetic fields in vacuum chambers?**
    - A) Superconducting Qubits
    - B) Photonic Qubits
    - C) Ion Trap Qubits
    - D) Quantum Dots
    - **A:** C
6. **Q: How are quantum information stored in ion trap quantum computers?**
    - A) Polarization of photons
    - B) Internal states of the ions
    - C) Superconducting circuit oscillations
    - D) Electron spin
    - **A:** B
7. **Q: What is a key advantage of ion trap qubits in terms of their performance characteristics?**
    - A) Fast gate speeds
    - B) Room-temperature operation
    - C) Very low error rates and long coherence times
    - D) Natural compatibility with quantum networks
    - **A:** C
8. **Q: What is a primary challenge in scaling up ion trap quantum systems?**
    - A) Maintaining superconductivity
    - B) Minimizing photon loss
    - C) Controlling and addressing individual ions
    - D) Achieving quantum supremacy
    - **A:** C
9. **Q: Which type of quantum computer uses photons as qubits?**
    - A) Superconducting Qubits
    - B) Ion Trap Qubits
    - C) Photonic Quantum Computers
    - D) Neutral Atom Qubits
    - **A:** C
10. **Q: In photonic quantum computers, what properties of photons are used to encode quantum information?**
    - A) Temperature and pressure
    - B) Polarization, time-bin, or path
    - C) Voltage and current
    - D) Frequency and wavelength
    - **A:** B
11. **Q: What is a significant advantage of photonic quantum computers compared to superconducting and ion trap systems?** * A) Faster gate speeds * B) Higher fidelity * C) Room-temperature operation * D) Easier scaling * **A:** C
12. **Q: What is a major challenge in implementing photonic quantum computers?** * A) Maintaining ion traps * B) Achieving ultra-low temperatures * C) Photon loss and inefficient entangling gates * D) Controlling Josephson junctions * **A:** C

Noise, Decoherence, and Scalability

13. **Q: What is a major source of noise that affects quantum systems?** * A) Perfect gates * B) Thermal noise * C) Error correction * D) Quantum simulation * **A:** B
14. **Q: How do minute disturbances affect quantum states?** * A) They have no effect * B) They make them more stable * C) They cause them to collapse * D) They cause errors * **A:** D
15. **Q: What is the process by which qubits lose their quantum properties over time?** * A) Quantum entanglement * B) Quantum superposition * C) Decoherence * D) Quantum tunneling * **A:** C
16. **Q: What does T1 (relaxation time) measure?** * A) How long a qubit maintains phase coherence * B) How long a qubit stays entangled * C) How long a qubit stays excited * D) How long a qubit stays in superposition * **A:** C
17. **Q: What does T2 (dephasing time) indicate?** * A) How long a qubit stays excited * B) How long a qubit retains phase coherence * C) How long a qubit maintains its energy * D) How long a qubit remains isolated * **A:** B
18. **Q: Why are short coherence times a limitation for quantum computing?** * A) They allow for more complex operations * B) They increase the number of errors * C) They make qubits more stable * D) They simplify quantum algorithms * **A:** B
19. **Q: What is a significant challenge in building practical quantum computers?** * A) Operating at room temperature * B) Scaling to millions of qubits * C) Achieving perfect gates * D) Avoiding superposition * **A:** B
20. **Q: What is a key issue in scaling quantum computers to larger sizes?** * A) Decreasing error rates * B) Simplifying entanglement * C) Managing error rates as systems grow * D) Reducing the need for cooling * **A:** C
21. **Q: What is being developed to address the scalability challenges in quantum computing?** * A) Classical error correction * B) Quantum simulation software * C) Modular quantum architectures, 3D integration, and quantum interconnects * D) Room-temperature superconductors * **A:** C

Quantum Hardware vs. Simulation

22. **Q: What is the primary difference between quantum hardware and quantum simulation?** * A) Hardware uses classical bits, simulation uses qubits * B) Hardware is physical, simulation is on classical computers * C) Hardware is error-free, simulation has errors * D) Hardware is faster, simulation is more accurate * **A:** B
23. **Q: Which of the following is an example of quantum hardware?** * A) Qiskit * B) Cirq * C) IBM Q * D) QuTiP * **A:** C
24. **Q: What are the primary limitations of quantum hardware compared to quantum simulators?** * A) Lack of accessibility and high cost * B) Subject to noise, decoherence, and hardware-specific constraints * C) Inability to perform complex calculations * D) Limited to small-scale systems * **A:** B
25. **Q: What is the main advantage of using quantum simulators?** * A) They capture real-world physical limitations * B) They are free of noise and errors * C) They can simulate an unlimited number of qubits * D) They are faster than quantum hardware * **A:** B

26. **Q: What is a major drawback of quantum simulators?** * A) They are difficult to use * B) They require specialized hardware * C) They scale exponentially with the number of qubits * D) They cannot simulate quantum phenomena * **A:** C
27. **Q: For what purpose is quantum hardware best suited?** * A) Debugging quantum circuits * B) Running error-free computations * C) Real-world testing of error correction and calibration * D) Simulating large quantum systems * **A:** C
28. **Q: What is a key advantage of quantum simulators in the development process?** * A) High fidelity * B) Real-time performance * C) Debug-friendly and accessible * D) Low operating costs * **A:** C
29. **Q: When running a quantum algorithm like Grover's algorithm, what difference would you expect between the results from a simulator and real quantum hardware?** * A) Simulator: noisy results; Hardware: perfect results * B) Simulator: slow results; Hardware: fast results * C) Simulator: perfect results; Hardware: noisy results * D) Simulator: incomplete results; Hardware: complete results * **A:** C
30. **Q: Which tool or platform is used for quantum simulation?** * A) Quantum computer * B) Qiskit or Cirq * C) Oscilloscope * D) Dilution refrigerator * **A:** B

20 short questions and answers on Quantum Computing:

Types of Quantum Computers

1. **Q: What are IBM and Google using for their quantum computers?**
   - **A:** Superconducting qubits.
2. **Q: What do ion trap computers use?**
   - **A:** Trapped ions.
3. **Q: What do photonic quantum computers use?**
   - **A:** Photons.
4. **Q: What is a key advantage of superconducting qubits?**
   - **A:** Fast gate times.
5. **Q: What is a key advantage of ion trap qubits?**
   - **A:** Low error rates.
6. **Q: What is a key advantage of photonic quantum computers?**
   - **A:** Room-temperature operation.

Noise, Decoherence, and Scalability

7. **Q: What affects quantum states?**
   - **A:** Noise.
8. **Q: What is the loss of quantum properties called?**
   - **A:** Decoherence.
9. **Q: What does T1 measure?**
   - **A:** Relaxation time.
10. **Q: What does T2 measure?**
    - **A:** Dephasing time.

11. **Q: What is a major challenge for quantum computers?**
    - **A:** Scalability.
12. **Q: What are researchers developing to address the scaling challenge?** * **A:** Modular architectures.

Quantum Hardware vs. Simulation

13. **Q: What are real quantum processors called?**
    - **A:** Quantum hardware.
14. **Q: Are quantum processors subject to noise?**
    - **A:** Yes.
15. **Q: What do we call simulations of quantum circuits on classical computers?**
    - **A:** Quantum simulation.
16. **Q: Are quantum simulations free of noise?**
    - **A:** Yes.
17. **Q: Do quantum simulations scale exponentially?**
    - **A:** Yes.
18. **Q: Do quantum simulations capture real-world limitations?**
    - **A:** No.
19. **Q: Which is better for real-world testing: hardware or simulation?**
    - **A:** Hardware.
20. **Q: Which is more accessible: hardware or simulation?**
    - **A:** Simulation.

10 medium-size questions with answers on Quantum Computing:

Types of Quantum Computers

1. **Q: Compare superconducting and ion trap qubits. Discuss their physical implementation, and contrast their advantages and disadvantages in terms of coherence times and gate speeds.**
    - **A:** Superconducting qubits use cooled circuits, offering fast gate speeds but shorter coherence. Ion traps use trapped ions, with slower gate speeds but very long coherence.
2. **Q: Explain how photonic quantum computers work. What are the benefits of using photons as qubits, and what are the primary challenges in developing this technology?**
    - **A:** Photonic computers use photons, encoding information in their properties. Benefits include room-temperature operation and compatibility with quantum networks. Challenges include photon loss and implementing entangling gates.

Noise, Decoherence, and Scalability

3. **Q: Describe the phenomenon of decoherence in quantum systems. Explain the concepts of T1 and T2 times, and discuss why long coherence times are crucial for quantum computation.**

- **A:** Decoherence is the loss of quantum properties due to environmental interaction. T1 is relaxation time, and T2 is dephasing time. Long coherence times are crucial to perform sufficient operations before errors occur.

4. **Q: Discuss the challenges associated with scaling quantum computers to a large number of qubits. What are the main obstacles in terms of error rates, entanglement, and physical implementation?**
   - **A:** Scaling challenges include managing increasing error rates, efficiently entangling many qubits, and the physical difficulties of cooling and controlling large-scale systems.

Quantum Hardware vs. Simulation

5. **Q: Compare and contrast quantum hardware and quantum simulators. What are the key advantages and disadvantages of each approach in the context of developing and testing quantum algorithms?**
   - **A:** Quantum hardware is physical, subject to noise, and used for real-world testing. Simulators are classical, noise-free, and used for algorithm development, but they scale exponentially.
6. **Q: Explain the limitations of quantum simulators in accurately representing real quantum systems. How do noise and decoherence, which are present in quantum hardware, affect the performance of quantum algorithms?**
   - **A:** Simulators don't account for noise and decoherence, which are inherent in real hardware. These factors cause errors in real-world quantum computations, making error correction essential.
7. **Q: Describe how superconducting quantum computers are cooled and why such low temperatures are necessary. What is a dilution refrigerator, and how does it work?**
   - **A:** Superconducting computers are cooled to near absolute zero to suppress thermal noise and maintain superconductivity. Dilution refrigerators are cryogenic devices that use mixtures of helium isotopes to achieve these temperatures.
8. **Q: What is quantum supremacy (or quantum advantage), and what are the challenges in demonstrating it for practical applications? Use Google's Sycamore as an example.**
   - **A:** Quantum supremacy is when a quantum computer solves a problem that's practically impossible for classical computers. Google's Sycamore showed this for a specific task, but demonstrating it for useful applications is ongoing.
9. **Q: Discuss the potential applications of quantum computers across different industries. How might the strengths and weaknesses of different quantum computing architectures (superconducting, ion trap, photonic) make them more suitable for certain applications?**
   - **A:** Applications include materials science, drug discovery, and finance. Superconducting is suited for speed-demanding tasks, ion traps for high-precision computations, and photonics for quantum networking.
10. **Q: Explain the concept of quantum volume. What does it measure, and why is it an important metric for evaluating the overall performance and progress of quantum computers?**

- **A:** Quantum volume measures the size and complexity of the largest square quantum circuit that a computer can successfully run. It combines qubit count and error rate, and it is an important metric.

CHAPTER 11: QUANTUM PROGRAMMING WITH QISKIT

◆ Overview

Qiskit (Quantum Information Science Kit) is an open-source quantum computing framework developed by **IBM**. It enables users to:

- Build and simulate **quantum circuits**
- Run experiments on **real quantum devices** via the IBM Quantum Lab
- Visualize, analyze, and debug quantum programs

You write Qiskit programs in **Python**, making it accessible to students and researchers with basic programming skills.

Introduction to Qiskit and IBM Quantum Lab

Qiskit and IBM Quantum Lab provide a comprehensive platform for learning, experimenting, and programming quantum computers. Let's break them down:

✅ What is Qiskit?

Qiskit (Quantum Information Software Kit) is an open-source software development kit (SDK) for working with quantum computers. It provides tools for creating, manipulating, and executing quantum programs. Qiskit is designed to work with various quantum hardware backends and simulators. It's composed of several key components:

- **Qiskit Terra:**
    - **Purpose:** This is the foundation of Qiskit. It provides the essential building blocks for creating quantum circuits.
    - It handles:
        - Defining quantum circuits
        - Composing quantum gates
        - Managing quantum data
        - Optimizing circuits for execution on different backends (simulators or real quantum hardware).
- **Qiskit Aer:**
    - **Purpose:** Aer is Qiskit's high-performance quantum circuit simulator.
    - It allows you to:
        - Simulate quantum circuits on your classical computer.
        - Test your quantum programs without needing access to actual quantum hardware.

        - Model realistic noise models to better understand how quantum programs behave on real devices.
- **Qiskit IBMQ Provider:**
    - **Purpose:** This component provides the tools to access IBM Quantum's quantum computers and simulators.
    - It enables you to:
        - Connect to IBM's quantum systems via the cloud.
        - Submit quantum circuits for execution on real quantum hardware.
        - Retrieve and analyze the results of your quantum computations.
- **Qiskit Visualizations:**
    - **Purpose:** This module offers various tools for visualizing quantum circuits and quantum states.
    - It helps you to:
        - Visualize the structure of your quantum circuits.
        - Understand the evolution of quantum states during computation.
        - Analyze the output of quantum programs in a clear and intuitive way.

✅ IBM Quantum Lab

IBM Quantum Lab is a cloud-based platform that provides an interactive environment for working with quantum computers. You can access it at quantum.ibm.com. It's designed to make quantum computing more accessible and user-friendly.

- **Key Features:**
    - **Run circuits on real quantum computers:** IBM Quantum Lab allows you to execute your quantum circuits on IBM's actual quantum hardware, giving you hands-on experience with real quantum systems.
    - **Jupyter Notebooks:** The platform is based on Jupyter Notebooks, a popular tool for interactive computing. This provides a flexible environment for writing and running your quantum programs, combining code, text, and visualizations in a single document.
    - **Analyze execution results:** IBM Quantum Lab provides tools for analyzing the results of your quantum computations, whether they were run on a simulator or on real quantum hardware. You can visualize the output, examine the statistics, and gain insights into the behavior of your quantum programs.

Writing Quantum Circuits in Python with Qiskit

Let's start with a simple quantum circuit using Qiskit.

✅ Installation

Before we begin, you'll need to install Qiskit. You can do this using pip:

```
pip install qiskit
```

This command will install the core Qiskit components, including Terra, Aer, and others.

✅ Example 1: Hello Quantum World (Superposition)

This example demonstrates how to create a quantum circuit, apply a Hadamard gate to put a qubit into superposition, measure the qubit, and visualize the results.

```
from qiskit import QuantumCircuit, Aer, execute
from qiskit.visualization import plot_histogram
import matplotlib.pyplot as plt

# Step 1: Create a quantum circuit with 1 qubit and 1 classical bit
qc = QuantumCircuit(1, 1)

# Step 2: Apply Hadamard gate to create superposition
qc.h(0)  # Apply H gate to qubit 0

# Step 3: Measure the qubit
qc.measure(0, 0)  # Measure qubit 0 and store the result in classical bit 0

# Step 4: Execute using simulator
simulator = Aer.get_backend('qasm_simulator')  # Choose the simulator backend
result = execute(qc, simulator, shots=1024).result()  # Run the circuit 1024
times
counts = result.get_counts()  # Get the measurement counts

# Step 5: Visualize
plot_histogram(counts)  # Plot a histogram of the measurement results
plt.show()
```

Explanation:

1. **Import Libraries:**
    - `QuantumCircuit`: For creating quantum circuits.
    - `Aer` and `execute`: For running circuits on a simulator.
    - `plot_histogram`: For visualizing the measurement results.
    - `matplotlib.pyplot`: For showing the plot.
2. **Create a Quantum Circuit:**
    - `qc = QuantumCircuit(1, 1)`: Creates a quantum circuit named `qc` with one qubit and one classical bit.
        - A qubit is the quantum bit, which can be in a superposition of states.
        - A classical bit stores the result of a measurement. After measurement, the qubit's state collapses to either |0> or |1>, and that classical bit will then be 0 or 1.
3. **Apply Hadamard Gate:**

- `qc.h(0)`: Applies the Hadamard gate (H gate) to qubit 0. The H gate puts the qubit into an equal superposition of the |0⟩ and |1⟩ states.

4. **Measure the Qubit:**
   - `qc.measure(0, 0)`: Measures qubit 0 and stores the result in classical bit 0.
     - When a qubit is measured, its superposition collapses to either |0⟩ or |1⟩.
     - The classical bit stores the outcome of that measurement (0 or 1).
5. **Execute the Circuit:**
   - `simulator = Aer.get_backend('qasm_simulator')`: Selects the `qasm_simulator` backend from Aer. This is a software simulator that mimics a quantum computer.
   - `result = execute(qc, simulator, shots=1024).result()`: Executes the quantum circuit `qc` on the simulator.
     - `shots=1024`: The circuit is run 1024 times. Each run (or "shot") produces a measurement outcome. Running multiple shots allows us to gather statistics.
   - `counts = result.get_counts()`: Retrieves the counts of each measurement outcome (e.g., how many times we measured '0' and how many times we measured '1').
6. **Visualize the Results:**
   - `plot_histogram(counts)`: Creates a histogram showing the probability of measuring each state.
   - `plt.show()`: Displays the histogram.

📌 **Output:**

The output of this program is a histogram. Because the Hadamard gate creates an equal superposition, you'll see that the histogram shows roughly a 50% probability of measuring '0' and a 50% probability of measuring '1'. This demonstrates the probabilistic nature of quantum mechanics.

Simulation and Real-device Execution with Qiskit

You can run the same quantum circuit on a real quantum computer by connecting to IBM's cloud. This allows you to experience the behavior of quantum hardware firsthand.

✅ A. Accessing IBM Quantum Devices

To access IBM's quantum computers, you need an IBM Quantum account and your API token.

```
from qiskit import IBMQ

# Save your API token once (get it from the IBM Quantum dashboard)
# IMPORTANT: Replace 'YOUR_IBM_QUANTUM_TOKEN' with your actual token.
# This should only be done once on your machine.  The token is stored
```

```
# securely by Qiskit for future sessions.
# IBMQ.save_account('YOUR_IBM_QUANTUM_TOKEN')

# Load your account
IBMQ.load_account()

# Get the provider
#  hub='ibm-q' is the default, but you might need to specify it
#  if you are in a different group.
provider = IBMQ.get_provider(hub='ibm-q')

# Choose a real backend (a specific quantum device)
# 'ibmq_quito' is an example.  You can list available backends
# and choose one that is currently available.
backend = provider.get_backend('ibmq_quito')  # 5-qubit device
```

Explanation:

1. **`Import IBMQ`**: This module provides the tools to interact with IBM Quantum services.
2. **Save your API token:**
   - `IBMQ.save_account('YOUR_IBM_QUANTUM_TOKEN')`: This line saves your unique API token. You can find this token on the IBM Quantum website (quantum.ibm.com) in your account settings.
   - **Important:** You only need to run this `save_account` line *once* on your computer. Qiskit securely stores the token for future sessions.
   - **Security Note:** Treat your API token like a password. Do not share it with others.
3. **Load your account:**
   - `IBMQ.load_account()`: This line loads your saved account information, allowing you to access IBM Quantum resources.
4. **Get the provider:**
   - `provider = IBMQ.get_provider(hub='ibm-q')`: This retrieves the provider, which gives you access to the available quantum systems.
     - The `hub` parameter specifies which group of systems you want to access. The default is 'ibm-q'.
5. **Choose a backend:**
   - `backend = provider.get_backend('ibmq_quito')`: This selects a specific quantum device (a real quantum computer) to use.
     - `'ibmq_quito'` is just an example. You can use `provider.backends()` to get a list of available backends and their status. Choose one that is operational (not currently down for maintenance or heavily queued).
     - The number of qubits varies between devices (e.g., 'ibmq_quito' has 5 qubits).

✅ B. Running Your Circuit on Real Hardware

Once you've accessed a real quantum device, you can run your quantum circuit on it:

```
# Assuming 'qc' is your quantum circuit from the previous example
```

```
# Execute the circuit on the real quantum device
job = execute(qc, backend=backend, shots=1024)  # Run on the real device
result = job.result()  # Get the results
counts = result.get_counts()  # Get the measurement counts

# Visualize the results
plot_histogram(counts)  # Plot the histogram
```

Explanation:

1. **Execute the circuit:**
   - `job = execute(qc, backend=backend, shots=1024)`: This line runs your quantum circuit (`qc`) on the chosen real quantum computer (`backend`).
     - `shots=1024`: As with the simulator, we run the circuit multiple times (1024 times here) to get statistics.
2. **Get the results:**
   - `result = job.result()`: This retrieves the results of the execution from the quantum computer. This process may take some time, as your job is queued and executed on a remote device.
3. **Get the measurement counts:**
   - `counts = result.get_counts()`: This extracts the counts of each measurement outcome.
4. **Visualize the results:**
   - `plot_histogram(counts)`: This displays a histogram of the measurement probabilities.

Important Observation:

When you run your circuit on a real quantum computer, you'll likely notice that the results are different from the simulation. Specifically:

- **Noise and Imbalance:** The histogram will not show a perfect 50/50 split between '0' and '1' as in the ideal simulation. Instead, you'll see some imbalance, and there might be some counts for outcomes that are not expected in an ideal quantum computation.
- **Decoherence and Hardware Errors:** This deviation from the ideal result is due to the inherent noise and errors present in real quantum hardware. These errors arise from:
  - **Decoherence:** The loss of quantum coherence.
  - **Gate errors:** Imperfect quantum gate operations.
  - **Measurement errors:** Inaccuracies in the measurement process.

This difference between simulation and real-device execution highlights the challenges of building and working with quantum computers. Quantum error correction and other techniques are crucial for mitigating these errors and achieving reliable quantum computation.

Let's build a few practical mini-labs to help students explore key quantum concepts.

✓ Lab 1: Quantum Entanglement

This lab demonstrates the fascinating phenomenon of quantum entanglement by creating a Bell state.

```
from qiskit import QuantumCircuit, Aer, execute
from qiskit.visualization import plot_histogram

qc = QuantumCircuit(2, 2)  # Create a circuit with 2 qubits and 2 classical
bits

# Create entanglement
qc.h(0)     # Put qubit 0 into a superposition
qc.cx(0, 1)  # Apply a CNOT gate to entangle qubit 0 and qubit 1

qc.measure([0, 1], [0, 1])  # Measure both qubits and store results in
classical bits

simulator = Aer.get_backend('qasm_simulator')  # Choose the simulator
result = execute(qc, simulator, shots=1024).result()  # Run the circuit
counts = result.get_counts()  # Get the measurement counts

plot_histogram(counts)  # Visualize the results
```

Explanation:

1. **Create Quantum Circuit:**
    - `qc = QuantumCircuit(2, 2)`: Creates a quantum circuit with two qubits and two classical bits.
2. **Create Entanglement:**
    - `qc.h(0)`: Applies a Hadamard gate to qubit 0, putting it into a superposition of $|0\rangle$ and $|1\rangle$.
    - `qc.cx(0, 1)`: Applies a Controlled-NOT (CNOT) gate.
        - Qubit 0 is the control qubit.
        - Qubit 1 is the target qubit.
        - If qubit 0 is $|0\rangle$, nothing happens to qubit 1.
        - If qubit 0 is $|1\rangle$, qubit 1 is flipped (its state is changed).
    - This sequence of gates creates the Bell state: $(|00\rangle + |11\rangle) / \sqrt{2}$
        - This state is maximally entangled. The qubits are correlated such that if you measure qubit 0 as $|0\rangle$, you *always* measure qubit 1 as $|0\rangle$, and if you measure qubit 0 as $|1\rangle$, you *always* measure qubit 1 as $|1\rangle$.
3. **Measure Qubits:**
    - `qc.measure([0, 1], [0, 1])`: Measures both qubits.
        - The measurement results are stored in the corresponding classical bits.
4. **Execute and Visualize:**

- The circuit is executed on the simulator, and the results are visualized as a histogram.

📌 **Expected Output:**

The histogram will show only two possible outcomes:

- '00': Both qubits are measured as $|0\rangle$.
- '11': Both qubits are measured as $|1\rangle$.

The probabilities of '00' and '11' will be approximately equal (around 50% each). The outcomes '01' and '10' will *never* occur. This demonstrates the perfect correlation between the entangled qubits. Even though each qubit is in a superposition, their measurement outcomes are perfectly linked.

✅ Lab 2: Grover's Algorithm (2-qubit search)

This lab introduces students to Grover's algorithm, a quantum algorithm for searching an unstructured database. Here, we'll use it to search a 2-qubit space.

```
from qiskit.circuit.library import GroverOperator, ZGate
from qiskit.algorithms import AmplificationProblem, Grover
from qiskit import QuantumCircuit

# Define the oracle that marks |11⟩ as the solution
oracle = QuantumCircuit(2)
oracle.cz(0, 1)  # Apply a CZ gate, which flips the phase of |11>
oracle = oracle.to_gate(label="Oracle") #convert the circuit to a gate

# Build Grover Operator
grover_op = GroverOperator(oracle)

# Set up the problem
problem = AmplificationProblem(oracle=oracle, is_good_state=lambda bitstring:
bitstring == '11')

# Run Grover's algorithm
grover = Grover()
result = grover.amplify(problem)

print("Most likely solution:", result.top_measurement)
```

Explanation:

1. **Define Oracle:**
   - `oracle = QuantumCircuit(2)`: Creates a 2-qubit quantum circuit.
   - `oracle.cz(0, 1)`: Applies a Controlled-Z (CZ) gate. The CZ gate flips the phase of the $|11\rangle$ state. This CZ gate is our "oracle" -- it marks the state $|11\rangle$, which is the solution we are searching for.

   - `oracle = oracle.to_gate(label="Oracle")`: Converts the circuit into a gate.
2. **Build Grover Operator:**
   - `grover_op = GroverOperator(oracle)`: Constructs the Grover operator, which consists of the oracle and a diffusion operator.
3. **Set up Problem:**
   - `problem = AmplificationProblem(oracle=oracle, is_good_state=lambda bitstring: bitstring == '11')`: Sets up the search problem.
     - `oracle=oracle`: Specifies the oracle circuit.
     - `is_good_state`: A function that defines what constitutes a "good" state (the solution). In this case, the good state is $|11\rangle$.
4. **Run Grover's Algorithm:**
   - `grover = Grover()`: Creates a Grover's algorithm object.
   - `result = grover.amplify(problem)`: Runs Grover's algorithm to find the solution.
   - `print("Most likely solution:", result.top_measurement)`: Prints the most likely solution, which will be '11'.

Expected Output:

The output will be:

```
Most likely solution: 11
```

Grover's algorithm finds the state $|11\rangle$ with a high probability. In a 2-qubit search space, Grover's algorithm finds the solution in a single iteration.

✅ Lab 3: Visualizing Bloch Sphere

This lab uses Qiskit to visualize the state of a single qubit on the Bloch sphere.

```
from qiskit.quantum_info import Statevector
from qiskit.visualization import plot_bloch_multivector
from qiskit import QuantumCircuit

qc = QuantumCircuit(1)  # Create a 1-qubit quantum circuit
qc.h(0)  # Apply a Hadamard gate to qubit 0

state = Statevector.from_instruction(qc)  # Get the statevector of the
circuit
plot_bloch_multivector(state)  # Plot the state on the Bloch sphere
```

Explanation:

1. **Create Circuit:**
   - `qc = QuantumCircuit(1)`: Creates a quantum circuit with one qubit.

2. **Apply Hadamard Gate:**
   - `qc.h(0)`: Applies a Hadamard gate to qubit 0, putting it into an equal superposition of |0⟩ and |1⟩: |+⟩ = (|0⟩ + |1⟩) / √2
3. **Get Statevector:**
   - `state = Statevector.from_instruction(qc)`: Calculates the quantum state of the qubit after applying the gates. The statevector represents the qubit's state as a vector in Hilbert space.
4. **Plot on Bloch Sphere:**
   - `plot_bloch_multivector(state)`: Visualizes the qubit's state on the Bloch sphere.

✅ **Expected Output:**

The Bloch sphere will be displayed, and the arrow representing the qubit's state will point along the X-axis. This is because the +⟩ state corresponds to a point on the equator of the Bloch sphere, pointing in the positive X direction. This visualization clearly shows that the qubit is in a superposition of |0⟩ and |1⟩.

✅ Summary

Feature	Description
Qiskit	Python SDK for quantum programming
IBM Quantum Lab	Cloud access to real quantum machines
Simulators	Ideal for testing circuits without noise
Real-device execution	Offers practical exposure with real hardware
Hands-on labs	Builds intuitive understanding via code

10 practical questions with detailed explanation answers on Introduction to Qiskit and IBM Quantum Lab:

Introduction to Qiskit and IBM Quantum Lab

1. **Q: What is Qiskit, and what are its main components? Describe the purpose of Qiskit Terra, Qiskit Aer, and Qiskit IBMQ Provider.**
   - **A:** Qiskit is an open-source SDK for working with quantum computers. Its main components are:
     - **Qiskit Terra:** For creating and optimizing quantum circuits.
     - **Qiskit Aer:** For simulating quantum circuits.
     - **Qiskit IBMQ Provider:** For accessing IBM Quantum hardware.

2. **Q: What is IBM Quantum Lab, and how does it facilitate quantum computing experimentation? What are the key features and benefits of using this platform?**
   - **A:** IBM Quantum Lab is a cloud-based environment (quantum.ibm.com) for running quantum circuits on real quantum computers. Key features: Jupyter Notebooks, access to IBM hardware, and tools for result analysis. Benefits: hands-on experience, interactive programming.

Writing Quantum Circuits in Python

3. **Q: Write a Qiskit code snippet to create a quantum circuit with two qubits and two classical bits. Then, apply a Hadamard gate to the first qubit and a CNOT gate with the first qubit as control and the second qubit as target.**
   - **A:**

```
from qiskit import QuantumCircuit
qc = QuantumCircuit(2, 2)   # 2 qubits, 2 classical bits
qc.h(0)   # Apply H to qubit 0
qc.cx(0, 1)   # CNOT: control qubit 0, target qubit 1
print(qc)
```

4. **Q: Explain the role of the execute function in Qiskit. Provide a code example of how to use it to run a quantum circuit on a simulator and retrieve the measurement counts.**
   - **A:** The `execute` function runs a quantum circuit on a backend (simulator or real hardware).

```
from qiskit import Aer, execute, QuantumCircuit
qc = QuantumCircuit(1, 1)
qc.h(0)
qc.measure(0, 0)
simulator = Aer.get_backend('qasm_simulator')
job = execute(qc, simulator, shots=1024)
counts = job.result().get_counts()
print(counts)
```

Simulation and Real-device Execution

5. **Q: How do you access IBM Quantum's real quantum computers using Qiskit? Provide a code snippet and explain the steps involved in connecting to a real backend.**
   - **A:**

```
from qiskit import IBMQ
IBMQ.load_account()   # Load account (ensure token is saved)
provider = IBMQ.get_provider(hub='ibm-q')
backend = provider.get_backend('ibmq_quito')   # Example device
print(backend)
```

6. **Q: What is the purpose of the shots parameter in the execute function? Explain why we need to run a quantum circuit multiple times (with a non-zero number of shots) to get meaningful results.**

- **A:** The `shots` parameter specifies the number of times to run the circuit. We need multiple shots because quantum measurements are probabilistic. Running many times gives us statistics to estimate probabilities.

7. **Q: Write a Qiskit code snippet to run a quantum circuit on a real quantum device (assuming you have an IBM Quantum account) and visualize the measurement results using plot_histogram.**
   - **A:**

```
from qiskit import IBMQ, execute, QuantumCircuit
from qiskit.visualization import plot_histogram
import matplotlib.pyplot as plt
IBMQ.load_account()
provider = IBMQ.get_provider(hub='ibm-q')
backend = provider.get_backend('ibmq_quito')  # Choose a device
qc = QuantumCircuit(1, 1)
qc.h(0)
qc.measure(0, 0)
job = execute(qc, backend=backend, shots=1024)
counts = job.result().get_counts()
plot_histogram(counts)
plt.show()
```

8. **Q: What are the key differences you might observe when running the same quantum circuit on a simulator versus a real quantum device? Explain the reasons for these differences.**
   - **A:** Simulator results are ideal (e.g., perfect 50/50 for a Hadamard). Real devices show noise and deviations from ideal due to decoherence, gate errors, and measurement errors.

9. **Q: Explain how to visualize the state of a single qubit using Qiskit's plot_bloch_multivector function. Provide a code example that creates a qubit in the |+⟩ state and plots it on the Bloch sphere.**
   - **A:**

```
from qiskit import QuantumCircuit
from qiskit.quantum_info import Statevector
from qiskit.visualization import plot_bloch_multivector
import matplotlib.pyplot as plt
qc = QuantumCircuit(1)
qc.h(0)  # Create |+> state
state = Statevector.from_instruction(qc)
plot_bloch_multivector(state)
plt.show()
```

10. **Q: Describe how to implement Grover's algorithm for a 2-qubit search problem using Qiskit. Explain the role of the oracle and the Grover class in this implementation.**
    - **A:**

```
from qiskit.circuit.library import GroverOperator
from qiskit.algorithms import AmplificationProblem, Grover
from qiskit import QuantumCircuit

oracle = QuantumCircuit(2)
oracle.cz(0, 1)  # Oracle marks |11>
```

```
oracle_gate = oracle.to_gate(label="Oracle")

problem = AmplificationProblem(oracle=oracle_gate, is_good_state=lambda bitstring: bitstring == '11')
grover = Grover()
result = grover.amplify(problem)
print("Most likely solution:", result.top_measurement)
```

30 multiple-choice questions with answers on Introduction to Qiskit and IBM Quantum Lab:

Introduction to Qiskit and IBM Quantum Lab

1. **Q: What is Qiskit?**
   - A) A quantum computer
   - B) A quantum programming language
   - C) An open-source quantum computing SDK
   - D) A quantum simulator
   - **A:** C
2. **Q: Which Qiskit component is used for creating quantum circuits?**
   - A) Qiskit Aer
   - B) Qiskit Terra
   - C) Qiskit IBMQ
   - D) Qiskit Visualizations
   - **A:** B
3. **Q: Which Qiskit component is used for simulating quantum circuits?**
   - A) Qiskit Aer
   - B) Qiskit Terra
   - C) Qiskit IBMQ
   - D) Qiskit Visualizations
   - **A:** A
4. **Q: Which Qiskit component is used to access IBM Quantum hardware?**
   - A) Qiskit Aer
   - B) Qiskit Terra
   - C) Qiskit IBMQ Provider
   - D) Qiskit Visualizations
   - **A:** C
5. **Q: Which platform allows you to run quantum circuits on real IBM quantum computers?**
   - A) Qiskit Aer
   - B) Qiskit Terra
   - C) IBM Quantum Lab
   - D) Jupyter Notebook
   - **A:** C
6. **Q: IBM Quantum Lab is a...**
   - A) Local software application
   - B) Cloud-based environment
   - C) Quantum simulator

- D) Quantum programming language
- **A:** B

7. **Q: IBM Quantum Lab uses...**
   - A) Python scripts
   - B) C++ code
   - C) Jupyter Notebooks
   - D) Quantum Assembly Language
   - **A:** C
8. **Q: Which Qiskit component provides tools to visualize quantum circuits and states?**
   - A) Qiskit Aer
   - B) Qiskit Terra
   - C) Qiskit IBMQ
   - D) Qiskit Visualizations
   - **A:** D
9. **Q: Which is NOT a component of Qiskit?**
   - A) Qiskit Terra
   - B) Qiskit Aer
   - C) Qiskit Runtime
   - D) Qiskit IBMQ Provider
   - **A:** C
10. **Q: Where can you find your API token for IBM Quantum?**
    - A) Qiskit documentation
    - B) Python console
    - C) IBM Quantum website
    - D) Jupyter Notebook
    - **A:** C

Writing Quantum Circuits in Python

11. **Q: In Qiskit, what is used to create a quantum circuit?**
    - A) `QuantumProgram`
    - B) `QuantumCircuit`
    - C) `Qubit`
    - D) `ClassicalBit`
    - **A:** B
12. **Q: What Qiskit function is used to apply a Hadamard gate to a qubit?**
    - A) `qc.x()`
    - B) `qc.y()`
    - C) `qc.h()`
    - D) `qc.z()`
    - **A:** C
13. **`Q: What does the qc.measure(0, 0) command do in Qiskit?`**
    - A) Measures qubit 0 and stores the result in classical bit 0
    - B) Measures qubit 0 and stores the result in classical bit 1
    - C) Applies a measurement gate to qubit 0
    - D) Measures classical bit 0

- **A:** A

14. **Q: Which library is used for creating histograms in Qiskit?**
    - A) `matplotlib.pyplot`
    - B) `qiskit.visualization`
    - C) `qiskit.tools`
    - D) `qiskit.utils`
    - **A:** A
15. **Q: What is the output of applying a Hadamard gate to a qubit initialized in the |0⟩ state?**
    - A) The |0⟩ state
    - B) The |1⟩ state
    - C) A superposition of |0⟩ and |1⟩
    - D) An equal superposition of |0⟩ and |1⟩
    - **A:** D
16. **Q: What does the first argument in `QuantumCircuit(2, 2)` represent?**
    - A) Number of classical bits
    - B) Number of qubits
    - C) Number of gates
    - D) Number of measurements
    - **A:** B
17. **Q: What does the second argument in `QuantumCircuit(2, 2)` represent?**
    - A) Number of classical bits
    - B) Number of qubits
    - C) Number of gates
    - D) Number of measurements
    - **A:** A
18. **Q: Which gate creates entanglement between two qubits?**
    - A) Hadamard gate
    - B) Pauli-X gate
    - C) CNOT gate
    - D) Phase gate
    - **A:** C
19. **Q: What does `qc.cx(0, 1)` do?**
    - A) Applies X-gate to qubit 0 controlled by qubit 1
    - B) Applies X-gate to qubit 1 controlled by qubit 0
    - C) Applies CNOT to qubit 0 and 1
    - D) Applies CZ to qubit 0 and 1
    - **A:** B
20. **Q: What is the purpose of `plot_histogram(counts)`?**
    - A) To visualize the quantum circuit
    - B) To visualize the measurement results
    - C) To display the Bloch sphere
    - D) To print the quantum code
    - **A:** B

Simulation and Real-device Execution

21. **Q: Which Qiskit module provides quantum simulators?**
   - A) Qiskit Terra
   - B) Qiskit Aer
   - C) Qiskit IBMQ
   - D) Qiskit Visualizations
   - **A:** B
22. **Q: What function is used to execute a quantum circuit in Qiskit?**
   - A) `run()`
   - B) `simulate()`
   - C) `execute()`
   - D) `process()`
   - **A:** C
23. **Q: To run a circuit on a real quantum computer, you need to use...**
   - A) Qiskit Aer
   - B) Qiskit Terra
   - C) IBMQ Provider
   - D) Qiskit Visualizations
   - **A:** C
24. **Q: What information is needed to access IBM Quantum devices?**
   - A) System password
   - B) API token
   - C) Device IP address
   - D) Quantum code
   - **A:** B
25. **`Q: What does the shots parameter in the execute() function specify?`**
   - A) The number of qubits
   - B) The number of classical bits
   - C) The number of times the circuit is run
   - D) The number of quantum gates
   - **A:** C
26. **Q: Why do results from a real quantum computer differ from a simulation?**
   - A) Simulators are always incorrect
   - B) Real computers have noise and errors
   - C) Real computers are faster
   - D) Simulators use different algorithms
   - **A:** B
27. **Q: What is a typical source of error in real quantum computers?**
   - A) Perfect gates
   - B) Decoherence
   - C) Infinite coherence time
   - D) Error-free measurements
   - **A:** B
28. **Q: Which backend is used for simulation in Qiskit?**
   - A) ibmq_quito
   - B) aer_simulator
   - C) qasm_simulator

- D) Any real device
- **A:** C

29. **Q:** `What does IBMQ.load_account() do?`
    - A) Loads a quantum circuit
    - B) Loads a simulator
    - C) Loads your IBM Quantum account
    - D) Loads visualization tools
    - **A:** C
30. **Q:** `What is the purpose of provider.get_backend('ibmq_quito')?`
    - A) To get a simulator
    - B) To get a quantum circuit
    - C) To get a specific quantum device
    - D) To get the provider
    - **A:** C

20 short questions and answers on Introduction to Qiskit and IBM Quantum Lab:

Introduction to Qiskit and IBM Quantum Lab

1. **Q: What is Qiskit?**
    - **A:** Quantum SDK.
2. **Q: What does Qiskit Terra do?**
    - **A:** Circuit creation.
3. **Q: What does Qiskit Aer do?**
    - **A:** Simulation.
4. **Q: What does Qiskit IBMQ do?**
    - **A:** Access IBM hardware.
5. **Q: What is IBM Quantum Lab?**
    - **A:** Cloud-based platform.

Writing Quantum Circuits in Python

6. **Q: What Qiskit class creates circuits?**
    - **A:** QuantumCircuit.
7. **Q: What applies a Hadamard gate?**
    - **A:** qc.h().
8. **Q: What measures a qubit?**
    - **A:** qc.measure().
9. **Q: What library visualizes results?**
    - **A:** matplotlib.pyplot.
10. **Q: What gate creates superposition?**
    - **A:** Hadamard.

Simulation and Real-device Execution

11. **Q: Which Qiskit module simulates?**

- **A:** Aer.

12. **Q: What function executes circuits?**
    - **A:** execute().
13. **Q: How to access IBM hardware?**
    - **A:** IBMQ Provider.
14. **Q: What is needed to use IBMQ?**
    - **A:** API token.
15. **Q: What does 'shots' mean?**
    - **A:** Number of runs.
16. **Q: Are real device results noisy?**
    - **A:** Yes.
17. **Q: What causes errors in real devices?**
    - **A:** Decoherence.
18. **Q: Which backend simulates?**
    - **A:** qasm_simulator.
19. **Q: What loads your IBMQ account?**
    - **A:** IBMQ.load_account().
20. **Q: What gets a quantum device?**
    - **A:** provider.get_backend().

10 medium-size questions with answers on Introduction to Qiskit and IBM Quantum Lab:

Introduction to Qiskit and IBM Quantum Lab

1. **Q: Describe Qiskit and its core components. Explain the role of Qiskit Terra, Qiskit Aer, and Qiskit IBMQ Provider in the quantum computing workflow.**
    - **A:** Qiskit is an open-source SDK. Terra creates circuits, Aer simulates them, and IBMQ Provider accesses IBM's hardware.
2. **Q: Explain IBM Quantum Lab. How does it simplify access to quantum computing resources, and what are its main features for users?**
    - **A:** IBM Quantum Lab is a cloud platform with Jupyter Notebooks. It simplifies access to IBM's quantum computers and provides tools for running experiments and analyzing results.

Writing Quantum Circuits in Python

3. **Q: Write a Python code snippet using Qiskit to create a quantum circuit with two qubits and two classical bits. Apply a Hadamard gate to the first qubit, followed by a CNOT gate. Explain the purpose of each step.**
    - **A:**

```
from qiskit import QuantumCircuit
qc = QuantumCircuit(2, 2)   # 2 qubits, 2 classical bits
qc.h(0)   # Apply H to qubit 0
qc.cx(0, 1)   # CNOT: control qubit 0, target qubit 1
```

This creates a Bell state.

4. **Q: Explain how to execute a quantum circuit on a simulator using Qiskit. Include a code example and describe the purpose of the execute function and the shots parameter.**
   - **A:**
   - `from qiskit import Aer, execute, QuantumCircuit`
   - `qc = QuantumCircuit(1, 1)`
   - `qc.h(0)`
   - `qc.measure(0, 0)`
   - `simulator = Aer.get_backend('qasm_simulator')`
   - `job = execute(qc, simulator, shots=1024)  # shots = repetitions`
   - `counts = job.result().get_counts()`

Simulation and Real-device Execution

5. **Q: Describe the process of accessing and using IBM Quantum's real quantum computers through Qiskit. Include a code snippet demonstrating how to connect to a backend.**
   - **A:**
   - `from qiskit import IBMQ`
   - `IBMQ.load_account()  # Load account`
   - `provider = IBMQ.get_provider()`
   - `backend = provider.get_backend('ibmq_quito')  # Example device`

6. **Q: What are the key differences between running a quantum circuit on a simulator and on real quantum hardware? Explain why the results might vary.**
   - **A:** Simulators are ideal; real hardware has noise and errors (decoherence, gate errors), leading to different results.
7. **Q: Explain how to visualize the output of a quantum circuit in Qiskit. Provide a code example that runs a simple circuit and displays the measurement results as a histogram.**
   - **A:**
   - `from qiskit import QuantumCircuit, Aer, execute`
   - `from qiskit.visualization import plot_histogram`
   - `import matplotlib.pyplot as plt`
   - `qc = QuantumCircuit(1, 1)`
   - `qc.h(0)`
   - `qc.measure(0, 0)`
   - `.simulator = Aer.get_backend('qasm_simulator')`
   - `job = execute(qc, simulator, shots=1024)`
   - `counts = job.result().get_counts()`
   - `plot_histogram(counts)`
   - `plt.show()`

8. **Q: Describe how to visualize the state of a single qubit using Qiskit and the Bloch sphere. Provide a code example.**
   - **A:**
   - `from qiskit import QuantumCircuit`
   - `from qiskit.quantum_info import Statevector`
   - `from qiskit.visualization import plot_bloch_multivector`

- `import matplotlib.pyplot as plt`
-
- `qc = QuantumCircuit(1)`
- `qc.h(0)   # Create |+> state`
- `state = Statevector.from_instruction(qc)`
- `plot_bloch_multivector(state)`
- `plt.show()`

9. **Q: Explain how to implement Grover's algorithm for a 2-qubit search problem using Qiskit. What is the role of the oracle in this algorithm?**
   - **A:** Grover's algorithm finds a marked state. The oracle marks the solution (e.g., $|11\rangle$ by flipping its phase). Qiskit's `Grover` class is used.
10. **Q: Describe the process of saving and loading your IBM Quantum account in Qiskit. Why is this necessary, and how is the API token used?**
    - **A:** `IBMQ.save_account()` saves your API token (from the IBM Quantum website) locally, allowing Qiskit to access your IBM Quantum account and use the hardware. This is only done once. `IBMQ.load_account()` loads the saved account for subsequent use.

CHAPTER 12: OTHER QUANTUM PLATFORMS

Google's Cirq

Cirq is an open-source framework developed by Google for working with quantum computers. It provides tools for creating, editing, and executing quantum circuits.

✅ What is Cirq?

Cirq is a Python library specifically designed for working with Noisy Intermediate-Scale Quantum (NISQ) devices. These are quantum computers that have a limited number of qubits and are still susceptible to noise. Cirq is tailored to address the challenges and opportunities presented by these early-stage quantum computers, such as Google's own Sycamore processor.

✅ Key Features

Cirq offers several important features:

- **Native support for quantum gates and noise modeling:** Cirq provides a wide range of built-in quantum gates, including standard gates like Hadamard (H), Pauli-X, Y, and Z, as well as more specialized gates relevant to specific hardware architectures. Crucially, Cirq also allows you to model noise, which is essential for simulating how quantum circuits will behave on real-world NISQ devices.
- **Integration with TensorFlow Quantum:** Cirq is designed to work seamlessly with TensorFlow Quantum (TFQ), a library for building quantum machine learning models. This integration allows researchers to combine the power of quantum computing with the capabilities of TensorFlow, Google's popular machine learning framework.
- **Optimized for hardware-specific execution:** Cirq is designed with the constraints and capabilities of specific quantum hardware in mind. For example, it is optimized for Google's Sycamore processor, taking into account its particular qubit connectivity and gate operations. This hardware awareness is important for achieving the best possible performance on real quantum devices.

✅ Example: Creating a Bell State in Cirq

Here's an example of how to use Cirq to create a Bell state, a fundamental example of quantum entanglement:

```
import cirq

# Step 1: Define two qubits
qubit_0 = cirq.LineQubit(0)
qubit_1 = cirq.LineQubit(1)

# Step 2: Create a quantum circuit
circuit = cirq.Circuit()
```

```
# Step 3: Add gates to create a Bell state
circuit.append([cirq.H(qubit_0), cirq.CNOT(qubit_0, qubit_1)])

# Step 4: Measure the qubits
circuit.append([cirq.measure(qubit_0), cirq.measure(qubit_1)])

# Step 5: Simulate the circuit
simulator = cirq.Simulator()
result = simulator.run(circuit, repetitions=100)

print("Measurement Results:\n", result)
```

Explanation:

1. **Define two qubits:**
   - `qubit_0 = cirq.LineQubit(0)` and `qubit_1 = cirq.LineQubit(1)`: These lines create two qubits, labeled 0 and 1, arranged in a line. Cirq provides different ways to define qubit arrangements, reflecting the physical layout of qubits on various hardware.
2. **Create a quantum circuit:**
   - `circuit = cirq.Circuit()`: This creates an empty quantum circuit.
3. **Add gates to create a Bell state:**
   - `circuit.append([cirq.H(qubit_0), cirq.CNOT(qubit_0, qubit_1)])`: This line adds two quantum gates to the circuit:
     - `cirq.H(qubit_0)`: Applies a Hadamard gate to qubit 0, putting it into a superposition of $|0\rangle$ and $|1\rangle$.
     - `cirq.CNOT(qubit_0, qubit_1)`: Applies a Controlled-NOT (CNOT) gate. Qubit 0 is the control qubit, and qubit 1 is the target qubit. This gate creates entanglement between the two qubits.
4. **Measure the qubits:**
   - `circuit.append([cirq.measure(qubit_0), cirq.measure(qubit_1)])`: This line adds measurement operations to the circuit. It measures both `qubit_0` and `qubit_1`.
5. **Simulate the circuit:**
   - `simulator = cirq.Simulator()`: Creates a Cirq simulator object.
   - `result = simulator.run(circuit, repetitions=100)`: Runs the quantum circuit on the simulator 100 times (repetitions).
   - `print("Measurement Results:\n", result)`: Prints the measurement results.

📌 **Expected result:**

When you run this code, you should see that the simulator produces two outcomes with roughly equal probability:

- '00': Both qubits are measured as $|0\rangle$.
- '11': Both qubits are measured as $|1\rangle$.

The outcomes '01' and '10' will occur very rarely (ideally, never). This demonstrates the entanglement between the two qubits in the Bell state. The measurement outcomes are correlated: if one qubit is measured to be in the $|0\rangle$ state, the other qubit is guaranteed to be in the $|0\rangle$ state as well, and similarly for the $|1\rangle$ state.

Microsoft Q#

Q# is a domain-specific programming language developed by Microsoft for writing quantum programs. It's a key part of Microsoft's Quantum Development Kit (QDK), a suite of tools for quantum computing.

✅ What is Q#?

Q# is designed to provide a high-level way to express quantum algorithms. It's not a general-purpose language like Python or C++; instead, it's focused specifically on quantum operations and control flow. Q# is strongly-typed, which helps catch errors early in the development process, and it supports modular programming, making it easier to write and maintain large quantum programs. It's integrated with the .NET platform and can be used with development environments like Visual Studio or VS Code.

✅ Key Features

Q# offers several important features for quantum programming:

- **Rich support for quantum control structures:** Q# provides control flow constructs that are essential for quantum algorithms, such as:
    - Loops (for iterating over quantum operations)
    - Conditional statements (for performing different operations based on measurement outcomes)
    - Functions and operations (for defining reusable quantum subroutines)
- **Integration with the .NET platform:** Q# programs can be called from and can call classical .NET programs (in languages like C# or F#). This allows you to combine classical and quantum processing, which is often necessary in quantum algorithms.
- **Simulators:** The QDK includes several different quantum simulators:
    - **Full-state simulator:** This simulator can simulate small quantum systems (typically up to 30 qubits) and provides a detailed view of the quantum state.
    - **Toffoli-only simulator:** This simulator can simulate quantum circuits that use only Toffoli gates, which are a type of classical reversible gate. This simulator can handle larger numbers of qubits but is limited to certain types of quantum computations.
    - **Resource estimator:** This tool estimates the resources (number of qubits, gate count, etc.) that would be required to run a Q# program on a real quantum

computer. This is useful for understanding the feasibility of different quantum algorithms.

✅ Example: Deutsch-Jozsa Algorithm in Q#

Here's an example of the Deutsch-Jozsa algorithm, a quantum algorithm that can distinguish between constant and balanced functions, implemented in Q#:

```
operation DeutschJozsaAlgorithm() : Result[] {
    using (qubits = Qubit[3]) {

        // Apply X and H to the last qubit
        X(qubits[2]);
        H(qubits[2]);

        // Apply H to the first two qubits
        H(qubits[0]);
        H(qubits[1]);

        // Oracle for constant function (does nothing)
        // Normally, you'd insert a U_f gate here, representing the function
        // For a balanced function, you'd have different gates.
        // This example shows the constant function case.

        // Apply H again
        H(qubits[0]);
        H(qubits[1]);

        // Measure
        return [M(qubits[0]), M(qubits[1])];
    }
}
```

Explanation:

- **`operation DeutschJozsaAlgorithm() : Result[]`**: This defines a Q# operation (similar to a function) called `DeutschJozsaAlgorithm`. It returns an array of `Result` values (the results of measurements).
- **`using (qubits = Qubit[3]) { ... }`**: This block allocates three qubits. The `using` statement ensures that the qubits are automatically released when the operation finishes.
- **`X(qubits[2]); H(qubits[2]);`**: These lines apply an X gate and then a Hadamard gate to the third qubit (`qubits[2]`). This prepares the qubit in the |-> state.
- **`H(qubits[0]); H(qubits[1]);`**: These lines apply Hadamard gates to the first two qubits (`qubits[0]` and `qubits[1]`), putting them into a superposition.
- **`// Oracle for constant function (does nothing)`**: This is a comment indicating where the oracle (the function being tested) would normally be inserted. The Deutsch-Jozsa algorithm works by querying this oracle. In this example, the oracle is for a *constant* function (it does nothing to the qubits). For a *balanced* function, the oracle would apply different gates.

- `H(qubits[0]); H(qubits[1]);`: These lines apply Hadamard gates again to the first two qubits. This is part of the algorithm's interference step.
- `return [M(qubits[0]), M(qubits[1])];`: These lines measure the first two qubits and return the measurement results. `M(qubit)` measures a qubit and returns a `Result` (either `Zero` or `One`).

📌 **Running the code:**

To run this Q# code, you would typically:

1. Write the code in a `.qs` file (e.g., `DeutschJozsa.qs`).
2. Create a host program (in C#, for example) to call the Q# operation.
3. Use the Q# simulator (provided with the QDK) to execute the program. This can be done from within Visual Studio, VS Code, or from the command line.

The output of the Deutsch-Jozsa algorithm will tell you whether the function represented by the oracle is constant or balanced.

Comparative Features and Ecosystem: Qiskit, Cirq, and Q#

Here's a comparison of Qiskit, Cirq, and Q#, highlighting their key features and ecosystems:

Feature	Qiskit (IBM)	Cirq (Google)	Q# (Microsoft)
Language	Python	Python	Q# (new DSL)
IDE Integration	Jupyter, VS Code	Jupyter, Colab	Visual Studio, VS Code
Real Hardware Access	IBM Quantum	Google Sycamore (private)	Azure Quantum (limited)
Simulation	Aer	cirq.Simulator()	Full State + Resource Est.
Learning Curve	Easy (Python)	Easy (Python)	Medium (new language)
Visualization Tools	Strong	Moderate	Limited (but improving)
Libraries	Aqua, Terra, Ignis	Cirq, TensorFlow Quantum	QDK

Detailed Explanation:

- **Language:**
  - **Qiskit and Cirq:** Both are Python-based, making them relatively easy to learn for those familiar with Python. Python's popularity in the scientific and machine learning communities also benefits these frameworks.

    - **Q#:** Q# is a new, domain-specific language (DSL) designed specifically for quantum programming. This means it has syntax and features tailored to quantum operations, but it requires learning a new language.
- **IDE Integration:**
    - All three frameworks offer integration with popular IDEs:
        - **Qiskit and Cirq:** Work well with Jupyter Notebooks, which are widely used for interactive computing and data analysis. Cirq also works in Google Colab, a cloud-based notebook environment.
        - **Q#:** Integrates with Microsoft's Visual Studio and VS Code, providing a more traditional integrated development environment.
- **Real Hardware Access:**
    - Each framework provides access to different quantum hardware:
        - **Qiskit:** Primarily used to program and access IBM Quantum's fleet of quantum computers.
        - **Cirq:** Designed to work with Google's quantum hardware, particularly the Sycamore processor. Access to this hardware is generally through Google Cloud.
        - **Q#:** Provides access to a variety of quantum hardware through Microsoft's Azure Quantum service, which includes backends from IonQ, Quantinuum, and Rigetti.
- **Simulation:**
    - All frameworks include simulators for testing and debugging quantum circuits:
        - **Qiskit:** Provides Aer, a high-performance quantum circuit simulator.
        - **Cirq:** Includes a built-in simulator (`cirq.Simulator()`) for running circuits.
        - **Q#:** Offers a full-state simulator for detailed simulation of small quantum systems and a resource estimator for analyzing the hardware requirements of quantum programs.
- **Learning Curve:**
    - **Qiskit and Cirq:** Have a relatively gentle learning curve for those who already know Python, which is a widely-used language.
    - **Q#:** Has a steeper learning curve because it requires learning a new language (Q#) with its own syntax and paradigms.
- **Visualization Tools:**
    - **Qiskit:** Provides strong visualization tools for displaying quantum circuits, quantum states (e.g., Bloch sphere), and measurement results.
    - **Cirq:** Offers moderate visualization capabilities.
    - **Q#:** Has more limited visualization tools, although they are improving.
- **Libraries:**
    - Each framework has its own set of libraries and tools:
        - **Qiskit:** Includes Aqua (for quantum algorithms), Terra (for circuit construction), and Ignis (for quantum error correction).
        - **Cirq:** Works with TensorFlow Quantum (TFQ) for quantum machine learning.
        - **Q#:** Comes with the Quantum Development Kit (QDK), which provides tools and libraries for quantum programming.

✓ When to Use What?

Here's a guide to help you choose the right framework for different use cases:

Use Case	Best Platform
Beginner learning & visualization	Qiskit
Hardware-specific optimization	Cirq (Sycamore)
Large-scale modular programming	Q#
Quantum + Machine Learning	Cirq + TensorFlow Quantum
Cross-platform experiments	Try all (via Azure Quantum)

Detailed Explanation:

- **Beginner learning & visualization:** Qiskit is a good choice for beginners due to its Python base, extensive documentation, and strong visualization tools.
- **Hardware-specific optimization:** Cirq is well-suited for researchers and developers working with Google's Sycamore hardware, as it is designed to take advantage of its specific architecture.
- **Large-scale modular programming:** Q# is designed for writing large, complex quantum programs with a focus on modularity and scalability.
- **Quantum + Machine Learning:** Cirq's integration with TensorFlow Quantum makes it a natural choice for quantum machine learning applications.
- **Cross-platform experiments:** Azure Quantum provides a unified platform for experimenting with Qiskit, Cirq, and Q#, allowing you to compare different hardware and software solutions.

🔎 Practical Tip: Azure Quantum

Microsoft's Azure Quantum is a valuable resource for exploring different quantum computing platforms. It allows you to:

- Run Qiskit and Cirq code on various quantum hardware.
- Submit jobs to quantum computers from IonQ, Quantinuum, and Rigetti.
- Compare the performance of different quantum hardware and software platforms.

10 practical questions with detailed explanation answers on Google's Cirq, Microsoft Q#, and Comparative Features and Ecosystem:

Google's Cirq

1. **Q: Write a Cirq code snippet to create a quantum circuit that prepares a qubit in the state (|0⟩ + i|1⟩)/√2 and then measures it in the X basis. Explain each step.**
   - **A:**
   - `import cirq`
   - `import numpy as np`

```
# Define a qubit
q = cirq.LineQubit(0)

# Create a circuit
circuit = cirq.Circuit()

# Apply gates to prepare the state (|0> + i|1>)/sqrt(2)
circuit.append(cirq.H(q))  # Hadamard gate
circuit.append(cirq.S(q))  # S gate (phase gate)

# Measure in the X basis
circuit.append(cirq.H(q))  # Apply Hadamard before measurement

# Simulate the circuit
simulator = cirq.Simulator()
result = simulator.run(circuit, repetitions=1000)
print(result)

# Print the circuit
print(circuit)
```

- **Explanation:**
  - We import `cirq` and `numpy`.
  - A qubit is defined.
  - A `cirq.Circuit` is created.
  - An H-gate is applied to put the qubit in superposition.
  - An S-gate is applied, which adds a phase of *i*.
  - Another H-gate is applied *before* measurement. Measuring in the X basis is equivalent to applying a Hadamard and then measuring in the Z basis.
  - The circuit is simulated, and the results are printed. The circuit is also printed to the console.

2. **Q: How do you define a custom quantum gate in Cirq, and how would you use it in a quantum circuit? Provide an example.**
   - **A:**

```
import cirq
import numpy as np

class MyPhaseGate(cirq.Gate):
    def __init__(self, phase):
        self._phase = phase

    def _unitary_(self):
        return np.array([[1, 0], [0, np.exp(1j * self._phase)]])

    def _circuit_diagram_info_(self, args):
        return f"P({self._phase})"

# Define a qubit
q = cirq.LineQubit(0)
# Create a circuit
```

```
circuit = cirq.Circuit()
# Use the custom gate
phase_gate = MyPhaseGate(np.pi / 4)
circuit.append(phase_gate(q))
circuit.append(cirq.measure(q))

# Simulate
simulator = cirq.Simulator()
result = simulator.run(circuit, repetitions=100)
print(result)
print(circuit)
```

- **Explanation:**
  - A class is defined inheriting from `cirq.Gate`.
  - `__init__` takes the phase parameter.
  - `_unitary_` returns the unitary matrix of the gate.
  - `_circuit_diagram_info_` provides a label for the gate in circuit diagrams.
  - An instance is created, and the gate is applied to a qubit in a circuit.

Microsoft Q#

3. **Q: Write a Q# operation that creates a Bell state using two qubits. Explain the Q# syntax and the quantum operations used.**
   - **A:**

```
operation CreateBellState(q1 : Qubit, q2 : Qubit) : Unit {
    H(q1);
    CNOT(q1, q2);
}

operation RunBellState() : (Result, Result) {
    use (qubits = Qubit[2]) {
        CreateBellState(qubits[0], qubits[1]);
        let result1 = M(qubits[0]);
        let result2 = M(qubits[1]);
        return (result1, result2);
    }
}
```

- **Explanation:**
  - `CreateBellState` takes two qubits as input.
  - `H(q1)` applies a Hadamard gate to the first qubit.
  - `CNOT(q1, q2)` applies a CNOT gate with `q1` as control and `q2` as target.
  - `RunBellState` allocates two qubits, calls `CreateBellState`, measures them, and returns the results as a tuple.
  - The `using` statement ensures the qubits are released after use.

4. **Q: How do you simulate a Q# operation, and how do you estimate the resources required to run a Q# program on a real quantum computer?**
   - **A:**
     - **Simulation:** Q# operations are typically called from a host program (C#, Python). The QDK provides simulators (full-state, etc.) that can be used from the host program to execute Q# code.
     - **Resource Estimation:** The QDK includes a resource estimator that analyzes Q# code and provides estimates of the number of qubits, gates, and other resources needed to run it on a quantum computer. This is done via a simulator configured for resource estimation.

Comparative Features and Ecosystem

5. **Q: Compare Qiskit and Cirq in terms of their strengths and weaknesses for quantum algorithm development. Which framework would you choose for developing a quantum algorithm for a specific hardware architecture, and why?**
   - **A:**
     - **Qiskit:** Strengths: Strong visualization, broad community, good for general-purpose quantum programming. Weaknesses: Can be less hardware-focused than Cirq.
     - **Cirq:** Strengths: Hardware-aware, optimized for Google's hardware, good for NISQ algorithms. Weaknesses: Less extensive visualization than Qiskit.
     - For hardware-specific algorithm development, Cirq is often preferred when targeting Google hardware due to its design philosophy.
6. **Q: Discuss the advantages and disadvantages of using Python (as in Qiskit and Cirq) versus a domain-specific language like Q# for quantum programming. Which approach is better suited for large-scale quantum software development?**
   - **A:**
     - **Python (Qiskit, Cirq):** Advantages: Easy to learn, large ecosystem, good for rapid prototyping. Disadvantages: Can be less expressive for specific quantum operations.
     - **Q#:** Advantages: Designed specifically for quantum programming, strong typing, better suited for large-scale modular projects. Disadvantages: Steeper learning curve, smaller community.
     - Q# is arguably better suited for large-scale development due to its strong typing and modularity.
7. **Q: Compare the quantum hardware access provided by Qiskit, Cirq, and Q#. Which platform offers the most diverse range of quantum hardware options, and what are the implications of this for quantum algorithm developers?**
   - **A:**
     - **Qiskit:** Primarily provides access to IBM Quantum hardware.
     - **Cirq:** Primarily focuses on Google's Sycamore hardware.
     - **Q# (via Azure Quantum):** Offers access to a more diverse range of hardware from IonQ, Quantinuum, and Rigetti.

        - Azure Quantum offers the most diverse hardware options, allowing developers to test their algorithms on different architectures and compare performance.
8. **Q: Explain how TensorFlow Quantum (TFQ) integrates with Cirq. What types of quantum-classical hybrid algorithms can be implemented using this combination, and what are the potential applications in quantum machine learning?**
    - **A:** TFQ allows you to build quantum circuits within TensorFlow and use them as layers in neural networks. This enables the creation of hybrid quantum-classical algorithms. Applications include:
        - Quantum neural networks
        - Variational quantum eigensolver (VQE) for quantum chemistry
        - Quantum approximate optimization algorithm (QAOA)
        - Using quantum circuits to process or generate quantum data.
9. **Q: You want to develop a quantum algorithm and test it on different quantum hardware providers. Which platform would you choose, and why?**
    - **A:** Azure Quantum. Azure Quantum allows you to write code in Qiskit or Cirq and run it on hardware from IonQ, Quantinuum, and Rigetti. This makes it the best choice for cross-platform testing and benchmarking.
10. **Q: A team is developing a complex quantum application with many modules and reusable components. Which language, Qiskit's Python or Microsoft's Q#, would be more suitable for this project, and why?**
    - **A:** Q# is likely more suitable. Q# is designed for modularity and scalability, with strong typing and features that make it easier to manage large codebases. While Python can be used for large projects, Q#'s design makes it a better fit for complex, modular quantum applications.

✅ Summary

- Cirq and Q# are **powerful alternatives** to Qiskit, each with unique strengths.
- Cirq is Pythonic, hardware-oriented, and great for research.
- Q# is scalable, modular, and integrates well with enterprise-grade systems.
- Cross-platform experience strengthens understanding of **quantum software diversity**.

30 multiple-choice questions with answers on Google's Cirq, Microsoft Q#, and Comparative Features and Ecosystem:

Google's Cirq

1. **Q: Cirq is primarily designed for...**
    - A) General-purpose programming
    - B) Classical simulation

- C) NISQ devices
- D) Quantum machine learning only
- **A:** C

2. **Q: Cirq is developed by...**
   - A) IBM
   - B) Microsoft
   - C) Google
   - D) Amazon
   - **A:** C
3. **Q: Which language is Cirq based on?**
   - A) Q#
   - B) C++
   - C) Python
   - D) Java
   - **A:** C
4. **Q: Cirq integrates well with...**
   - A) .NET
   - B) QDK
   - C) TensorFlow Quantum
   - D) Azure Quantum
   - **A:** C
5. **Q: Cirq provides native support for...**
   - A) Classical data structures
   - B) Quantum gates and noise modeling
   - C) Web development
   - D) Database management
   - **A:** B
6. **Q: In Cirq, qubits can be defined using...**
   - A) `Qubit()`
   - B) `QuantumBit()`
   - C) `cirq.LineQubit()`
   - D) `cirq.Qubit()`
   - **A:** C
7. **Q: Which class is used to create a quantum circuit in Cirq?**
   - A) `QuantumCircuit`
   - B) `Circuit`
   - C) `cirq.Circuit`
   - D) `cirq.QuantumCircuit`
   - **A:** C
8. **Q: How do you simulate a Cirq circuit?**
   - A) Using Qiskit Aer
   - B) Using Q# simulator
   - C) Using `cirq.Simulator()`
   - D) Using TensorFlow
   - **A:** C
9. **Q: Which is a valid Cirq gate?**

- A) `q.H`
- B) `cirq.H`
- C) `H()`
- D) `cirq.H()`
- **A:** D

10. **Q: What is the expected output of a Bell State circuit in Cirq?**
    - A) Equal probability of |00> and |11>
    - B) Only |00>
    - C) Only |11>
    - D) Equal probability of |01> and |10>
    - **A:** A

Microsoft Q#

11. **Q: Q# is a...**
    - A) General-purpose language
    - B) Domain-specific language for quantum computing
    - C) Quantum simulator
    - D) Quantum hardware
    - **A:** B
12. **Q: Q# is developed by...**
    - A) IBM
    - B) Google
    - C) Microsoft
    - D) Amazon
    - **A:** C
13. **Q: Q# is part of...**
    - A) Cirq
    - B) Qiskit
    - C) Quantum Development Kit (QDK)
    - D) TensorFlow Quantum
    - **A:** C
14. **Q: Q# integrates with...**
    - A) Python
    - B) Java
    - C) .NET platform
    - D) CUDA
    - **A:** C
15. **Q: Q# provides rich support for...**
    - A) Classical data structures
    - B) Quantum control structures
    - C) Web development
    - D) Database management
    - **A:** B
16. **Q: In Q#, a quantum operation is defined using...**
    - A) `def`

- B) `operation`
- C) `qop`
- D) `function`
- **A:** B

17. **Q: Which simulator is included in QDK?**
    - A) Qiskit Aer
    - B) cirq.Simulator()
    - C) Full-state simulator
    - D) TensorFlow Quantum
    - **A:** C
18. **Q: Which IDE is commonly used with Q#?**
    - A) Jupyter Notebook
    - B) Google Colab
    - C) Visual Studio
    - D) Xcode
    - **A:** C
19. **Q: What is the purpose of the using statement in Q#?**
    - A) Import libraries
    - B) Define classical variables
    - C) Allocate and release qubits
    - D) Define quantum gates
    - **A:** C
20. **Q: What does the M() operation do in Q#?**
    - A) Applies Hadamard gate
    - B) Applies CNOT gate
    - C) Measures a qubit
    - D) Performs a unitary transformation
    - **A:** C

Comparative Features and Ecosystem

21. **Q: Which language is used in both Qiskit and Cirq?**
    - A) Q#
    - B) C++
    - C) Python
    - D) Java
    - **A:** C
22. **Q: Which IDE is commonly used with Q#?**
    - A) Jupyter
    - B) VS Code
    - C) Google Colab
    - D) PyCharm
    - **A:** B
23. **Q: Which platform provides access to IBM Quantum hardware?**
    - A) Cirq
    - B) Q#

- C) Qiskit
- D) Azure Quantum
- **A:** C

24. **Q: Which platform is optimized for Google Sycamore hardware?**
    - A) Qiskit
    - B) Q#
    - C) Cirq
    - D) Azure Quantum
    - **A:** C
25. **Q: Which platform uses a new domain-specific language?**
    - A) Qiskit
    - B) Cirq
    - C) Q#
    - D) TensorFlow Quantum
    - **A:** C
26. **Q: Which platform offers a full-state simulator?**
    - A) Qiskit
    - B) Cirq
    - C) Q#
    - D) TensorFlow Quantum
    - **A:** C
27. **Q: Which platform is known for its strong visualization tools?**
    - A) Qiskit
    - B) Cirq
    - C) Q#
    - D) TensorFlow Quantum
    - **A:** A
28. **Q: Which library is associated with Cirq for quantum machine learning?**
    - A) Aqua
    - B) Terra
    - C) TensorFlow Quantum
    - D) QDK
    - **A:** C
29. **Q: Which platform allows you to experiment with Qiskit, Cirq, and Q#?**
    - A) IBM Quantum Lab
    - B) Google Cloud Quantum Engine
    - C) Azure Quantum
    - D) AWS Braket
    - **A:** C
30. **Q: Which is best for beginner learning?**
    - A) Q#
    - B) Cirq
    - C) Qiskit
    - D) All are the same
    - **A:** C

20 short questions and answers on Google's Cirq, Microsoft Q#, and Comparative Features and Ecosystem:

Google's Cirq

1. **Q: What is Cirq?**
   - **A:** Google's quantum framework.
2. **Q: What language does Cirq use?**
   - **A:** Python.
3. **Q: What is Cirq optimized for?**
   - **A:** NISQ devices.
4. **Q: Does Cirq support noise modeling?**
   - **A:** Yes.
5. **Q: What does Cirq integrate with?**
   - **A:** TensorFlow Quantum.

Microsoft Q#

6. **Q: What is Q#?**
   - **A:** Microsoft's quantum language.
7. **Q: Is Q# a DSL?**
   - **A:** Yes.
8. **Q: What is Q# part of?**
   - **A:** Quantum Development Kit (QDK).
9. **Q: What IDEs support Q#?**
   - **A:** Visual Studio, VS Code.
10. **Q: Does Q# have a resource estimator?**
    - **A:** Yes.

Comparative Features and Ecosystem

11. **Q: Which frameworks use Python?**
    - **A:** Qiskit, Cirq.
12. **Q: Which uses a new language?**
    - **A:** Q#.
13. **Q: Which accesses IBM hardware?**
    - **A:** Qiskit.
14. **Q: Which accesses Google hardware?**
    - **A:** Cirq.
15. **Q: Which accesses multiple hardwares?**
    - **A:** Q#.
16. **Q: Which has the strongest visualization?**
    - **A:** Qiskit.
17. **Q: Which is best for quantum machine learning?**
    - **A:** Cirq.
18. **Q: Which is best for large-scale programming?**

- **A:** Q#.

19. **Q: Which platform offers IonQ, Quantinuum, and Rigetti?**
    - **A:** Azure Quantum.
20. **Q: Which framework is from IBM?**
    - **A:** Qiskit.

10 medium-size questions with detailed answers on Google's Cirq, Microsoft Q#, and Comparative Features and Ecosystem:

Google's Cirq

1. **Q: Explain how to create a quantum circuit and apply quantum gates in Cirq. Provide a code example that creates a 3-qubit GHZ state.**
    - **A:**

```
import cirq

q0, q1, q2 = cirq.LineQubit.range(3)   # Define 3 qubits
circuit = cirq.Circuit()
circuit.append(cirq.H(q0))             # Apply H to q0
circuit.append(cirq.CNOT(q0, q1))      # CNOT(q0, q1)
circuit.append(cirq.CNOT(q1, q2))      # CNOT(q1, q2)
circuit.append(cirq.measure(q0, q1, q2, key='result')) # Measure all
print(circuit)

simulator = cirq.Simulator()
result = simulator.run(circuit, repetitions=100)
print(result)
```

    This creates a GHZ state: (|000> + |111>)/sqrt(2)

2. **Q: How does Cirq handle quantum simulation, and how can you retrieve measurement results from a simulated circuit?**
    - **A:** Cirq uses `cirq.Simulator()`. You create a simulator object, run the circuit with `simulator.run(circuit, repetitions=...)`, and get results using the result object, which contains measurement counts.

Microsoft Q#

3. **Q: Describe the basic structure of a Q# program. Explain how to define a quantum operation and call it from another operation.**
    - **A:** Q# programs consist of operations and functions. An operation defines a quantum computation. Example:

```
operation MyHadamard(q : Qubit) : Unit { H(q); }   // Define
operation MyCircuit() : Unit {              // Call
    use (qubit = Qubit()) {
        MyHadamard(qubit); // Call the operation
        // ...
    }
```

- }

4. **Q: Explain how Q# integrates with classical .NET programs. Provide a high-level overview of how you would call a Q# operation from a C# program.**
   - **A:** Q# operations can be called from C# using the QDK. You create a C# project, reference the Q# project, and use the QDK libraries to create a simulator or target a hardware provider and run the Q# operation.

Comparative Features and Ecosystem

5. **Q: Compare Qiskit and Cirq in terms of their approach to defining quantum circuits and applying quantum gates. What are the key differences in their syntax and design philosophies?**
   - **A:** Both use Python. Qiskit's design is more general-purpose. Cirq is more hardware-aware, with gate definitions tailored to specific architectures. Cirq emphasizes explicit qubit placement.
6. **Q: Discuss the strengths and weaknesses of Q# as a domain-specific language for quantum programming. How does it compare to using Python with Qiskit or Cirq in terms of code readability and maintainability for large quantum projects?**
   - **A:** Q# strengths: Strong typing, modularity, designed for quantum. Weaknesses: Steeper learning curve, smaller ecosystem. For large projects, Q#'s modularity and strong typing are advantages. Python is more readable for those familiar with it, but can be less structured for quantum code.
7. **Q: Compare the simulation capabilities of Cirq and Q#. Which framework provides more advanced simulation features, such as noise modeling or resource estimation?**
   - **A:** Cirq excels in noise modeling. Q# provides a resource estimator, which is a unique feature for analyzing hardware requirements. Both have simulators. Q# has a full-state simulator.
8. **Q: You want to implement a quantum algorithm that combines quantum computation with classical machine learning. Which framework, Cirq or Q#, would be more suitable for this task, and why?**
   - **A:** Cirq, because of its integration with TensorFlow Quantum (TFQ). TFQ allows for building hybrid quantum-classical models, which is essential for many quantum machine learning applications.
9. **Q: Compare the quantum hardware access offered by Qiskit and Azure Quantum. What are the advantages and disadvantages of each platform in terms of the variety of hardware providers and the ease of accessing different quantum systems?**
   - **A:** Qiskit: Primarily IBM hardware. Advantage: Direct access to IBM's systems. Disadvantage: Limited to one provider. Azure Quantum: IonQ, Quantinuum, Rigetti. Advantage: Diverse hardware. Disadvantage: Access is through Azure.
10. **Q: A research team wants to benchmark a new quantum algorithm on several different quantum computing platforms. Which platform, Qiskit, Cirq, or Azure Quantum, would be the most efficient choice for this task, and why?**
    - **A:** Azure Quantum is the most efficient choice. It allows you to run code (Qiskit, Cirq) on hardware from multiple providers (IonQ, Quantinuum, Rigetti) from a single platform, simplifying cross-platform benchmarking.

CHAPTER 13: QUANTUM MACHINE LEARNING

◆ Introduction

Quantum Machine Learning (QML) leverages quantum computing to enhance machine learning models, especially for high-dimensional and complex data patterns. While today's quantum devices are still in the NISQ era, hybrid approaches are already showing promise.

Hybrid Quantum-Classical Algorithms

Hybrid quantum-classical algorithms are a crucial approach in the NISQ (Noisy Intermediate-Scale Quantum) era. They leverage the strengths of both quantum and classical computing to tackle problems that are difficult for either type of computer alone.

✅ What Are They?

These algorithms combine the power of quantum circuits with classical optimization techniques. The basic idea is to divide a computational problem into parts that are best suited for each type of processor:

- **Quantum Circuit:** A quantum circuit is used to perform specific quantum operations, such as:
  - Encoding the problem's data into quantum states.
  - Applying a sequence of quantum gates to transform these states.
  - Creating complex quantum superpositions and entanglements.
- **Classical Optimizer:** A classical computer runs an optimization algorithm (like gradient descent) to:
  - Control the parameters of the quantum circuit.
  - Analyze the measurement results obtained from the quantum circuit.
  - Determine how to adjust the parameters to improve the solution.

In essence, the quantum computer acts as a specialized co-processor, performing the parts of the computation that benefit most from quantum mechanics, while the classical computer handles the overall control and optimization.

✅ Example: Variational Quantum Eigensolver (VQE)

A prominent example of a hybrid quantum-classical algorithm is the Variational Quantum Eigensolver (VQE). VQE is used to approximate the ground-state energy of a quantum system, which is a fundamental problem in quantum chemistry and materials science.

Here's how VQE works:

1. **Prepare a Parameterized Quantum Circuit (Ansatz):**
   - A parameterized quantum circuit, also known as an *ansatz*, is designed. This circuit contains a set of adjustable parameters.
   - The ansatz is designed to create a quantum state that is a candidate for the ground state of the system.
   - The parameters control the specific state that the circuit prepares.
2. **Measure an Observable (Energy):**
   - The quantum circuit is executed on a quantum computer (or a simulator).
   - The output of the circuit is measured to determine the expectation value of an observable, which in this case represents the energy of the system.
   - The energy is calculated based on the measurement results.
3. **Use a Classical Computer to Optimize the Circuit Parameters:**
   - The classical computer receives the measured energy value from the quantum computer.
   - A classical optimization algorithm (e.g., gradient descent, Nelder-Mead) is used to adjust the parameters of the quantum circuit.
   - The goal of the optimization is to find the set of parameters that minimizes the energy. The parameters are adjusted iteratively to find a lower energy.
4. **Iteration:**
   - Steps 1-3 are repeated in a loop.
   - In each iteration, the classical optimizer suggests a new set of parameters, the quantum circuit is run with these parameters, the energy is measured, and the classical optimizer updates the parameters again.
   - This process continues until the energy converges to a minimum value, which is an approximation of the ground-state energy.

In VQE, the quantum computer efficiently explores a space of possible quantum states, while the classical computer guides the search for the state with the lowest energy. This combination allows VQE to approximate ground-state energies for molecules and materials that are too complex to be solved using purely classical methods.

Variational Quantum Circuits (VQCs)

Variational Quantum Circuits (VQCs) are a specific type of quantum circuit that plays a central role in many hybrid quantum-classical algorithms.

✅ What Is a VQC?

A VQC is a quantum circuit with tunable parameters. These parameters are typically rotation angles applied to the qubits within the circuit. The key idea is that instead of designing a fixed quantum circuit, we create a circuit structure with adjustable parameters, and then use classical optimization techniques to find the best values for those parameters.

VQCs are used in a variety of applications, including:

- **Classification:** VQCs can be designed to classify data points into different categories.
- **Regression:** VQCs can be used to learn a function that maps input data to continuous output values.
- **Quantum Neural Networks (QNNs):** VQCs form the building blocks of quantum neural networks, where the tunable parameters act like the weights in a classical neural network.

✅ Example: Binary Classifier with VQC (Qiskit)

Here's an example of how to create a simple VQC for binary classification using Qiskit:

```
from qiskit import QuantumCircuit, Aer, execute
from qiskit.circuit import Parameter
import numpy as np

# Define parameters
theta = Parameter('θ')
phi = Parameter('φ')

# Create a 1-qubit variational circuit
qc = QuantumCircuit(1)
qc.ry(theta, 0)  # Apply a rotation around the Y-axis
qc.rz(phi, 0)    # Apply a rotation around the Z-axis
qc.measure_all()  # Measure the qubit

# Substitute values for the parameters.  These would normally come from an
optimizer.
bound_circuit = qc.bind_parameters({theta: np.pi / 4, phi: np.pi / 2})

# Simulate
backend = Aer.get_backend('qasm_simulator')
result = execute(bound_circuit, backend, shots=1000).result()
counts = result.get_counts()

print("Counts:", counts)
```

Explanation:

1. **Define Parameters:**
   - `theta = Parameter('θ')` and `phi = Parameter('φ')`: These lines define symbolic parameters named 'θ' and 'φ'. These parameters will be the tunable knobs of our VQC.
2. **Create a 1-Qubit Variational Circuit:**
   - `qc = QuantumCircuit(1)`: Creates a quantum circuit with one qubit.
   - `qc.ry(theta, 0)`: Applies a rotation around the Y-axis to qubit 0, with the angle specified by the parameter 'θ'.
   - `qc.rz(phi, 0)`: Applies a rotation around the Z-axis to qubit 0, with the angle specified by the parameter 'φ'.

- `qc.measure_all()`: Measures the qubit.

3. **Substitute Values:**
   - `bound_circuit = qc.bind_parameters({theta: np.pi / 4, phi: np.pi / 2})`: This line assigns specific numerical values to the symbolic parameters. In a real application, these values would be determined by a classical optimizer. Here, we just set them to example values. The `bind_parameters` method creates a new circuit where the parameters are no longer symbolic, but have concrete values.
4. **Simulate:**
   - The circuit with the bound parameters is then simulated, and the measurement counts are printed.

📌 **Classical Optimization:**

In a typical VQC application, you would use a classical optimizer (from libraries like `scipy.optimize` in Python) to adjust the values of 'θ' and 'φ'. The optimizer's goal is to minimize a *loss function*, which measures how well the VQC is performing its task (e.g., how accurately it's classifying data). The optimizer would try different values of the parameters, run the quantum circuit, evaluate the loss function, and then update the parameters in a direction that reduces the loss. This iterative process continues until the loss function reaches a minimum.

✅ Use in Quantum Neural Networks (QNNs)

VQCs are the core component of Quantum Neural Networks (QNNs). Libraries like Qiskit Machine Learning and PennyLane provide tools to build QNNs using parameterized gates, much like the layers in a classical neural network. In a QNN:

- The parameters of the VQC act like the weights of a neural network.
- The structure of the VQC defines the architecture of the QNN.
- Classical optimization algorithms are used to train the QNN by adjusting these parameters to minimize a cost function.

Applications in Data Science and AI

Quantum computing has the potential to revolutionize data science and AI by enabling the development of new algorithms and models that can solve problems intractable for classical computers. Here are some key application areas:

✅ A. Quantum-enhanced Classification

Quantum classifiers leverage the principles of quantum mechanics, such as superposition and entanglement, to learn complex patterns in data. These patterns might be too subtle or high-dimensional for classical models to capture effectively.

Example: Iris Dataset (2D version)

A common example used to illustrate quantum classification is the Iris dataset. While the full dataset has 4 features, we can consider a simplified 2D version for visualization.

- **Process:**
  - **Amplitude Encoding:** The data points (e.g., sepal length and petal length) are encoded into the amplitudes of a quantum state. This means that each data point's features are represented by the probability amplitudes of the quantum state.
  - **Classification using VQC:** A Variational Quantum Circuit (VQC) is used to process the encoded quantum states. The VQC has tunable parameters that are optimized using classical techniques to separate the different classes of Iris flowers.

✅ B. Quantum Kernel Methods

Kernel methods are a powerful technique in classical machine learning, particularly with Support Vector Machines (SVMs). Quantum computers can be used to calculate kernel values in a fundamentally different way than classical computers.

- **Quantum Kernel:** A quantum kernel is defined as the squared overlap between the quantum states representing two input data points:
- `Quantum Kernel = |⟨ψ(x1)|ψ(x2)⟩|^2`

  Where:

  - `x1` and `x2` are two input data points.
  - `|ψ(x1)⟩` and `|ψ(x2)⟩` are the quantum states representing those data points after some quantum encoding.
  - This kernel measures the similarity between the quantum representations of the two inputs.
- **Use Case:** By using a quantum computer to calculate these kernel values, we can create SVM-like classifiers that can potentially capture more complex relationships in the data than classical kernels.
- **Libraries:** Libraries like `qiskit_machine_learning.kernels` provide tools for building and using quantum kernels.

✅ C. Generative Models (Quantum GANs)

Generative Adversarial Networks (GANs) are a class of machine learning frameworks designed by Ian Goodfellow and his colleagues in 2014. Two neural networks contest with each other in a zero-sum game framework.

- **QGANs:** Quantum Generative Adversarial Networks (QGANs) are a quantum version of GANs.

    - They use quantum circuits as the generator, which creates synthetic data.
    - They use a classical neural network as the discriminator, which tries to distinguish between real data and the synthetic data generated by the quantum circuit.
- **Applications:** QGANs have potential applications in:
    - Image synthesis
    - Financial modeling
    - Cybersecurity (e.g., generating adversarial examples)

✅ D. Reinforcement Learning

Reinforcement learning (RL) is an area of machine learning where an agent learns to make decisions in an environment to maximize a reward.

- **Quantum Reinforcement Learning:** Quantum computing may offer advantages in reinforcement learning by:
    - Enabling the design of more efficient quantum policies.
    - Speeding up the process of updating the agent's state.
- **Current Status:** This is a highly experimental area, and practical quantum advantages in RL are still being explored.

◆ Comparison with Classical ML

Here's a comparison of classical and quantum machine learning:

Aspect	Classical ML	Quantum ML
Speed on large data	Efficient	Promising for very high-dim data
Interpretability	High (e.g., trees, linear models)	Still emerging
Model Types	SVM, NN, Trees	QNN, VQC, Quantum Kernels
Hardware Requirement	Classical CPUs/GPUs	Quantum + Classical hybrid
Readiness	Production-ready	Early-stage but growing fast

✅ Summary

Concept	Description
Hybrid Algorithms	Quantum circuit + classical optimizer loop
VQC	Parameterized circuits acting like neural nets
QML Applications	Classification, kernel methods, GANs, RL
Libraries to Explore	Qiskit ML, PennyLane, TensorFlow Quantum

10 practical questions with detailed explanation answers on Hybrid Quantum-Classical Algorithms:

Hybrid Quantum-Classical Algorithms

1. **Q: Explain the fundamental concept of a hybrid quantum-classical algorithm. Why are they important in the NISQ era?**
   - **A:** Hybrid algorithms use both quantum circuits for specific tasks and classical computers for control and optimization. They're important in the NISQ era because current quantum computers are limited, and these algorithms make the most of both classical and quantum resources.
2. **Q: Describe the general workflow of a hybrid quantum-classical algorithm. What are the roles of the quantum processor and the classical processor?**
   - **A:**
     - Quantum processor: Executes a parameterized quantum circuit.
     - Classical processor: Optimizes the circuit's parameters based on measurement results from the quantum processor. This involves iterative feedback.

Variational Quantum Circuits (VQCs)

3. **Q: What is a Variational Quantum Circuit (VQC)? How are the parameters in a VQC optimized?**
   - **A:** A VQC is a quantum circuit with tunable parameters. These parameters are optimized using classical optimization algorithms (e.g., gradient descent) to minimize a cost function.
4. **Q: Design a simple VQC for a 2-qubit system with two tunable parameters. Show the quantum circuit diagram and explain how you would use it in a hybrid algorithm.**
   - **A:**
   - `q0: —Ry(θ1)—CNOT—Ry(θ2)—M—`
   - `q1: —Ry(θ3)—CNOT—Ry(θ4)—M—`

     - This circuit has 4 parameters (θ1, θ2, θ3, θ4). A classical optimizer would adjust these angles to minimize a cost function calculated from the measurements (M).

Applications in Data Science and AI

5. **Q: Explain how quantum computers can be used for classification tasks. What are the potential advantages of quantum classifiers over classical ones?**
   - **A:** Quantum classifiers use VQCs to learn decision boundaries. Advantages: Potential to learn more complex patterns, especially in high-dimensional data, due to entanglement and superposition.
6. **Q: What are quantum kernel methods? How do they differ from classical kernel methods, and what are their potential benefits?**

    - **A:** Quantum kernels are calculated using quantum circuits. They measure the similarity between quantum states. Potential benefits: Can capture different data relationships than classical kernels, potentially leading to better classification or regression.
7. **Q: Describe the architecture of a Quantum Generative Adversarial Network (QGAN). What are the roles of the quantum and classical components in a QGAN?**
    - **A:** QGANs use a quantum circuit as the generator and a classical neural network as the discriminator. The quantum generator creates synthetic data, and the classical discriminator evaluates its quality.
8. **Q: How might quantum computing enhance reinforcement learning? What are some of the challenges in applying quantum computing to RL?**
    - **A:** Potential enhancements: More efficient policies, faster state updates. Challenges: Still highly experimental, requires efficient ways to represent states and actions in a quantum system.
9. **Q: Compare and contrast classical and quantum machine learning in terms of data requirements, model interpretability, and computational resources.**
    - **A:**
        - Classical ML: Can use large datasets, often interpretable, runs on CPUs/GPUs.
        - Quantum ML: May require new data encoding, interpretability is emerging, requires hybrid quantum-classical systems.
10. **Q: Choose one application of quantum computing in data science or AI (e.g., VQE for materials science, QGANs for image generation). Explain in detail the potential impact of quantum computing in that area and the current limitations.**

```
* **A:** VQE for materials science:
    * Potential impact: More accurate simulations of molecular properties, leading to discovery of new materials.
    * Current limitations: Requires larger, less noisy quantum computers to handle complex molecules.
```

30 multiple-choice questions with answers on Hybrid Quantum-Classical Algorithms:

Hybrid Quantum-Classical Algorithms

1. **Q: Hybrid quantum-classical algorithms combine...**
    - A) Two quantum computers
    - B) Quantum circuits and classical computation
    - C) Two classical computers
    - D) Quantum and classical data
    - **A:** B
2. **Q: In a hybrid algorithm, the quantum circuit is used for...**
    - A) Classical optimization
    - B) Data storage
    - C) Encoding and transforming data
    - D) Displaying results
    - **A:** C

3. **Q: In a hybrid algorithm, the classical optimizer is used for...**
   - A) Running quantum gates
   - B) Tuning parameters
   - C) Data storage
   - D) Quantum simulation
   - **A:** B
4. **Q: Which is a common classical optimization technique used in hybrid algorithms?**
   - A) Quantum Fourier Transform
   - B) Gradient descent
   - C) Quantum annealing
   - D) Shor's algorithm
   - **A:** B
5. **Q: Hybrid algorithms are particularly relevant in the...**
   - A) Fault-tolerant quantum computing era
   - B) NISQ era
   - C) Classical computing era
   - D) Analog computing era
   - **A:** B

Variational Quantum Circuits (VQCs)

6. **Q: What is a Variational Quantum Circuit (VQC)?**
   - A) A fixed quantum circuit
   - B) A quantum circuit with tunable parameters
   - C) A classical circuit
   - D) A circuit with no gates
   - **A:** B
7. **Q: The tunable parameters in a VQC are typically...**
   - A) Qubit types
   - B) Gate types
   - C) Rotation angles
   - D) Measurement bases
   - **A:** C
8. **Q: VQCs are used in...**
   - A) Quantum key distribution
   - B) Classification and regression
   - C) Quantum error correction
   - D) Quantum teleportation
   - **A:** B
9. **Q: In a VQC, the parameters are optimized using...**
   - A) Quantum gates
   - B) Classical techniques
   - C) Random search
   - D) Quantum annealing
   - **A:** B
10. **Q: VQCs are a key component of...**

- A) Quantum Fourier Transform
- B) Quantum neural networks
- C) Shor's algorithm
- D) Quantum teleportation
- **A:** B

Applications in Data Science and AI

11. **Q: Quantum classifiers use...**
    - A) Classical bits
    - B) Entangled states and superposition
    - C) Classical neural networks
    - D) Quantum annealing
    - **A:** B
12. **Q: In quantum-enhanced classification, data is often encoded into...**
    - A) Classical bits
    - B) Qubit indices
    - C) Quantum state amplitudes
    - D) Gate sequences
    - **A:** C
13. **Q: Quantum kernel methods calculate kernel values based on...**
    - A) Classical data
    - B) Qubit indices
    - C) Overlap of quantum states
    - D) Gate sequences
    - **A:** C
14. **Q: A quantum kernel measures the...**
    - A) Distance between qubits
    - B) Similarity between quantum representations of inputs
    - C) Number of quantum gates
    - D) Energy of a quantum system
    - **A:** B
15. **Q: QGAN stands for...**
    - A) Quantum General Algorithm Network
    - B) Quantum Gate Array Network
    - C) Quantum Generative Adversarial Network
    - D) Quantum Global Area Network
    - **A:** C
16. **Q: In a QGAN, the generator is a...**
    - A) Classical neural network
    - B) Quantum circuit
    - C) Classical circuit
    - D) Quantum computer
    - **A:** B
17. **Q: In a QGAN, the discriminator is a...**
    - A) Quantum circuit

- B) Classical neural network
- C) Quantum computer
- D) Classical computer
- **A:** B

18. **Q: Quantum reinforcement learning aims to improve...**
    - A) Classical data storage
    - B) Quantum gate design
    - C) Agent policies and state updates
    - D) Quantum simulation accuracy
    - **A:** C
19. **Q: Compared to classical ML, quantum ML's speed on large data is...**
    - A) Less efficient
    - B) More efficient
    - C) The same
    - D) Promising for very high-dimensional data
    - **A:** D
20. **Q: The interpretability of quantum ML models is...**
    - A) High
    - B) Low
    - C) Still emerging
    - D) Always better than classical ML
    - **A:** C
21. **Q: An example of a classical ML model type is...** * A) QNN * B) VQC * C) Quantum Kernel * D) SVM * **A:** D
22. **Q: An example of a quantum ML model type is...** * A) SVM * B) Decision Tree * C) QNN * D) Linear Regression * **A:** C
23. **Q: Classical ML primarily requires...** * A) Quantum computers * B) Classical CPUs/GPUs * C) Qubits * D) Superposition * **A:** B
24. **Q: Quantum ML primarily requires...** * A) Classical CPUs/GPUs * B) Quantum computers * C) A hybrid of quantum and classical hardware * D) Only qubits * **A:** C
25. **Q: The readiness of classical ML is...** * A) Early-stage * B) Growing fast * C) Production-ready * D) Experimental * **A:** C
26. **Q: The readiness of quantum ML is...**
    - A) Production-ready
    - B) Early-stage but growing fast
    - C) Mature
    - D) Obsolete
    - **A:** B
27. **Q: Which algorithm is used for approximating ground-state energies?**
    - A) Grover's Algorithm
    - B) VQE
    - C) Shor's Algorithm
    - D) Quantum Fourier Transform
    - **A:** B
28. **Q: What does VQE stand for?**
    - A) Variational Quantum Encoder

- B) Variational Quantum Eigensolver
- C) Variable Quantum Estimator
- D) Vector Quantum Engine
- **A:** B

29. **Q: In VQE, a classical computer optimizes...**
    - A) Qubit states
    - B) Circuit parameters
    - C) Gate types
    - D) Measurement basis
    - **A:** B
30. **Q: Which library provides tools to build QNNs?**
    - A) TensorFlow
    - B) PyTorch
    - C) Qiskit Machine Learning
    - D) NumPy
    - **A:** C

20 short questions and answers on Hybrid Quantum-Classical Algorithms:

Hybrid Quantum-Classical Algorithms

1. **Q: What do hybrid algorithms combine?**
    - **A:** Quantum circuits and classical computation.
2. **Q: What does the quantum part do?**
    - **A:** Encodes and transforms data.
3. **Q: What does the classical part do?**
    - **A:** Tunes parameters.
4. **Q: Are they important in the NISQ era?**
    - **A:** Yes.
5. **Q: Give an example of a hybrid algorithm.**
    - **A:** VQE.

Variational Quantum Circuits (VQCs)

6. **Q: What are VQCs?**
    - **A:** Quantum circuits with tunable parameters.
7. **Q: What are the tunable parameters?**
    - **A:** Rotation angles.
8. **Q: How are VQC parameters optimized?**
    - **A:** Classically.
9. **Q: Are VQCs used in QNNs?**
    - **A:** Yes.
10. **Q: What is a VQC used for?**
    - **A:** Classification, regression.

Applications in Data Science and AI

11. **Q: What do quantum classifiers use?**
    - **A:** Entangled states.
12. **Q: How is data encoded in quantum classifiers?**
    - **A:** Amplitude encoding.
13. **Q: What do quantum kernels calculate?**
    - **A:** Overlap of quantum states.
14. **Q: What do quantum kernels measure?**
    - **A:** Similarity.
15. **Q: What are QGANs?**
    - **A:** Quantum Generative Adversarial Networks.
16. **Q: What is the generator in a QGAN?**
    - **A:** Quantum circuit.
17. **Q: What is the discriminator in a QGAN?**
    - **A:** Classical network.
18. **Q: What is enhanced in quantum RL?**
    - **A:** Policies.
19. **Q: Is quantum ML production-ready?**
    - **A:** No.
20. **Q: Is quantum ML growing fast?**
    - **A:** Yes.

10 medium-size questions with detailed answers on Hybrid Quantum-Classical Algorithms:

Hybrid Quantum-Classical Algorithms

1. **Q: Describe the core idea behind hybrid quantum-classical algorithms. Explain why they are considered a promising approach for near-term quantum computing.**
    - **A:** Hybrid algorithms combine quantum circuits for specific computational tasks with classical computers that handle control and optimization. They are promising for the NISQ era because they can leverage limited quantum resources by offloading complex control and optimization to classical computers.
2. **Q: Explain the typical workflow of a hybrid quantum-classical algorithm, detailing the interaction between the quantum and classical components.**
    - **A:** 1. A parameterized quantum circuit is prepared. 2. The circuit is executed on a quantum processor, and measurements are taken. 3. A classical computer uses the measurement results to calculate a cost function. 4. A classical optimization algorithm updates the parameters of the quantum circuit to minimize the cost function. 5. Steps 1-4 are repeated until convergence.

Variational Quantum Circuits (VQCs)

3. **Q: What are Variational Quantum Circuits (VQCs)? Explain their role in hybrid quantum-classical algorithms and how they differ from fixed quantum circuits.**
    - **A:** VQCs are quantum circuits with adjustable parameters. Unlike fixed circuits, their parameters are optimized classically. They are crucial in hybrid algorithms

as they provide a flexible quantum circuit structure that can be adapted to specific problems.

4. **Q: Describe how a VQC can be used for a simple binary classification problem. Include the steps involved in setting up the circuit and training it.**
   - **A:** 1. Encode data into a quantum state. 2. Apply a VQC to the state. 3. Measure the output. 4. Use the measurement results to calculate a loss function (e.g., classification error). 5. Use a classical optimizer to adjust the VQC's parameters to minimize the loss. Repeat until the classification accuracy is satisfactory.

Applications in Data Science and AI

5. **Q: Explain how quantum computing can be applied to enhance classification tasks in machine learning. What are the potential advantages of quantum classifiers?**
   - **A:** Quantum classifiers use VQCs to create complex decision boundaries. Potential advantages include the ability to learn highly entangled representations of data, which may be beneficial for high-dimensional or complex datasets, and the potential for increased expressivity with fewer parameters.
6. **Q: What are quantum kernel methods, and how do they work? Describe how they can be used to improve Support Vector Machines (SVMs).**
   - **A:** Quantum kernel methods use a quantum computer to calculate the kernel function, which measures the similarity between data points in a feature space. By using quantum circuits to define this feature space, quantum kernels can capture different relationships in the data than classical kernels, potentially improving the performance of SVMs.
7. **Q: Describe the architecture and working principle of Quantum Generative Adversarial Networks (QGANs). What are some potential applications of QGANs?**
   - **A:** QGANs consist of a quantum generator and a classical discriminator. The quantum generator creates synthetic data, and the classical discriminator tries to distinguish between real and synthetic data. Applications include image synthesis, financial modeling, and generating training data for other machine learning models.
8. **Q: How might quantum computing be used to improve reinforcement learning algorithms? What are the potential benefits and challenges in this area?**
   - **A:** Quantum computing may enable more efficient exploration of state spaces, the design of more complex and expressive policies, and faster convergence. Challenges include representing states and actions efficiently in a quantum system and developing quantum algorithms for policy optimization.
9. **Q: Compare and contrast classical and quantum machine learning in terms of their strengths, weaknesses, and potential applications. Provide examples of tasks where each approach excels.**
   - **A:** Classical ML: Strengths: Mature, efficient for many tasks, interpretable. Weaknesses: Struggles with very high-dimensional data. Quantum ML: Strengths: Potential for handling very high-dimensional data, new model types. Weaknesses: Early stage, limited hardware, interpretability challenges. Classical ML excels at tasks with large datasets and well-defined features. Quantum ML may excel at problems with complex, high-dimensional correlations.

10. **Q: Choose one application of quantum computing in data science or AI and discuss its current state of development, potential impact, and the key challenges that need to be overcome.**
    - **A:** Quantum-enhanced Classification: Current state: Early stage, with small-scale demonstrations. Potential impact: Improved accuracy and efficiency for complex classification problems. Key challenges: Developing efficient methods for encoding classical data into quantum states, designing expressive and trainable VQCs, and scaling to larger datasets.

CHAPTER 14: QUANTUM CRYPTOGRAPHY AND POST-QUANTUM SECURITY

◆ Introduction

Quantum computers have the potential to **break widely used cryptographic systems** like RSA and ECC (Elliptic Curve Cryptography), which rely on problems like integer factorization and discrete logarithms—both solvable using **Shor's algorithm**. This chapter introduces:

- **Quantum-based security mechanisms** like QKD
- **Quantum attacks** on classical systems
- **Post-quantum cryptographic** solutions like lattice-based cryptography

---

Quantum Key Distribution (QKD)

Quantum Key Distribution (QKD) is a groundbreaking technique that uses the principles of quantum mechanics to secure the exchange of cryptographic keys between two parties, traditionally called Alice and Bob.

✅ What is QKD?

QKD allows Alice and Bob to generate a shared, secret key that can then be used to encrypt and decrypt messages using a classical encryption algorithm (like AES). What makes QKD special is that its security is not based on the computational difficulty of mathematical problems (like factoring large numbers, as in RSA), but on the fundamental laws of quantum physics.

The security of QKD relies on two key principles:

- **No-cloning theorem:** This theorem states that it is impossible to create an identical copy of an arbitrary quantum state. If an eavesdropper (Eve) tries to intercept and copy the quantum information being transmitted between Alice and Bob, she will inevitably alter the state of the qubits.
- **Observation causes disturbance:** In quantum mechanics, the act of measuring a quantum state changes that state. If Eve tries to measure the qubits being exchanged by Alice and Bob, her measurement will disturb the qubits, and this disturbance can be detected by Alice and Bob.

✅ Key Properties

QKD has some unique and powerful properties:

- **Detects eavesdropping automatically:** The most important feature of QKD is its ability to detect any attempt at eavesdropping. If Eve tries to intercept or measure the quantum information, she will introduce errors into the transmission. Alice and Bob can then use these errors to determine whether the key exchange has been compromised and discard the key if necessary.

- **Does not encrypt data, only secures the key exchange:** It's crucial to understand that QKD itself does *not* encrypt the actual data being transmitted. Instead, it provides a secure way for Alice and Bob to agree on a secret key. This key can then be used with a classical symmetric-key encryption algorithm (like AES) to encrypt and decrypt the data. In other words, QKD solves the key distribution problem, which is a major challenge in classical cryptography.

BB84 Protocol (Bennett and Brassard, 1984)

The BB84 protocol, named after its inventors Charles Bennett and Gilles Brassard, is the first and most famous Quantum Key Distribution (QKD) protocol. It provides a method for two parties, Alice and Bob, to establish a shared secret key using quantum mechanics.

✅ Overview

BB84 uses the properties of quantum states to ensure secure key exchange. It relies on the following key elements:

- **Two bases:** The protocol employs two mutually unbiased bases for encoding and measuring quantum information:
    - **Rectilinear (+) basis:** This basis consists of the horizontal ($|0\rangle$) and vertical ($|1\rangle$) polarization states.
    - **Diagonal (×) basis:** This basis consists of the diagonal right ($|+\rangle$) and diagonal left ($|-\rangle$) polarization states.
- **Random polarization states for encoding bits:** Alice encodes classical bits (0 or 1) into photons with specific polarization states. The choice of polarization state depends on both the bit value and the randomly chosen basis.

Here's a table summarizing the relationship between bits, bases, and photon states in BB84:

Bit	Basis (+)	Photon State	Basis (×)	Photon State
0	+	→ (horizontal)	×	↘ (diagonal right)
1	+	↑ (vertical)	×	↗ (diagonal left)

✅ Protocol Steps

The BB84 protocol involves the following steps:

1. **Alice generates a random bit string and a random basis string:** Alice creates two random sequences: one representing the bits she wants to send and the other representing the bases she will use to encode those bits.
2. **Alice sends photons encoded in those bases:** Alice encodes each bit from her bit string into a photon's polarization state, using the corresponding basis from her basis string. She then sends these photons to Bob through a quantum channel (e.g., an optical fiber).
3. **Bob measures photons using random bases:** Bob independently chooses a random basis for each received photon and measures its polarization state. He records the measurement result and the basis he used.
4. **Alice and Bob compare bases (not bits) over a public channel:** Alice and Bob communicate over a classical, public channel (which is assumed to be insecure). They compare the bases they used for each photon. They do *not* reveal the actual bit values.
5. **They discard mismatched results → remaining bits = raw key:** For each photon, if Alice and Bob used the same basis, their measurements will be correlated. They keep the corresponding bit. If they used different bases, the measurement results are random, and they discard that bit. The remaining bits form the "raw key," which is a shared, but potentially noisy, secret key.
6. **Use error correction & privacy amplification to form final key:**
   - **Error correction:** Because of noise in the quantum channel or potential eavesdropping, the raw key may contain some errors. Alice and Bob use classical error correction techniques (exchanging some information over the public channel) to identify and correct these errors.
   - **Privacy amplification:** Even after error correction, an eavesdropper (Eve) might have gained some partial information about the key. Alice and Bob use a technique called privacy amplification to reduce Eve's information to a negligible level, resulting in the final, secure shared secret key.

✅ Example

Here's a simplified example of the BB84 protocol:

Alice wants to send the bit sequence: `1 0 1 0`

Alice chooses the basis sequence: + × + ×

Bob chooses the basis sequence: × × + +

Position	Alice Bit	Alice Basis	Bob Basis	Keep?
1	1	+	×	No
2	0	×	×	Yes
3	1	+	+	Yes
4	0	×	+	No

□ **Final raw key = 0 1**

In this example, Alice and Bob keep the bits at positions 2 and 3 because they used the same basis. The resulting raw key is `0 1`. They would then proceed with error correction and privacy amplification to obtain the final secure key.

Quantum Attacks on Classical Cryptography

Quantum computers, while still in their early stages of development, pose a significant threat to many of the cryptographic systems that we rely on today. Two quantum algorithms, in particular, Shor's algorithm and Grover's algorithm, have the potential to break widely used classical cryptographic schemes.

✅ A. Shor's Algorithm

Shor's algorithm, developed by Peter Shor in 1994, is a quantum algorithm that can efficiently solve two mathematical problems:

- **Integer factorization:** Given a large integer N, find its prime factors.
- **Discrete logarithm problem:** Given numbers a, b, and N, find x such that ax ≡ b (mod N).

These two problems are the foundation of the security of several widely used public-key cryptosystems, including:

- **RSA:** RSA relies on the difficulty of factoring large numbers. A quantum computer running Shor's algorithm could factor the large numbers used in RSA, allowing it to derive the private key from the public key.
- **Diffie-Hellman key exchange:** Diffie-Hellman relies on the difficulty of the discrete logarithm problem. Shor's algorithm could efficiently solve the discrete logarithm problem, allowing an attacker to compute the shared secret key.

Impact:

The implications of Shor's algorithm are profound. If a sufficiently large and fault-tolerant quantum computer were built, it could break the RSA and Diffie-Hellman systems that are used to secure a vast amount of online communication, including:

- Secure websites (HTTPS)
- Email encryption
- Digital signatures
- Virtual Private Networks (VPNs)

For example, RSA with 2048-bit keys, which is currently considered secure, would become vulnerable to attack by a quantum computer running Shor's algorithm.

✅ B. Grover's Algorithm

Grover's algorithm, developed by Lov Grover in 1996, is another quantum algorithm that poses a threat to classical cryptography, although its impact is different from Shor's algorithm. Grover's algorithm can speed up the search of an unsorted database. In the context of cryptography, this "database" can be thought of as the space of all possible keys.

Impact on Symmetric Encryption:

Grover's algorithm can be used to speed up brute-force attacks on symmetric encryption algorithms, such as:

- **AES (Advanced Encryption Standard):** AES is a widely used symmetric encryption algorithm. A brute-force attack involves trying every possible key until the correct one is found.
- **Other symmetric ciphers:** DES, 3DES, and other symmetric ciphers are also vulnerable to brute-force attacks, and Grover's algorithm can speed these up.

Key Strength Reduction:

Grover's algorithm reduces the effective key strength of a symmetric cipher by a factor of two (in terms of the number of operations required for an attack). This means that:

- A 256-bit AES key would offer approximately the same level of security as a 128-bit key against a quantum brute-force attack.

Mitigation:

While Grover's algorithm does reduce the security of symmetric ciphers, they are not completely broken. The primary way to mitigate the threat from Grover's algorithm is to:

- **Double the key size:** For example, using a 256-bit AES key provides a level of security equivalent to 128-bit AES against a quantum attack, which is still considered very secure.

In summary, Shor's algorithm poses a catastrophic threat to public-key cryptography, while Grover's algorithm poses a less severe but still significant threat to symmetric cryptography, which can be mitigated by increasing key sizes.

Post-Quantum Cryptographic Solutions

As we've seen, quantum computers pose a serious threat to many of our current cryptographic systems. To prepare for the "quantum era," we need to develop new cryptographic methods that are resistant to attacks from both classical and quantum computers. This field of study is called Post-Quantum Cryptography (PQC).

✅ Why Do We Need Post-Quantum Cryptography?

The primary reason for developing PQC is to ensure the long-term security of our digital infrastructure. We need encryption methods that:

- **Are resistant to quantum attacks:** The algorithms must be secure against known quantum algorithms, such as Shor's algorithm and Grover's algorithm.
- **Can run on classical hardware:** These new cryptographic methods need to be implementable and efficient on classical computers, as we will rely on classical hardware for the foreseeable future.

✅ A. Lattice-Based Cryptography

One of the most promising areas of PQC research is lattice-based cryptography. This approach relies on the mathematical difficulty of solving certain problems related to *lattices*.

- **Lattices:** In this context, a lattice is a mathematical structure consisting of a regular, repeating arrangement of points in space.

Lattice-based cryptography uses hard problems in lattices, such as:

- **Shortest Vector Problem (SVP):** Given a lattice, find the shortest non-zero vector in the lattice.
- **Learning With Errors (LWE):** Given a set of noisy linear equations, find the secret values.

The security of lattice-based cryptography is based on the fact that these problems are believed to be computationally hard, even for quantum computers. There are no known efficient quantum algorithms that can solve them.

🔐 Examples:

Some prominent examples of cryptographic schemes based on lattices include:

- **Kyber (Key encapsulation):** Kyber is a key-encapsulation mechanism (KEM), which is a way to securely exchange a secret key between two parties. Kyber is designed to be efficient and secure against quantum attacks.
- **Dilithium (Digital signatures):** Dilithium is a digital signature scheme that provides a way to verify the authenticity and integrity of digital messages. Like Kyber, Dilithium is designed to be resistant to quantum attacks.

✅ B. Code-Based, Multivariate, and Hash-Based Cryptography

Here's an overview of three other important branches of Post-Quantum Cryptography:

Type	Example	Notes
Code-Based	McEliece	Large keys, fast encryption
Multivariate Polynomials	Rainbow	Used in digital signatures
Hash-Based	SPHINCS+	Stateless, relatively long signatures

Code-Based Cryptography

- **Example:** McEliece cryptosystem
- **How it works:** Code-based cryptography relies on the difficulty of decoding a general linear code. The McEliece cryptosystem, for instance, uses a special type of code (a Goppa code) that is easy to decode if you know the code's structure, but hard to decode if you don't. The public key is a scrambled version of this code, while the private key is the original, easily decodable structure.
- **Pros:** Fast encryption.
- **Cons:** Very large key sizes, which can be a practical challenge.

Multivariate Polynomial Cryptography

- **Example:** Rainbow
- **How it works:** This approach uses systems of multivariate polynomial equations. The idea is to create a system of equations that is easy to solve if you know the secret structure used to create them, but very difficult to solve in general. The public key is the set of polynomial equations, and the private key is the secret structure.
- **Use:** Primarily used for digital signatures.
- **Example:** Rainbow is a signature scheme based on solving multivariate polynomial equations.

Hash-Based Cryptography

- **Example:** SPHINCS+
- **How it works**: Hash-based cryptography uses cryptographic hash functions (like SHA-256 or SHA-3) to build cryptographic schemes. The security relies on the properties of hash functions: they are one-way (easy to compute in one direction, hard to reverse) and collision-resistant (hard to find two inputs that produce the same output).
- **Pros:** Very conservative approach (relies on well-understood hash functions), relatively simple to understand.
- **Cons:** Can result in relatively long signatures.
- **Stateless:** SPHINCS+ is a "stateless" hash-based signature scheme, meaning the signer doesn't need to keep track of any state between signing different messages.

✅ Summary Table

Aspect	Classical Crypto	Quantum-Safe Alternative
RSA, ECC	Vulnerable to Shor	Lattice-based (Kyber, Dilithium)
AES	Partially affected	Larger key sizes (AES-256)
Key Distribution	DH vulnerable	QKD (BB84), Lattice KEMs
Signature Schemes	RSA, ECDSA	Dilithium, SPHINCS+, Rainbow

🔎 Suggested Exercises

Here are detailed explanations and examples for the suggested exercises:

1. Simulate BB84 using Python (qubit state preparation and basis measurement).

This exercise involves simulating the BB84 protocol using Python. You'll need to represent qubits and quantum operations. Here's a breakdown:

- **Qubit Representation:** You can represent a qubit's state using a complex-valued vector in Python. For example, the $|0\rangle$ state can be represented as `[1, 0]` and the $|1\rangle$ state as `[0, 1]`. Superpositions can be represented as linear combinations of these, like `[1/sqrt(2), 1/sqrt(2)]` for the $|+\rangle$ state.
- **Basis Representation:** Represent the rectilinear (+) basis as `0` and the diagonal (×) basis as `1`.
- **State Preparation:**
  - If Alice wants to send 0 in the + basis, prepare the qubit in the $|0\rangle$ state.
  - If Alice wants to send 1 in the + basis, prepare the qubit in the $|1\rangle$ state.
  - If Alice wants to send 0 in the × basis, prepare the qubit in the $|+\rangle$ state: `[1/sqrt(2), 1/sqrt(2)]`.
  - If Alice wants to send 1 in the × basis, prepare the qubit in the $|-\rangle$ state: `[1/sqrt(2), -1/sqrt(2)]`.
- **Measurement:**
  - To measure in the + basis, project the qubit state onto $|0\rangle$ and $|1\rangle$. The probability of measuring 0 is the square of the amplitude of the $|0\rangle$ component, and similarly for 1.
  - To measure in the × basis, project the qubit state onto $|+\rangle$ and $|-\rangle$.
- **Error Introduction:** To simulate noise or an eavesdropper (Eve), you can introduce errors by randomly flipping the qubit state with a certain probability.

Python Example (Conceptual):

```
import numpy as np

def prepare_qubit(bit, basis):
    """Prepares a qubit state based on bit and basis."""
    if basis == 0:  # + basis
        if bit == 0:
            return np.array([1, 0])  # |0>
        else:
            return np.array([0, 1])  # |1>
    else:  # x basis
        if bit == 0:
            return np.array([1/np.sqrt(2), 1/np.sqrt(2)]) # |+>
        else:
            return np.array([1/np.sqrt(2), -1/np.sqrt(2)]) # |->

def measure_qubit(state, basis):
  """Measures a qubit in the given basis."""
  if basis == 0: # + basis
    prob_0 = np.abs(state[0])**2
    if np.random.random() < prob_0:
      return 0
    else:
      return 1
  else: # x basis
    plus_state = np.array([1/np.sqrt(2), 1/np.sqrt(2)])
    minus_state = np.array([1/np.sqrt(2), -1/np.sqrt(2)])
    prob_plus = np.abs(np.dot(plus_state, state))**2
    if np.random.random() < prob_plus:
      return 0 # |+> maps to 0
    else:
      return 1 # |-> maps to 1

# Example usage
alice_bits = [1, 0, 1, 0]
alice_bases = [0, 1, 0, 1]  # 0: +, 1: x
bob_bases =   [1, 1, 0, 0]
key = []

for i in range(len(alice_bits)):
    qubit = prepare_qubit(alice_bits[i], alice_bases[i])
    # Simulate channel (potential eavesdropping)
    # qubit = simulate_eavesdropping(qubit)
    measured_bit = measure_qubit(qubit, bob_bases[i])
    if alice_bases[i] == bob_bases[i]:
        key.append(measured_bit)

print("Shared Key:", key)
```

2. Compare RSA and Kyber in terms of key sizes and performance.

- **RSA:**
    - Key Sizes: RSA key sizes are typically 2048 bits or 3072 bits for strong security.

- Performance: RSA is relatively slow for both encryption and decryption, especially with larger key sizes.
- **Kyber:**
    - Key Sizes: Kyber's key sizes are much smaller than RSA's. For example, Kyber512 has public keys of 800 bytes and private keys of 1632 bytes.
    - Performance: Kyber is designed to be very efficient, with significantly faster encryption and decryption speeds compared to RSA.

Comparison: Kyber offers much smaller key sizes and significantly better performance than RSA, making it a more practical choice for many applications, especially in a post-quantum world.

3. Implement lattice encryption using Python libraries like PQCrypto or pycryptodome.

- **PQCrypto:** This is a Python library specifically designed for post-quantum cryptography. You can install it using pip: `pip install pqcrypto`
- **PyCryptodome:** While primarily for classical cryptography, it might have some limited PQC support or be usable in conjunction with other libraries. Install via: `pip install pycryptodome`

Example using PQCrypto (Conceptual):

```
import pqcrypto.kem.kyber as kyber

# Generate keys
public_key, private_key = kyber.generate_keypair(variant='Kyber512')

# Alice encrypts
ciphertext, shared_secret = kyber.encrypt(public_key, b"My secret message")

# Bob decrypts
decrypted_secret = kyber.decrypt(private_key, ciphertext)

print("Original secret:", b"My secret message")
print("Decrypted secret:", decrypted_secret)
print(f"Public Key Size: {len(public_key)} bytes")
print(f"Private Key Size: {len(private_key)} bytes")
```

4. Research post-quantum algorithms shortlisted by NIST.

The National Institute of Standards and Technology (NIST) is in the process of standardizing post-quantum cryptographic algorithms. Research the algorithms that have been shortlisted in this process. Look for information on:

- **Algorithm Name:** (e.g., Kyber, Dilithium, Falcon, SPHINCS+)
- **Category:** (e.g., Key Encapsulation Mechanism, Digital Signature Algorithm)
- **Cryptographic Primitive:** (e.g., Lattice-based, Hash-based)
- **Security Strength:** (e.g., NIST security level 1-5)

- **Key Sizes:** (Public and private keys)
- **Performance:** (Encryption/decryption speed, signature generation/verification speed)

You can find the latest information on the NIST Post-Quantum Cryptography Standardization process on the NIST website.

10 practical questions with detailed answers and explanations on Quantum Key Distribution (QKD):

Quantum Key Distribution (QKD)

1. **Q: Explain the fundamental difference between how QKD and classical cryptography achieve security. Why is QKD considered "future-proof"?**
    - **A:** Classical cryptography relies on the *computational difficulty* of mathematical problems (like factoring large numbers in RSA). QKD, on the other hand, relies on the fundamental *laws of quantum mechanics* (like the no-cloning theorem and the uncertainty principle).
    - QKD is considered "future-proof" because its security is not based on assumptions about the computational power of future computers. Even if powerful quantum computers are built, the laws of quantum mechanics will still hold, ensuring the security of QKD. Classical crypto is vulnerable to new mathematical breakthroughs and quantum computers.
2. **Q: Describe a scenario where QKD would be highly advantageous compared to traditional public-key cryptography (like RSA).**
    - **A:** Secure government communications: Imagine two government agencies exchanging highly sensitive information (e.g., diplomatic secrets, military plans). QKD would be advantageous here because:
        - The information needs to remain secure not only today but also decades into the future.
        - The risk of eavesdropping by powerful adversaries (nation-states) is very high.
        - QKD provides a level of security that is independent of future computing capabilities.

BB84 Protocol

3. **Q: In the BB84 protocol, Alice sends a series of qubits to Bob. Explain how Alice encodes the bits 0 and 1 onto these qubits, considering both the rectilinear (+) and diagonal (×) bases.**
    - **A:** In BB84, Alice uses two bases:
        - Rectilinear (+):
            - To send 0, Alice encodes the qubit in the horizontal polarization state ($|0\rangle$ or →).
            - To send 1, Alice encodes the qubit in the vertical polarization state ($|1\rangle$ or ↑).
        - Diagonal (×):

        - To send 0, Alice encodes the qubit in the diagonal right polarization state (|+⟩ or ↘).
        - To send 1, Alice encodes the qubit in the diagonal left polarization state (|−⟩ or ↗).
    - Alice randomly chooses either the + or × basis for each bit she wants to transmit.
4. **Q: Bob receives the qubits from Alice in the BB84 protocol. Explain how Bob measures these qubits and why it's crucial for him to choose his measurement basis randomly.**
    - **A:** Bob, like Alice, randomly chooses to measure each received qubit in either the + or × basis.
    - If Bob chooses the same basis as Alice, he will measure the correct bit value (0 or 1) with high probability.
    - If Bob chooses a different basis, his measurement result will be random (50% chance of 0, 50% chance of 1).
    - It's crucial for Bob to choose his basis randomly because this is what allows QKD to detect eavesdropping. If Eve intercepts the qubits and measures them, she also has to randomly choose a basis. With 50% probability, Eve will choose the wrong basis, disturbing the state of the qubit. This disturbance introduces errors that Alice and Bob can detect.

Quantum Attacks on Classical Cryptography

5. **Q: Explain how Shor's algorithm poses a threat to RSA cryptography. What specific mathematical problem does Shor's algorithm solve efficiently, and how does this undermine RSA's security?**
    - **A:** RSA's security relies on the difficulty of factoring large numbers. Shor's algorithm is a quantum algorithm that can factor large numbers exponentially faster than the best-known classical algorithms.
    - If a quantum computer running Shor's algorithm were available, it could factor the large number that is the public key in RSA, allowing it to calculate the private key. This would enable the quantum computer to decrypt any RSA-encrypted message.
6. **Q: Describe how Grover's algorithm can be used to attack symmetric encryption algorithms like AES. How does Grover's algorithm affect the effective key length of AES, and what is the recommended countermeasure?**
    - **A:** Grover's algorithm can speed up a brute-force attack on symmetric ciphers. Instead of trying every possible key sequentially, Grover's algorithm can find the correct key in approximately the square root of the time it would take classically.
    - This effectively halves the key length. For example, a 256-bit AES key would have a security level equivalent to a 128-bit key against a quantum attack.
    - The recommended countermeasure is to double the key size. Using AES-256 provides security against quantum computers equivalent to AES-128 in the classical world.

Lattice-based and Post-Quantum Solutions

7. **Q: What is Post-Quantum Cryptography (PQC), and why is it important to develop PQC algorithms?**
   - **A:** PQC is the development of cryptographic algorithms that are secure against both classical and quantum computers.
   - It's important to develop PQC because quantum computers threaten the security of widely used public-key cryptosystems (like RSA and ECC). We need to transition to new algorithms that will remain secure in the quantum era to protect our digital infrastructure.
8. **Q: Explain the basic idea behind lattice-based cryptography. What mathematical problem related to lattices is considered hard, even for quantum computers?**
   - **A:** Lattice-based cryptography relies on the difficulty of solving certain problems related to mathematical structures called lattices (regular arrangements of points in space).
   - A key hard problem is the *Learning With Errors* (LWE) problem. In LWE, given a set of noisy linear equations, the goal is to find the secret values. This problem is believed to be hard for both classical and quantum computers.
9. **Q: Describe the key features and applications of the Kyber cryptosystem. Why is Kyber considered a promising candidate for post-quantum key exchange?**
   - **A:** Kyber is a key-encapsulation mechanism (KEM) based on lattice problems.
   - Key Features:
     - Efficient: Fast encryption and decryption.
     - Compact: Relatively small key sizes compared to other PQC schemes.
     - Secure: Believed to be secure against quantum attacks.
   - Kyber is a promising candidate because it offers a good balance of security, efficiency, and practicality, making it suitable for replacing current key exchange methods like RSA and Diffie-Hellman.
10. **Q: Briefly describe two other categories of post-quantum cryptography besides lattice-based cryptography, and provide an example of a cryptographic scheme from each category.**
    - **A:**
      - **Code-Based Cryptography:** Relies on the difficulty of decoding general linear codes.
        - Example: McEliece cryptosystem (fast encryption, large keys).
      - **Hash-Based Cryptography:** Uses cryptographic hash functions.
        - Example: SPHINCS+ (stateless, relatively long signatures, relies on well-understood hash functions).

30 multiple-choice questions on Quantum Key Distribution (QKD), covering the BB84 protocol, quantum attacks on classical cryptography, and post-quantum solutions.

- **What is the primary purpose of Quantum Key Distribution (QKD)?**

- a) To encrypt messages
- b) To distribute encryption keys securely
- c) To transmit quantum information
- d) To create quantum computers

- Answer: b

- **Which principle of quantum mechanics is fundamental to QKD?**
    - a) Heisenberg Uncertainty Principle
    - b) Pauli Exclusion Principle
    - c) Schrödinger's Equation
    - d) Bohr's Model
    - Answer: a

- **In QKD, what are the basic units of information transmitted?**
    - a) Bits
    - b) Qubits
    - c) Bytes
    - d) Photons
    - Answer: b

- **What does BB84 stand for?**
    - a) Bell, Bennett, 1984
    - b) Bennett, Brassard, 1984
    - c) Bose, Bennett, 1984
    - d) Bohr, Brassard, 1984
    - Answer: b

- **In the BB84 protocol, how many different polarization bases are used?**
    - a) 1
    - b) 2
    - c) 3
    - d) 4
    - Answer: b

- **Which polarization states are commonly used in the BB84 protocol?**
    - a) Linear and circular
    - b) Horizontal/vertical and diagonal
    - c) Spin up/spin down
    - d) Left and right
    - Answer: b

- **What is the purpose of "basis reconciliation" in BB84?**
    - a) To correct errors in the quantum transmission
    - b) To agree on a shared secret key

- c) To determine if an eavesdropper is present
- d) To amplify the quantum signal
- Answer: c

- **What is "quantum bit error rate" (QBER)?**

  - a) The rate at which qubits are generated
  - b) The probability of a bit flip in classical communication
  - c) The error rate in the shared key due to noise or eavesdropping
  - d) The speed of quantum key distribution
  - Answer: c

- **If the QBER is too high in a BB84 implementation, what does it indicate?**

  - a) The communication is perfectly secure
  - b) The communication channel is noisy or an eavesdropper is present
  - c) The quantum computer is malfunctioning
  - d) The encryption algorithm is weak
  - Answer: b

- **What is the process of "privacy amplification" in QKD?**

  - a) Increasing the intensity of the quantum signal
  - b) Reducing the length of the key to enhance security
  - c) Extracting a shorter, more secure key from a partially secure one
  - d) Amplifying the quantum state
  - Answer: c

- **Which attack on classical cryptography does QKD aim to prevent?**

  - a) Brute-force attack
  - b) Man-in-the-middle attack
  - c) Chosen-plaintext attack
  - d) Eavesdropping attack
  - Answer: d

- **What is an "intercept-resend" attack in the context of QKD?**

  - a) An attack on the classical communication channel
  - b) An eavesdropping attack where the attacker measures and resends qubits
  - c) A denial-of-service attack on the QKD system
  - d) An attack that exploits flaws in the key generation algorithm
  - Answer: b

- **Why is an intercept-resend attack detectable in QKD?**

- a) Because the attacker does not have the correct basis
- b) Because the attacker destroys the key
- c) Due to the no-cloning theorem
- d) Because the attacker changes the message
- Answer: c

- **What does the no-cloning theorem state?**

  - a) Quantum information cannot be perfectly copied
  - b) Quantum information can be transmitted faster than light
  - c) Quantum computers cannot be built
  - d) Quantum keys cannot be distributed
  - Answer: a

- **In QKD, who are the two parties that want to establish a secure key?**

  - a) Alice and Bob
  - b) Sender and Receiver
  - c) Cryptographer and Analyst
  - d) Encoder and Decoder
  - Answer: a

- **What is the role of Eve in QKD?**

  - a) To facilitate communication between Alice and Bob
  - b) To eavesdrop on the quantum channel
  - c) To generate the quantum key
  - d) To verify the security of the key
  - Answer: b

- **Which type of quantum attack involves Eve storing the intercepted qubits and measuring them later?**

  - a) Intercept-resend attack
  - b) Man-in-the-middle attack
  - c) Storage attack
  - d) Trojan horse attack
  - Answer: c

- **What is a "measurement" in quantum mechanics?**

  - a) The process of encoding information into qubits
  - b) The process of transmitting qubits
  - c) The process of extracting classical information from a qubit
  - d) The process of amplifying a quantum signal
  - Answer: c

- **How does measurement affect a qubit?**
    - a) It leaves the qubit unchanged
    - b) It collapses the qubit into a definite state
    - c) It entangles the qubit with another qubit
    - d) It destroys the qubit
    - Answer: b
- **Which mathematical structure is used in lattice-based cryptography?**
    - a) Groups
    - b) Rings
    - c) Lattices
    - d) Fields
    - Answer: c
- **Why are lattice-based cryptographic systems considered post-quantum?**
    - a) They are based on quantum mechanics
    - b) They are resistant to attacks from quantum computers
    - c) They use quantum key distribution
    - d) They are very old cryptographic systems
    - Answer: b
- **What is a "lattice" in mathematics?**
    - a) A set of points in space generated by a set of basis vectors
    - b) A type of quantum gate
    - c) A classical encryption algorithm
    - d) A method for quantum error correction
    - Answer: a
- **Which problem is believed to be hard for both classical and quantum computers in lattice-based cryptography?**
    - a) Integer factorization
    - b) Discrete logarithm problem
    - c) Shortest Vector Problem (SVP)
    - d) Quantum entanglement
    - Answer: c
- **What does SVP stand for?**
    - a) Shortest Vector Projection
    - b) Smallest Vector Problem
    - c) Shortest Vector Problem

- d) Singular Value Problem
- Answer: c

- **Which cryptographic primitive can be built using lattice-based cryptography?**

  - a) Public-key encryption
  - b) Digital signatures
  - c) Key exchange
  - d) All of the above
  - Answer: d

- **Which is a key advantage of lattice-based cryptography?**

  - a) Simplicity of implementation
  - b) High speed of computation
  - c) Resistance to quantum computer attacks
  - d) Small key sizes
  - Answer: c

- **What is post-quantum cryptography (PQC)?**

  - a) Cryptography that uses quantum key distribution
  - b) Cryptography that is secure against quantum computers
  - c) Cryptography that uses quantum computers for encryption
  - d) Cryptography that is based on quantum mechanics
  - Answer: b

- **Which of the following is a post-quantum cryptographic algorithm?**

  - a) RSA
  - b) AES
  - c) McEliece
  - d) Diffie-Hellman
  - Answer: c

- **Which mathematical problem is the McEliece cryptosystem based on?**

  - a) Integer factorization
  - b) Decoding of general linear codes
  - c) Elliptic curve discrete logarithm problem
  - d) Shortest Vector Problem
  - Answer: b

- **Which post-quantum cryptographic algorithm is based on the difficulty of solving multivariate polynomial equations?**

- a) NTRU
- b) CRYSTALS-Kyber
- c) CRYSTALS-Dilithium
- d) Rainbow
- Answer: d

20 short question with answer

- **Q: What is Quantum Key Distribution (QKD)?**
  - **A:** A method for secure key distribution based on the principles of quantum mechanics.
- **Q: What type of information does QKD transmit?**
  - **A:** Qubits (quantum bits).
- **Q: What is the BB84 protocol?**
  - **A:** A specific QKD protocol that uses different polarization states of photons to transmit information.
- **Q: How many polarization bases are used in BB84?**
  - **A:** Two.
- **Q: Name the two polarization bases used in BB84.**
  - **A:** Rectilinear (horizontal/vertical) and diagonal.
- **Q: What principle ensures BB84's security?**
  - **A:** The Heisenberg Uncertainty Principle.
- **Q: What happens when a qubit is measured?**
  - **A:** It collapses into a definite state.
- **Q: What is QBER?**
  - **A:** Quantum Bit Error Rate, which indicates the level of errors (and potential eavesdropping) in a QKD system.
- **Q: What is "basis reconciliation"?**
  - **A:** The process where Alice and Bob compare their measurement bases to identify matching ones.

- **Q: What is "privacy amplification"?**
  - **A:** A process to distill a shorter, more secure key from a partially secure one.
- **Q: What is an "intercept-resend" attack?**
  - **A:** An eavesdropping attempt where the attacker measures transmitted qubits and resends them to the receiver.
- **Q: Why is an intercept-resend attack detectable?**
  - **A:** Because measuring a qubit alters its state, introducing errors.
- **Q: What does the no-cloning theorem state?**
  - **A:** It is impossible to create an exact copy of an arbitrary quantum state.
- **Q: Who are the two parties that establish a secure key in QKD?**
  - **A:** Alice and Bob.
- **Q: What is the role of Eve in QKD?**
  - **A:** The eavesdropper who tries to intercept the key.
- **Q: What is post-quantum cryptography (PQC)?**
  - **A:** Cryptography that is designed to be secure against attacks from quantum computers.
- **Q: What is a lattice in mathematics?**
  - **A:** A set of points in space generated by a set of basis vectors.
- **Q: Why is lattice-based cryptography considered post-quantum?**
  - **A:** Because it is believed to be resistant to attacks from quantum computers.
- **Q: What is the Shortest Vector Problem (SVP)?**
  - **A:** A hard mathematical problem on lattices that is the basis for some post-quantum cryptography.
- **Q: Name one post-quantum cryptographic algorithm.**
  - **A:** CRYSTALS-Kyber, CRYSTALS-Dilithium, or McEliece.

10 MID SIZE QUESTION WITH ANSWER • **Q: Explain the BB84 protocol in detail, including the steps involved in key generation and how it ensures security.**

- **A:** The BB84 protocol, developed by Bennett and Brassard in 1984, is a QKD protocol that enables two parties (Alice and Bob) to establish a shared secret key. Here's how it works:
    - **Quantum Transmission:**
        - Alice prepares qubits (typically photons) in one of four polarization states: horizontal (0°), vertical (90°), diagonal (45°), or anti-diagonal (135°). These states represent bits 0 and 1 in two different bases: the rectilinear basis (0° and 90°) and the diagonal basis (45° and 135°).
        - Alice randomly chooses one of the four states for each qubit and sends it to Bob.
    - **Qubit Measurement:**
        - Bob randomly chooses to measure each incoming qubit in either the rectilinear or the diagonal basis.
        - If Bob chooses the correct basis, he measures the qubit accurately (e.g., a 0° photon will be read as a 0). If he chooses the wrong basis, he gets a random result (0 or 1).
    - **Basis Reconciliation:**
        - Alice and Bob communicate over a classical channel. Alice tells Bob which basis she used for each qubit, and Bob tells Alice which basis he used for each measurement.
        - They discard the bits where Bob used the wrong basis. The remaining bits are correlated.
    - **Error Estimation:**
        - Alice and Bob compare a subset of their shared bits over the classical channel.
        - If the error rate (QBER) is below a certain threshold, they assume the communication was not significantly affected by eavesdropping. If the error rate is too high, they discard the key and start over.
    - **Privacy Amplification:**
        - If the error rate is acceptable, Alice and Bob apply a process called privacy amplification. This reduces any partial information an eavesdropper (Eve) might have gained, resulting in a shorter, highly secure shared secret key.
- **Security:** The security of BB84 relies on the principles of quantum mechanics:
    - **Qubit Measurement:** Measuring a qubit collapses its superposition, changing its state. If Eve tries to measure the photons, she'll disturb them, and Alice and Bob can detect the errors this introduces.
    - **No-Cloning Theorem:** This theorem states that it's impossible to create an identical copy of an unknown quantum state. Eve cannot copy the photons to measure them without altering the originals.

• **Q: Describe the key differences between classical key distribution and Quantum Key Distribution (QKD).**

- **A:** Classical key distribution and QKD differ fundamentally in how they achieve security:
    - **Classical Key Distribution:**
        - Relies on mathematical algorithms and computational complexity. For example, in RSA, the difficulty of factoring large numbers secures the key exchange.
        - Vulnerable to advances in computing power. If a faster algorithm or a quantum computer is developed, current classical methods could be compromised.
        - Does not provide a way to detect eavesdropping during the key exchange itself.
    - **Quantum Key Distribution (QKD):**
        - Relies on the laws of quantum mechanics, such as the Heisenberg Uncertainty Principle and the no-cloning theorem.
        - Offers security against any eavesdropping attempt, regardless of the eavesdropper's computational power. The act of trying to measure the quantum states disturbs them, which is detectable.
        - Provides a mechanism to detect if an eavesdropper is present during the key exchange.
- In essence, classical cryptography's security is based on the *difficulty* of solving a problem, while QKD's security is based on the *fundamental laws of physics*.

• Q: Explain how the Heisenberg Uncertainty Principle is used to ensure the security of the BB84 protocol.

- **A:** The Heisenberg Uncertainty Principle states that certain pairs of physical properties, like position and momentum, or in the case of BB84, certain pairs of polarization states, cannot both be known with perfect accuracy.
- In BB84, this principle is applied to the polarization of photons. There are two mutually incompatible bases for measuring polarization: the rectilinear basis (horizontal/vertical) and the diagonal basis (45°/135°).
- Alice encodes her bits onto photons polarized in one of these four states, randomly choosing a basis for each photon. Bob then randomly chooses a basis to measure each incoming photon.
- An eavesdropper, Eve, attempting to intercept the photons and measure their polarization to learn the key, faces a crucial problem: she doesn't know which basis Alice used to encode each photon. If Eve measures a photon in the wrong basis, she'll get a random result, and more importantly, she'll *change* the photon's polarization state.
- When Bob receives the photon, its state will have been altered by Eve's measurement. During the basis reconciliation step, Alice and Bob compare a subset of their measurements. If Eve is present, the error rate in these measurements will be higher than expected from just channel noise. This is because Eve's random measurements introduce errors.
- Therefore, the Heisenberg Uncertainty Principle guarantees that any attempt by Eve to gain information about the key will inevitably introduce detectable errors, alerting Alice and Bob to her presence.

- **Q: Describe the "intercept-resend" attack on QKD and explain how it can be detected.**
  - **A:** The "intercept-resend" attack is a basic eavesdropping strategy in QKD. Here's how it works:
    - Eve intercepts the qubits (photons) that Alice sends to Bob.
    - Eve measures each intercepted qubit to determine its state. Since she doesn't know the basis Alice used, she randomly chooses a basis for each measurement.
    - After measuring, Eve prepares new qubits in the states she measured and sends them to Bob.
    - Eve hopes that, statistically, some of her measurements will be correct, allowing her to gain partial knowledge of the key.
  - **Detection:** This attack is detectable due to the fundamental properties of quantum mechanics:
    - **Qubit Alteration:** When Eve measures a qubit, she collapses its superposition into a definite state. If she measures in the wrong basis, she alters the qubit's state.
    - **Error Introduction:** When Bob receives the altered qubits from Eve, his measurements won't perfectly correlate with Alice's original encodings, even when they use the same basis. This introduces errors into the shared key.
    - **Error Rate Analysis:** Alice and Bob compare a subset of their key bits over a classical channel to estimate the Quantum Bit Error Rate (QBER). If there's no eavesdropping, the QBER will be low, reflecting only the noise in the quantum channel. However, if Eve performs an intercept-resend attack, the QBER will be significantly higher.
    - **Threshold:** Alice and Bob set a threshold for the QBER. If the measured QBER exceeds this threshold, they know an attack has occurred, and they discard the key and start the QKD process again.
  - In summary, the intercept-resend attack is detected by analyzing the error rate in the key exchange. Eve's measurements introduce errors that are not due to natural channel noise, revealing her presence.

- **Q: What are the advantages and disadvantages of Quantum Key Distribution (QKD) compared to classical cryptography?**
  - **A:** QKD offers some compelling advantages but also has limitations compared to classical cryptography:
    - **Advantages of QKD:**
      - **Information-Theoretic Security:** QKD's security is based on the fundamental laws of quantum mechanics, not on the computational difficulty of mathematical problems. This means it's secure against any eavesdropper, regardless of their computational power, even future quantum computers.
      - **Eavesdropping Detection:** QKD allows the legitimate parties (Alice and Bob) to detect any attempt by an eavesdropper to intercept the key exchange. The very act of measuring quantum states introduces detectable disturbances.

        - **Forward Secrecy:** QKD can provide forward secrecy, meaning that even if an attacker compromises the system in the future, past communications remain secure.
    - **Disadvantages of QKD:**
        - **Limited Distance:** QKD's range is limited by signal loss in quantum channels, such as optical fibers. While repeaters can extend the distance, they add complexity and potential vulnerabilities.
        - **Specialized Hardware:** QKD requires specialized and often expensive hardware for transmitting and receiving quantum states.
        - **Key Exchange Only:** QKD only provides a mechanism for secure key exchange. The actual data encryption and decryption still typically rely on classical symmetric-key cryptography.
        - **Classical Channel Dependence:** QKD requires an authenticated classical channel for communication, which, while not needing to be secret, introduces a potential point of vulnerability.
        - **Integration Challenges:** Integrating QKD systems with existing communication infrastructures can be complex and costly.
    - **Classical Cryptography:**
        - **Advantages:**
            - **Scalability:** Classical cryptography is highly scalable and can be implemented in software on a wide range of devices.
            - **Long Distances:** Classical signals can be transmitted over long distances using repeaters and amplifiers.
            - **Versatility:** Classical cryptography provides solutions for various security needs, including encryption, digital signatures, and authentication.
            - **Efficiency:** Classical encryption and decryption are generally computationally efficient.
        - **Disadvantages:**
            - **Vulnerability to Quantum Computers:** Many widely used classical cryptographic algorithms (like RSA and ECC) are vulnerable to attacks from quantum computers.
            - **Dependence on Computational Hardness:** Its security relies on the assumption that certain mathematical problems are hard to solve, which may not always hold true.
            - **No Inherent Eavesdropping Detection:** Classical cryptography doesn't provide a built-in mechanism to detect if an eavesdropper has intercepted the key exchange.
- In summary, QKD offers superior security for key exchange but has limitations in distance, cost, and integration. Classical cryptography is more practical for many applications but is vulnerable to quantum computers.

• Q: Explain the concept of lattice-based cryptography and why it is considered a promising post-quantum solution.

- **A:** Lattice-based cryptography is an approach to building cryptographic systems that rely on the mathematical properties of lattices.
    - **Lattices:** A lattice is a geometric structure consisting of a regular array of points in n-dimensional space. These points are defined by a set of basis vectors.
    - **Hard Problems:** Lattice-based cryptography bases its security on the presumed difficulty of solving certain computational problems on lattices. One of the most important is the Shortest Vector Problem (SVP), which involves finding the shortest non-zero vector in a lattice. Another is the Closest Vector Problem (CVP), which involves finding the lattice point closest to a given point in space.
    - **Post-Quantum Promise:** Lattice-based cryptography is considered a promising post-quantum solution for several reasons:
        - **Resistance to Quantum Attacks:** Unlike many classical public-key cryptosystems (like RSA and ECC), lattice-based algorithms are not known to be efficiently solvable by quantum computers.
        - **Mathematical Foundation:** Lattices have a rich mathematical structure, which allows for the construction of a variety of cryptographic primitives.
        - **Versatility:** Lattice-based cryptography can be used to build public-key encryption schemes, digital signatures, key exchange protocols, and other cryptographic tools.
        - **Efficiency:** Some lattice-based schemes offer relatively efficient key sizes and computational speeds, making them practical for implementation.
- In summary, lattice-based cryptography leverages the hardness of lattice problems, which are believed to be difficult for both classical and quantum computers, making them a strong candidate for securing communications in a post-quantum world.

- **Q: How does lattice-based cryptography differ from traditional public-key cryptography like RSA and ECC?**

- **A:** Lattice-based cryptography differs from traditional public-key cryptography (like RSA and ECC) in its underlying mathematical foundation and its security properties:
    - **Mathematical Foundation:**
        - **RSA:** Relies on the difficulty of factoring large numbers.
        - **ECC:** Relies on the difficulty of solving the discrete logarithm problem on elliptic curves.
        - **Lattice-based cryptography:** Relies on the difficulty of solving problems like the Shortest Vector Problem (SVP) or the Closest Vector Problem (CVP) in mathematical structures called lattices.
    - **Security:**
        - **RSA and ECC:** Their security is based on the assumption that certain mathematical problems are computationally hard for classical computers. However, these problems are known to be efficiently solvable by quantum computers using Shor's algorithm.
        - **Lattice-based cryptography:** Its security is based on the hardness of lattice problems, which are believed to be difficult for both classical and quantum computers. This makes it a potential solution for post-quantum cryptography, secure in the age of quantum computing.

- **Key Size and Efficiency:**
    - **RSA:** Can have large key sizes, especially for higher security levels, which can impact performance.
    - **ECC:** Generally offers smaller key sizes compared to RSA for equivalent security, leading to better performance.
    - **Lattice-based cryptography:** Can offer a range of trade-offs between key size and efficiency. Some schemes may have larger key sizes than ECC but offer good computational performance.
- **Quantum Resistance:**
    - **RSA and ECC:** Vulnerable to attacks from quantum computers.
    - **Lattice-based cryptography:** Designed to resist attacks from both classical and quantum computers.

- In essence, the key difference lies in the mathematical problems on which they are based and their resilience to quantum computer attacks. Lattice-based cryptography is designed to address the quantum threat, while RSA and ECC are not.

- **Q: Explain the importance of post-quantum cryptography (PQC) and the role of NIST in its standardization.**

- **A: Importance of Post-Quantum Cryptography (PQC):**
    - Current public-key cryptographic systems, such as RSA and ECC, are widely used to secure digital communications and data. However, they are vulnerable to attacks from quantum computers, which are capable of efficiently solving the mathematical problems on which these systems rely.
    - The development of practical quantum computers poses a significant threat to the security of current cryptographic infrastructure.
    - Post-quantum cryptography (PQC) is crucial to ensure the long-term security of digital systems. PQC aims to develop cryptographic algorithms that are secure against both classical and quantum computers.
    - The transition to PQC is essential to protect sensitive data and communications that need to remain secure for many years, even after quantum computers become a reality. This is sometimes referred to as ""cryptographic agility"".
- **Role of NIST in PQC Standardization:**
    - The National Institute of Standards and Technology (NIST) plays a vital role in developing and standardizing cryptographic algorithms in the United States.
    - Recognizing the threat posed by quantum computers, NIST initiated a process to solicit, evaluate, and standardize PQC algorithms.
    - NIST's standardization effort aims to:
        - Identify and select promising PQC algorithms from the cryptographic community.
        - Subject these algorithms to rigorous security analysis and testing.
        - Develop standards for PQC algorithms that can be adopted by industry and government agencies.
    - The standardization process is crucial for ensuring that robust and interoperable PQC solutions are available for widespread use, facilitating a smooth transition to a quantum-safe future.

- By standardizing PQC, NIST helps to build confidence in these new cryptographic tools and promotes their adoption, mitigating the risks associated with the advent of quantum computing.

- **Q: Discuss the challenges in implementing Quantum Key Distribution (QKD) in real-world scenarios.**

- **A:** Implementing QKD in real-world scenarios faces several challenges:
  - **Distance Limitations:** QKD's range is limited by signal loss in quantum channels, particularly optical fibers. Photons, which are often used to transmit qubits, are absorbed or scattered, restricting transmission distances. While quantum repeaters can extend the range, they are complex and still under development.
  - **Cost:** QKD systems can be expensive to deploy and maintain. The specialized hardware required for single-photon sources, detectors, and precise control of quantum states adds to the overall cost.
  - **Integration with Existing Infrastructure:** Integrating QKD with current communication networks, which are primarily designed for classical signals, can be challenging. New protocols and interfaces may be needed.
  - **Classical Channel Requirement:** QKD requires an authenticated classical channel for communication, which introduces a potential vulnerability. Ensuring the security of this classical channel is crucial.
  - **Key Management:** Managing and storing the quantum-generated keys securely can be complex, especially in large networks. Efficient key management systems are needed.
  - **Device Imperfections:** Real-world QKD devices are not perfect and can deviate from the theoretical models. Imperfections in single-photon sources and detectors can create vulnerabilities that attackers can exploit (e.g., photon number splitting attacks).
  - **Repeaters:** Quantum repeaters, necessary for long-distance QKD, are still in the research and development phase. Building efficient and reliable quantum repeaters is a significant challenge.
  - **Complexity:** QKD systems are more complex to set up and maintain than classical cryptography systems, requiring specialized expertise.
  - **Speed:** The rate at which secure keys can be generated by QKD systems can be limited, which might not be sufficient for very high-bandwidth applications.
- Overcoming these challenges is crucial for the widespread adoption of QKD and the realization of its potential to provide truly secure communication.

- **Q: Compare and contrast Quantum Key Distribution (QKD) and post-quantum cryptography (PQC) as approaches to securing communications in the quantum era.**

- **A:** Both QKD and PQC aim to secure communications in the future when quantum computers may render current classical cryptography insecure, but they take different approaches:
  - **Quantum Key Distribution (QKD):**

- **Approach:** Uses the principles of quantum mechanics to distribute encryption keys securely.
- **Security Basis:** Relies on the laws of physics, such as the Heisenberg Uncertainty Principle and the no-cloning theorem.
- **Strengths:**
    - Provides information-theoretic security: secure against any eavesdropper, regardless of computational power.
    - Detects eavesdropping: any attempt to intercept the key exchange introduces detectable disturbances.
- **Weaknesses:**
    - Limited distance: signal loss restricts transmission range.
    - Specialized hardware: requires expensive and complex equipment.
    - Key exchange only: secures key distribution, not data encryption itself.
    - Requires a classical channel: this channel needs to be authenticated.

- **Post-Quantum Cryptography (PQC):**
    - **Approach:** Develops classical cryptographic algorithms that are resistant to attacks from both classical and quantum computers.
    - **Security Basis:** Relies on the computational hardness of mathematical problems that are believed to be difficult for quantum computers to solve.
    - **Strengths:**
        - Compatible with existing infrastructure: can be implemented using current hardware and software.
        - Versatile: provides solutions for encryption, digital signatures, and key exchange.
        - Long-distance communication: works over any distance that classical communication can reach.
        - More efficient: generally faster and more scalable than QKD.
    - **Weaknesses:**
        - Security relies on unproven assumptions: the hardness of the underlying mathematical problems could be challenged in the future.
        - Potential vulnerabilities: new attacks, both classical and quantum, may be discovered.
- **Comparison:**
    - **Security Foundation:** QKD's security is based on the laws of physics, while PQC's security is based on mathematical hardness.
    - **Quantum Resistance:** Both aim to be secure against quantum computer attacks.
    - **Implementation:** PQC is generally easier to implement with existing technology, while QKD requires specialized hardware.
    - **Range:** PQC can be used for long-distance communication, while QKD has distance limitations.

- **Use Cases:** QKD is best suited for secure key exchange in high-security applications over relatively short distances, while PQC offers broader applicability for various cryptographic needs across any distance.

Quantum Supremacy and Notable Experiments

Here's a more detailed explanation of quantum supremacy and some of the key experiments:

✓ What is Quantum Supremacy?

- **Definition:** Quantum supremacy, a term coined by John Preskill, refers to the point where a quantum computer can solve a problem that no classical computer can solve in a reasonable amount of time.
- **Key Idea:** It's about demonstrating a clear computational advantage of a quantum computer over the best possible classical approach, even if the problem itself doesn't have any immediate practical application.
- **Why it Matters:**
    - It's a milestone that shows quantum computers are fundamentally more powerful for certain tasks.
    - It validates the potential of quantum computing technology.
    - It drives further research and development in the field.
- **Example:** Imagine a very complex mathematical calculation. A classical computer might take years or even centuries to find the answer. If a quantum computer can solve the same problem in minutes or seconds, that's quantum supremacy.

✓ Google's Quantum Supremacy (2019)

- **Experiment:** Google's Sycamore processor, with 54 qubits, performed a specific computation.
- **Claimed Achievement:** The Sycamore processor completed the task in 200 seconds. Google claimed that the most powerful classical supercomputer at the time would have taken approximately 10,000 years to do the same calculation.
- **Task:** The computation involved sampling the output of a random quantum circuit.
    - A random quantum circuit is a sequence of quantum operations (gates) applied to qubits in a seemingly random way.
    - The goal was to generate a set of output probabilities.
    - Classical computers struggle to simulate the complex behavior of these random quantum circuits as the number of qubits increases.
- **Significance:**
    - Demonstrated that a quantum computer could perform a specific task far beyond the reach of classical computers.
    - Fueled debate and further research in the quantum computing field.
- **Important Note:** IBM, a competitor, argued that a classical supercomputer could perform the task in a few days with improved algorithms, challenging Google's claim. This highlights the difficulty in definitively proving quantum supremacy, as classical algorithms and hardware continue to improve.

✅ Other Notable Experiments

Here's a table expanding on the notable experiments you provided, with more context:

Year	Organization	Achievement
2020	USTC (China)	Boson Sampling with 76 photons using the Jiuzhang processor. - Boson sampling is a specific quantum computation involving photons (particles of light) passing through a network of beam splitters and mirrors. - Jiuzhang demonstrated a speedup over classical computers in simulating this process, showing a quantum advantage in a different type of computation.
2022	IBM	Introduced the 127-qubit Eagle processor. - This marked a significant increase in the number of qubits in a quantum processor, a crucial step towards building more powerful quantum computers. - While not a "supremacy" claim, it represented progress in quantum hardware development.
2023	IonQ	Demonstrated high-fidelity multi-qubit gates on trapped ions. - Trapped ion technology is another approach to building quantum computers. - High-fidelity gates are essential for reducing errors in quantum computations. This achievement is important for building more reliable quantum systems.
2024	IBM	Launched Condor (1000+ qubits), roadmap to 100,000 qubits by 2033. - Condor crossed the 1000-qubit barrier, another step towards scaling up quantum computers. - The roadmap towards 100,000 qubits is a long-term goal for achieving fault-tolerant quantum computers, which can perform complex computations with very low error rates.
2025	D-Wave Quantum	Demonstrated quantum supremacy on a useful, real-world problem by simulating magnetic materials in minutes. Classical computation would take one million years.

◆ 2. Current Research Trends and Roadblocks in Quantum Computing

Here's a breakdown of the trends and roadblocks in quantum computing research:

✅ A. Trends in Quantum Computing Research

- **Quantum Machine Learning (QML)**
    - **Concept:** QML is an interdisciplinary field that explores how quantum computers can enhance or accelerate machine learning tasks. It combines the principles of quantum computing with classical machine learning algorithms.
    - **Merging Classical AI with Quantum Circuits:** * Classical machine learning algorithms are translated into a series of quantum operations. * Quantum circuits are designed to process data in a fundamentally different way than classical computers, potentially offering advantages in speed and efficiency for specific tasks.
    - **Variational Quantum Classifiers (VQCs):** * VQCs are quantum circuits designed to classify data. * They have adjustable parameters that are optimized using classical computers to learn patterns in the data. * *Example:* A VQC could be used to classify images, where the image data is encoded into quantum states, and the quantum circuit learns to distinguish between different categories (e.g., cats vs. dogs).
    - **Quantum Generative Adversarial Networks (QGANs):** * QGANs are quantum versions of classical GANs, a framework for training generative models. * They involve two quantum networks: a generator that creates new data samples and a discriminator that evaluates their authenticity. * *Example:* A QGAN could be used to generate new quantum states with specific properties, potentially useful in materials science or drug discovery.
    - **Potential Benefits:** * Speedup for certain machine learning algorithms. * Ability to process high-dimensional quantum data. * Improved pattern recognition.
- **Quantum Error Correction (QEC)**
    - **Concept:** QEC is essential for building fault-tolerant quantum computers. It aims to protect quantum information from errors caused by noise and decoherence.
    - **Decoherence:** Qubits are very sensitive to environmental disturbances, which can cause them to lose their quantum state. This loss of information is called decoherence, and it's a major obstacle to quantum computation.
    - **Topological Codes:** * Topological codes encode quantum information in a way that is robust to local errors. * **Surface Code:** A prominent example is the surface code, where qubits are arranged on a 2D grid, and errors can be detected by measuring the interactions between neighboring qubits. * Information is stored in the overall topology of the code, making it less susceptible to individual qubit errors.
    - **Fault-Tolerant Architectures:** * These are quantum computer designs that can perform computations even in the presence of errors. * They combine QEC codes with fault-tolerant quantum gates, which are designed to operate reliably even if individual components fail.
    - **Importance:** QEC is crucial for performing long and complex quantum computations. Without it, errors accumulate and destroy the computation.
- **Quantum Networking**
    - **Concept:** Quantum networking aims to connect quantum computers and other quantum devices over long distances, enabling the transmission of quantum information.

- **Entanglement-Based Communication:** * Quantum networks rely on the phenomenon of quantum entanglement, where two or more qubits become interconnected in such a way that their fates are linked, regardless of the distance between them. * Entanglement can be used to perform secure communication, distributed quantum computing, and other quantum tasks.
- **Quantum Repeaters:** * Quantum repeaters are devices that extend the range of quantum communication. * Unlike classical repeaters, they cannot simply amplify quantum signals because of the no-cloning theorem. * Instead, they use techniques like entanglement swapping to create entanglement over longer distances.
- **Quantum Internet:** * The ultimate goal is to build a "Quantum Internet," a network that allows quantum devices anywhere in the world to communicate and share quantum information. * This would enable new applications such as distributed quantum computing, enhanced secure communication, and quantum key distribution on a global scale.

- **Post-Quantum Cryptography (PQC)**
  - **Concept:** PQC is a field of cryptography that focuses on developing encryption and digital signature methods that are secure against both classical computers and future quantum computers.
  - **Threat of Quantum Computers:** Quantum computers threaten the security of many widely used classical public-key cryptography algorithms, such as RSA and ECC.
  - **Lattice-Based Systems:** * Lattice-based cryptography is a promising approach to PQC. * It relies on the difficulty of solving certain mathematical problems related to lattices, which are believed to be hard for quantum computers. * *Example:* CRYSTALS-Kyber (key-encapsulation mechanism) and CRYSTALS-Dilithium (digital signature algorithm) are lattice-based algorithms selected by NIST for standardization.
  - **NIST Standardization:** * The National Institute of Standards and Technology (NIST) is leading an effort to standardize PQC algorithms. * NIST has selected several PQC algorithms, including lattice-based ones, for inclusion in cryptographic standards. * This will ensure that secure communication methods are available in the quantum era.
- **Quantum Simulation**
  - **Concept:** Quantum simulation uses quantum computers to model and study complex quantum systems that are difficult or impossible to simulate with classical computers.
  - **Applications:** * **Materials Science:** Simulating new materials with specific properties. * **Drug Discovery:** Simulating molecules and chemical reactions to design new drugs. * *Example:* Quantum computers could be used to simulate the behavior of proteins involved in Alzheimer's disease or cancer, helping researchers to develop targeted therapies. * **Fundamental Physics:** Studying the behavior of quantum systems, such as high-temperature superconductors or exotic quantum states.

- **Benefits:** * More accurate and efficient simulations of quantum systems. * Accelerated discovery of new materials and drugs. * Deeper understanding of fundamental physics.

✅ B. Roadblocks in Quantum Computing

- **Decoherence**
    - **Challenge:** Decoherence is the loss of quantum information due to interactions with the environment. Qubits are extremely sensitive to external noise, such as heat, electromagnetic radiation, and vibrations.
    - **Description:** These interactions cause qubits to lose their superposition and entanglement, which are essential for quantum computation.
    - **Impact:** Decoherence limits the amount of time a quantum computer can perform computations, restricting the complexity of the algorithms that can be executed.
- **Scalability**
    - **Challenge:** Building large-scale quantum computers with many qubits is a significant engineering challenge.
    - **Description:** As the number of qubits increases, it becomes more difficult to control and maintain their quantum states.
    - **Increased Error Rates:** Adding more qubits often leads to higher error rates, making it harder to perform reliable computations.
- **Error Rates**
    - **Challenge:** Quantum computations are inherently noisy.
    - **Description:** Real qubits are imperfect and prone to errors caused by various factors, including decoherence, control imprecision, and manufacturing defects.
    - **Impact:** High error rates limit the accuracy of quantum computations and make it difficult to achieve fault tolerance.
- **Resource Requirements (for QEC)**
    - **Challenge:** Quantum error correction requires a significant overhead in terms of the number of physical qubits.
    - **Description:** To protect one logical qubit (a fault-tolerant qubit) from errors, many physical qubits are needed.
    - **Example:** Surface code, a leading QEC technique, may require hundreds or even thousands of physical qubits to encode a single logical qubit.
    - **Impact:** This increases the complexity and cost of building fault-tolerant quantum computers.
- **Algorithm Limitations**
    - **Challenge:** While quantum computers offer the potential for exponential speedups, only a limited number of quantum algorithms have been developed that demonstrate a clear advantage over classical algorithms.
    - **Description:** Finding practical problems where quantum computers excel is an ongoing research area.
    - **Examples:** Shor's algorithm for factoring and Grover's algorithm for searching are two well-known quantum algorithms with proven speedups.

🎓 Real-World Analogy: Quantum Computer as an Orchestra

- **Coherence:** Like an orchestra where all instruments must play in perfect harmony and timing, a quantum computer requires its qubits to maintain their delicate quantum states (coherence). Any disturbance can throw off the harmony.
- **Error:** If a single instrument in the orchestra is out of tune or plays the wrong note, it disrupts the entire performance. Similarly, a single qubit error in a quantum computer can corrupt the entire computation.

◆ 3. Careers in Quantum Computing

Quantum computing is a rapidly growing field with a demand for professionals who possess a unique combination of skills. Here's a detailed look at some of the key career paths and the skills you'll need to develop:

✅ Career Paths

- **Quantum Software Engineer**
    - **Role:** Quantum software engineers design, develop, and implement software for quantum computers. They work on creating quantum algorithms, writing code to control quantum hardware, and building software tools for quantum computing.
    - **Skills Required:**
        - Proficiency in Python and quantum programming languages/frameworks like Qiskit (IBM), Cirq (Google), and/or Ocean (D-Wave).
        - Understanding of quantum algorithms and data structures.
        - Knowledge of quantum circuit design and optimization.
        - Familiarity with cloud-based quantum computing platforms (e.g., Amazon Braket).
        - Software development best practices, including version control, testing, and documentation.
    - **Example Tasks:**
        - Writing code to implement a quantum algorithm for a specific application (e.g., quantum simulation, optimization).
        - Developing a library of reusable quantum circuits.
        - Creating software tools to visualize and analyze the results of quantum computations.
        - Working with quantum hardware teams to ensure software compatibility.
    - **Sample Employers:** IBM, Amazon Braket, Xanadu, Rigetti Computing, Quantum software startups.
- **Quantum Physicist**
    - **Role:** Quantum physicists study the fundamental principles of quantum mechanics and explore new ways to harness quantum phenomena for technological applications. They often work in research settings, developing new quantum theories, designing experiments, and analyzing data.
    - **Skills Required:**

        - Deep understanding of quantum mechanics, quantum field theory, and related physics concepts.
        - Strong mathematical background, including linear algebra, differential equations, and complex analysis.
        - Experience with experimental techniques and data analysis.
        - Ability to conduct independent research and publish findings in scientific journals.
    - **Example Tasks:**
        - Designing and conducting experiments to test quantum phenomena.
        - Developing new theoretical models of quantum systems.
        - Analyzing experimental data and interpreting the results.
        - Collaborating with engineers to translate research findings into practical technologies.
    - **Sample Employers:** Universities (as professors or researchers), government research labs (e.g., NIST, NASA), private research institutions, some quantum hardware companies.
- **Quantum Hardware Engineer**
    - **Role:** Quantum hardware engineers design, build, and test the physical components of quantum computers. They work on developing and improving the hardware that makes quantum computation possible, such as qubits, control systems, and cryogenic technologies.
    - **Skills Required:**
        - Expertise in relevant areas of physics and engineering, such as:
            - **Cryogenics:** For superconducting quantum computers.
            - **Vacuum systems:** For trapped ion systems.
            - **Laser systems:** For photonic quantum computers.
            - **Microwave engineering:** For controlling superconducting qubits.
        - Knowledge of materials science, nanofabrication, and precision measurement techniques.
        - Ability to design and build complex experimental setups.
    - **Example Tasks:**
        - Designing and fabricating superconducting circuits for qubits.
        - Developing cryogenic systems to cool quantum processors to near absolute zero.
        - Building laser systems to control and manipulate trapped ions.
        - Testing and characterizing the performance of quantum hardware components.
    - **Sample Employers:** Rigetti Computing, IonQ, D-Wave Systems, Google Quantum AI, university research labs, national labs.
- **Quantum Research Scientist**
    - **Role:** Quantum research scientists focus on pushing the boundaries of quantum computing knowledge. They conduct cutting-edge research, develop new quantum algorithms, explore novel quantum computing architectures, and publish their findings in academic journals.
    - **Skills Required:**

        - A strong background in quantum physics, computer science, or a related field.
        - Extensive knowledge of quantum algorithms, quantum information theory, and quantum complexity theory.
        - Proficiency in programming languages like Python and quantum computing SDKs.
        - Excellent problem-solving skills and the ability to think creatively and independently.
        - Strong research and publication record.
    - **Example Tasks:**
        - Developing a new quantum algorithm that outperforms classical algorithms for a specific problem.
        - Exploring new ways to encode and manipulate quantum information.
        - Designing a novel quantum computer architecture.
        - Writing research papers and presenting findings at conferences.
    - **Sample Employers:** Google AI Quantum, Microsoft Quantum, Amazon Web Services (AWS), Universities, Research institutions.
- **Quantum Data Scientist**
    - **Role:** Quantum data scientists explore how quantum computers can be used to solve data-driven problems. They work on developing quantum machine learning algorithms, analyzing quantum data, and building hybrid quantum-classical models.
    - **Skills Required:**
        - Strong background in mathematics, statistics, and machine learning.
        - Knowledge of quantum mechanics and quantum information processing.
        - Experience with quantum machine learning (QML) libraries and frameworks.
        - Proficiency in Python and classical machine learning libraries (e.g., scikit-learn, TensorFlow).
        - Ability to design and implement both quantum and classical machine learning models.
    - **Example Tasks:**
        - Developing a quantum algorithm for a classification or regression problem.
        - Designing a hybrid quantum-classical neural network.
        - Analyzing the performance of quantum machine learning models on different datasets.
        - Working with domain experts to apply quantum machine learning to real-world problems.
    - **Sample Employers:** QC Ware, Zapata Computing, start-ups focused on Quantum Machine Learning.

✓ Skills to Develop

To prepare for a career in quantum computing, you should focus on developing a strong foundation in the following areas:

- **Mathematics:**
  - **Linear Algebra:** Essential for understanding quantum states, quantum operations, and quantum circuits.
  - **Probability and Statistics:** Crucial for analyzing quantum measurements, dealing with uncertainty, and developing quantum algorithms.
  - **Complex Numbers:** Quantum states are described using complex numbers.
- **Physics:**
  - **Quantum Mechanics:** The fundamental theory that governs quantum systems. You'll need to understand concepts like superposition, entanglement, and quantum measurement.
  - **Wave Functions:** Mathematical descriptions of the state of a quantum system.
  - **Quantum Measurement:** The process of extracting information from a quantum system.
- **Programming:**
  - **Python:** The most widely used programming language in quantum computing.
  - **Quantum SDKs:** Familiarity with quantum software development kits is essential:
    - **Qiskit (IBM):** For programming IBM's quantum computers.
    - **Cirq (Google):** For working with Google's quantum hardware.
    - **Ocean (D-Wave):** For programming D-Wave's quantum annealers.
- **Problem Solving:**
  - **Complexity Theory:** Understanding the limits of computation and how quantum computers can overcome them.
  - **Algorithm Analysis:** Evaluating the efficiency and performance of quantum algorithms.
- **Communication:**
  - **Writing Papers:** For researchers, the ability to clearly and concisely communicate findings in scientific publications is crucial.
  - **Presenting Findings:** Effectively presenting research results at conferences and to colleagues is an important skill.

◆ 4. Further Reading, MOOCs, and Research Labs

Here's a detailed guide to the resources you've listed, with additional context and examples:

✅ Books for Deeper Study

- **Quantum Computation and Quantum Information – Nielsen & Chuang:**
  - **The "Bible" of Quantum Computing:** Often referred to as "Mike and Ike" (after the authors' initials), this book is the standard textbook for quantum computing.
  - **Comprehensive Coverage:** It provides a thorough and rigorous treatment of quantum computation and quantum information theory.
  - **Content:**

        - Introduces the fundamentals of quantum mechanics.
        - Covers quantum gates, quantum circuits, and quantum algorithms in detail.
        - Explains quantum information concepts like entanglement, quantum teleportation, and quantum error correction.
        - Discusses quantum complexity theory and the limits of quantum computation.
    - **Target Audience:** Advanced undergraduates, graduate students, researchers.
    - **Why it's important:** It's the most cited book in the field, providing a strong theoretical foundation.
- **Dancing with Qubits – Robert S. Sutor:**
    - **More Accessible Introduction:** This book is designed to be more accessible to those with a background in classical computing and software development.
    - **Practical Focus:** It emphasizes the practical aspects of quantum computing and how to start programming quantum computers.
    - **Content:**
        - Introduces quantum computing concepts in a clear and intuitive way.
        - Provides hands-on examples and code snippets using Qiskit.
        - Explores potential applications of quantum computing in various industries.
    - **Target Audience:** Software engineers, programmers, and those with a basic understanding of computer science.
    - **Why it's important:** A great starting point for those who want to get into quantum programming quickly.
- **Quantum Computing for Computer Scientists – Yanofsky & Mannucci:**
    - **Rigorous and Formal:** This book provides a mathematically rigorous introduction to quantum computing, specifically tailored for computer scientists.
    - **Focus on Foundations:** It emphasizes the mathematical and logical foundations of quantum computation.
    - **Content:**
        - Covers the necessary mathematics, including category theory and topos theory.
        - Explains quantum mechanics from a computer science perspective.
        - Discusses quantum logic, quantum programming languages, and the philosophy of quantum mechanics.
    - **Target Audience:** Computer science students, researchers, and those interested in the theoretical foundations of quantum computing.
    - **Why it's important:** Provides a deeper understanding of the mathematical structures underlying quantum computation.

✓ Online Courses (MOOCs)

- **edX - Quantum Mechanics for Everyone (Georgetown University):**
    - **Focus:** Provides a comprehensive introduction to quantum mechanics, the fundamental theory behind quantum computing.
    - **Content:**

        - Covers the basic principles of quantum mechanics, including wave functions, superposition, and entanglement.
        - Explains quantum measurement, quantum operators, and quantum dynamics.
        - May include some discussion of quantum information and quantum computing.
    - **Why it's useful:** Provides the necessary physics background for understanding quantum computing.
- **Coursera - Quantum Computing (University of London):**
    - **Focus:** A broader introduction to the field of quantum computing.
    - **Content:**
        - Introduces the basic concepts of quantum computing.
        - Covers quantum algorithms, quantum circuits, and quantum information.
        - May explore different quantum computing platforms and applications.
    - **Why it's useful:** A good overview of the field.
- **Udemy - Qiskit: Quantum Programming (Independent Instructor):**
    - **Focus:** Hands-on learning of how to program quantum computers using Qiskit, IBM's quantum software development kit.
    - **Content:**
        - Teaches how to write quantum circuits using Qiskit.
        - Covers quantum gates, quantum algorithms, and quantum simulation.
        - Provides practical examples and exercises.
    - **Why it's useful:** Develops practical skills in quantum programming.
- **Brilliant - Quantum Computing Foundations:**
    - **Focus:** Interactive and visual way to learn the basics.
    - **Content:**
        - Introduces the fundamental concepts of quantum computing.
        - Uses interactive exercises and problem-solving to build understanding.
        - Covers topics like qubits, quantum gates, and simple quantum circuits.
    - **Why it's useful:** Makes complex concepts more intuitive, especially for visual learners.

✅ Free Resources

- **IBM Quantum Lab:**
    - **Cloud-Based Access:** Provides access to IBM's quantum computers and simulators through the cloud.
    - **Hands-on Experience:** Allows users to run quantum circuits, experiment with quantum algorithms, and explore quantum computing applications.
    - **Qiskit Integration:** Works seamlessly with Qiskit, IBM's quantum programming framework.
    - **Why it's important:** Offers a practical way to start experimenting with real quantum hardware.
- **Qiskit Textbook:**
    - **Online Learning Resource:** A free online resource that teaches quantum computing using Qiskit.

    - **Practical Focus:** Provides code examples, exercises, and explanations to help users learn how to program quantum computers.
    - **Community Driven:** Open-source and constantly updated.
    - **Why it's important:** A great way to learn Qiskit and quantum programming for free.
- **Quantum Country:**
    - **Spaced Repetition:** An interactive learning tool that uses spaced repetition to help users memorize and understand quantum computing concepts.
    - **Focus on Fundamentals:** Covers the core ideas of quantum mechanics and quantum information science.
    - **Unique Approach:** Combines explanations with flashcard-style questions to reinforce learning.
    - **Why it's important:** Helps to build a strong foundation in the essential concepts.
- **Microsoft Quantum Docs:**
    - **Documentation Hub:** Microsoft's official documentation for its quantum computing technologies and the Q# programming language.
    - **Comprehensive Information:** Provides tutorials, code samples, and conceptual explanations.
    - **Q# Focus:** A good resource for those interested in learning Microsoft's quantum programming language.
    - **Why it's useful:** Provides up-to-date information on Microsoft's quantum efforts.
- **Quantum Open Source Foundation (QOSF):**
    - **Community and Resources:** A non-profit organization dedicated to supporting the quantum open-source ecosystem.
    - **Open-Source Projects:** Provides access to various open-source quantum software projects.
    - **Educational Initiatives:** Offers educational resources, workshops, and hackathons.
    - **Why it's important:** A good place to connect with the quantum open-source community and find learning opportunities.

✅ Top Quantum Research Labs

- **IBM Quantum:**
    - **Focus:** A leading player in quantum hardware development, particularly with superconducting qubits. Strong emphasis on developing Qiskit and quantum error correction techniques.
    - **Contributions:**
        - Building increasingly powerful superconducting quantum processors.
        - Developing Qiskit, a widely used open-source quantum programming framework.
        - Researching quantum error correction to improve the reliability of quantum computers.
    - **Why it's important:** Pushing the boundaries of superconducting quantum hardware and software.
- **Google Quantum AI:**

- **Focus:** Strong emphasis on achieving quantum supremacy and developing quantum machine learning algorithms.
- **Contributions:**
  - Claimed to have achieved quantum supremacy with its Sycamore processor.
  - Researching quantum algorithms and applications, particularly in machine learning.
  - Developing superconducting qubits and quantum control systems.
- **Why it's important:** Driving innovation in quantum hardware and exploring the potential of quantum computation.

- **Microsoft Quantum:**
  - **Focus:** Developing topological qubits, which are believed to be inherently more resistant to noise, and the Q# quantum programming language.
  - **Contributions:**
    - Researching topological quantum computing, a promising approach for fault-tolerant quantum computation.
    - Developing the Q# programming language and the Quantum Development Kit (QDK).
    - Working on building a full-stack quantum computing system.
  - **Why it's important:** Pursuing a different approach to building stable qubits and creating a comprehensive quantum software platform.
- **MIT Center for Theoretical Physics:**
  - **Focus:** A leading center for theoretical quantum physics research, including quantum information theory, quantum simulation, and quantum complexity theory.
  - **Contributions:**
    - Conducting foundational research in quantum information science.
    - Developing new theoretical models and algorithms for quantum computation.
    - Exploring the fundamental limits of quantum computation.
  - **Why it's important:** Advancing the theoretical understanding of quantum computation.
- **QuTech (Netherlands):**
  - **Focus:** A world-leading research institute focused on developing quantum technologies, including quantum computers and a quantum internet.
  - **Contributions:**
    - Researching superconducting qubits and other quantum hardware platforms.
    - Developing quantum networking protocols and technologies.
    - Working towards building a quantum internet.
  - **Why it's important:** A major player in quantum internet research and quantum hardware development in Europe.
- **TIFR (India), IISc, IIT-Madras:**
  - **Focus:** These Indian institutions are actively involved in foundational quantum research, quantum information theory, and developing quantum technologies.
  - **Contributions:**

        - Researching quantum algorithms, quantum cryptography, and quantum materials.
        - Training the next generation of quantum scientists and engineers.
        - Contributing to the growing quantum ecosystem in India.
    - **Why it's important:** These institutions are making significant contributions to quantum research and education in India.

www.ingramcontent.com/pod-product-compliance
Lightning Source LLC
LaVergne TN
LVHW081752050326
832903LV00027B/1919

* 9 7 9 8 3 1 9 2 1 6 4 6 5 *